John Randolph Spears

Our Navy in the War with Spain

John Randolph Spears

Our Navy in the War with Spain

ISBN/EAN: 9783337243067

Printed in Europe, USA, Canada, Australia, Japan

Cover: Foto ©ninafisch / pixelio.de

More available books at **www.hansebooks.com**

REAR ADMIRAL GEORGE DEWEY.

OUR NAVY IN THE WAR WITH SPAIN

BY

JOHN R. SPEARS

AUTHOR OF "THE HISTORY OF OUR NAVY," ETC.

WITH MORE THAN ONE HUNDRED ILLUSTRATIONS

NEW YORK
CHARLES SCRIBNER'S SONS
1898

CONTENTS

                                                              PAGE
INTRODUCTION   xvii

CHAPTER I. THE DEMAND FOR INTERVENTION . 1

    Efforts to Subjugate the Insurgent Cubans that had Degenerated into a Pitiless War of Extermination Wherein even Women and Children were Deliberately Starved to Death—Where Intervention was a Duty and Non-intervention not only Cruel but Dastardly.

CHAPTER II. TEACHING SPAIN TO DESPISE US . 8

    When our Sense of Honor was so Low that American Ships were Seized on the High Seas by Foreign Men-of-war and we Permitted the Aggressor to Change the Real Issue—American Citizens Shot to Death Without Trial and an American Consul Confined to his Office by an Armed Guard—Two Striking Pictures of Spanish Diplomacy in the Histories of the *Aspinwall* and the *Virginius*.

CHAPTER III. THE WHITE SQUADRON   .   . 25

    Money Grudgingly Provided for a New Navy—The Advisory Board—A Frigate, Two Corvettes, and a Despatch-boat—What "Junketing" Did for the Navy—Discouraging the Younger Officers While Demanding Increased Service.

CHAPTER IV. ARMORED CRUISERS AND BATTLE-SHIPS 43

    Building of the Ill-fated *Maine*—The *New York* as an Era Maker—Our Battle-ships that had Part in the War with Spain were not Wholly Free from Mistakes—The Beginning of our Industrial Independence—The Hessian Plans for Cruisers.

CONTENTS

CHAPTER V. TREACHEROUS DESTRUCTION OF
THE *MAINE* 61

Our Early Efforts to Remove Anarchy from Cuba—The *Maine* Sent to Havana to Protect Americans—The Undisputed Conclusion of the Court of Inquiry Regarding the Loss of the *Maine*.

CHAPTER VI. THE DAYS JUST BEFORE THE
WAR 81

A Display of Power that was Without Effect Because of Spanish Obstinacy—$50,000,000 for Defence—A Fleet of Auxiliary War-ships—How we Learned that we Must Depend on our own Ship-yards—Sampson in Command—A Combination that Gave the Rest of the World Pause.

CHAPTER VII. THE WAR MESSAGE . . 103

Summary of Reasons for American Intervention in Cuban Affairs—Aggravating Proof of Work of Spanish Spies and Spanish Insincerity—Diplomatic Relations Ended—Threatening Movements of War-ships.

CHAPTER VIII. FIRST SHOT OF THE WAR . 115

Capture of the Spanish Merchantman *Buenaventura* by the Gunboat *Nashville*—His Flag Hoisted in Honor of the Fine American Squadron Betrayed Him—Official Proclamation of the Blockade of Cuban Ports.

CHAPTER IX. BRAVE WORK ALONG SHORE . 126

Cutting Cables Within Ninety Feet of the Beach at Cienfuegos Under the Fire of 1,000 Spanish Soldiers—Wounded who Suffered in Silence lest Groans Unnerve their Shipmates—The *Winslow* at Cardenas—A Torpedo-boat Sent to Cut a Gun-boat from the Piers of a Well-defended City—A Tale of Rare Heroism and Resourcefulness—Remarkable Tests of Courage in the Face of Superior Forces Afloat—Returning Fire from the Shore—At Matanzas and Cabáñas.

CHAPTER X. DEWEY AT MANILA . . . 154

Good Work of the *Baltimore's* Men Aided by the British in Hong Kong—Precautions on the Way to Manila—A Night Attack on our

Squadron—The Scene at Dawn—When Montojo Became Desperate
—Wretched Use of Mines and Torpedo-boats—A Striking Exhibit of
the Repose of Conscious Power—Christening of the Baby Battle-ship
—Spanish Views of the Conflict.

CHAPTER XI. SAMPSON'S FIRST SEARCH FOR
     CERVERA 194

A Squadron with the Speed of a Ton-of-coal Barges Sent in a Chase
of Twenty-knot Spanish Cruisers—The Bombardment of San Juan de
Porto Rico—Work of Inexperienced Men that Showed their Mettle
—Another Vain Cruise to Nicholas Channel.

CHAPTER XII. THE *OREGON'S* FAMOUS RUN . 213

A Race Against Time, 14,700 Miles Long with Never a Break or a
Loss of a Turn of her Wheels—Men who Worked for Twenty-four
Hours at a Stretch More than Once in that Cruise—A Boiler-maker in
a Live Furnace—Shots that Gave Life to Fainting Firemen—Alongshore Signal Service.

CHAPTER XIII. SCHLEY'S CRUISE TO SANTIAGO 221

Reasons for his Delay at Cienfuegos—Stopped Twenty Miles from
his Destination and then Started Back to Key West—Break on the
Collier—Dash of the *Marblehead*—When Schley saw Cervera's Ships
at Anchor Within Easy Range—A "Reconnaissance" at a Range of
from Four to Five Miles—A Blockading Squadron Ten Miles from
Port—Acts of Auxiliary Cruisers Described.

CHAPTER XIV. THE BLOCKADE OF SANTIAGO . 239

Disposition of the Squadron—The Story of Hobson's Futile Bravery—It was Another Proof that Culture and Cool Courage go Hand
in Hand—The Forts Bombarded—Good Work of the *Vesuvius*.

CHAPTER XV. THE MARINES AT GUANTANAMO 259

Our First Armed Force to Maintain a Hold on Cuban Soil—The
Bay Captured by the *Marblehead* and *Yankee*—It was Hot Work for
a Week—The Spaniards in the Brush—Assault on a Funeral *Cortège*
—Spanish Woods Station Captured, and Caimanera's Fort Destroyed
—A Torpedo in the Propeller of the *Texas*—Good Health of this
Force on Shore.

CHAPTER XVI. AUXILIARIES AND NAVAL MILI-
TIA 275

The Spook Fleet and its Effect on the Movement of the Army—Landing at Baiquiri—Killed by a Shell on the *Texas*—Two Good Fights Against Odds off San Juan de Porto Rico—The *St. Paul* and the *Yosemite* with Their Untrained Crews were a Credit to the Naval Officers in Charge of Them—First American Flag Raised over Cuban Soil—Good Work Alongshore.

CHAPTER XVII. DESTRUCTION OF CERVERA'S
SQUADRON 291

Luck was with the Spaniards, in a Way, for Two of our Big Ships had Left the Blockade—Their Smoke had Excited our Suspicion and our Lookouts were Alert—Quick Work with the Torpedo-boats and Two Cruisers—Eulate's Vain Effort to Catch the *Brooklyn*—A Record Race in Naval Warfare that Established the Fame of the Bull Dog *Oregon*—How Wainwright's Day Came at Last.

CHAPTER XVIII. SEAMEN OF THE SQUADRONS
CONTRASTED 324

Story of Spanish Treachery on a Good Ship They had Surrendered to us—Captain Chadwick's Remarkable Skill in Handling the *New York*—Our Men as Life-savers—Undaunted in the Presence of Fire and Exploding Magazines—Atrocious Conduct of Cuban Soldiers—The Squadrons Compared—Reward of a Commander who Breaks Down Through Overwork.

CHAPTER XIX. CAPTURE OF GUAM AND MA-
NILA 343

A Bombardment that was Mistaken for a Salute—The Emperor-William Germans were Inclined to Make Trouble, but Dewey was a Good Diplomat as Well as a Fighter—Our Friends, the British—Notable Voyage of Two Monitors.

CHAPTER XX. SURRENDER OF SANTIAGO AND
AFTERWARD 350

Deadly Accuracy in Firing at a Target Five Miles Away and out of Sight Behind the Hills—Our Ships at Manzanillo, and a Poetic

CONTENTS

Tribute to Three of Them—The Capture of Nipe—When Ensign Curtin of the *Wasp* Demanded and Obtained the Surrender of Ponce by Telephone.

PAGE

CHAPTER XXI. OUR NEW NAVAL PROGRAMME . 365

Vessels that were in the Ship-yard when the War Began—Two-story Turrets and Broadside Batteries—Smokeless Powder in Future, with Guns that for the Moment will Lead the World—Ships to Replace the *Maine*—The New Monitors—A Tale of a Torpedo-boat on the Blockade—A Splendid Flotilla to Come—A Word About the Naval Academy.

LIST OF ILLUSTRATIONS

REAR ADMIRAL GEORGE DEWEY,		*Frontispiece*
		PAGE
REAR ADMIRAL WILLIAM T. SAMPSON,	*Facing*	1
GOVERNOR-GENERAL WEYLER,		3
SAGASTA,		11
WALL AT SANTIAGO WHERE CREW OF THE *VIRGINIUS* WERE SHOT,		21
LAUNCH OF THE UNITED STATES STEAMSHIP *RALEIGH*,		29
PROTECTED CRUISER *ATLANTA*,		35
DESPATCH-BOAT *DOLPHIN*,		37
THE WHITE SQUADRON AT SEA,		39
WILLIAM C. WHITNEY,		44
PROTECTED CRUISER *CHARLESTON*,		45
SECOND-CLASS BATTLE-SHIP *MAINE*,		47
ARMORED CRUISER *NEW YORK*,		50
BENJAMIN F. TRACY,		54
A BARBETTE BEFORE IT IS INSTALLED,		55
ONE-POUNDER ON A BATTLE-SHIP'S SUPERSTRUCTURE,		57
PROTECTED COMMERCE-DESTROYER *COLUMBIA*,		58
CRUISER *COLUMBIA* ON DRY DOCK,		59
THE *MAINE* ENTERING THE HARBOR OF HAVANA,		65
THEODORE ROOSEVELT,		67
HON. JOHN D. LONG,		68
CHART OF HAVANA HARBOR,		70
CAPTAIN SIGSBEE,		71

LIST OF ILLUSTRATIONS

	PAGE
THE WRECK OF THE *MAINE*,	73
COURT OF INQUIRY ON THE DESTRUCTION OF THE *MAINE*,	77
ARMORED CRUISER *BROOKLYN*,	87
SECOND-CLASS BATTLE-SHIP *TEXAS*,	89
PROTECTED CRUISER *NEW ORLEANS*,	94
ARMSTRONG GUN ON THE *NEW ORLEANS*,	96
A SIX-INCH GUN ON THE *NEW ORLEANS*,	97
ADMIRAL SICARD,	98
CAPTAIN ROBLEY D. EVANS,	101
GUN-BOAT *NASHVILLE*,	116
CAPTAIN MAYNARD,	117
TORPEDO-BOAT *FOOTE*,	120
CAPTAIN CHADWICK,	122
THE FIRST PRIZE OF THE WAR, *BUENAVENTURA*,	124
CHART OF MATANZAS BAY,	129
THE *BANCROFT* AND *HELENA* ON THE BLOCKADE,	131
A COLT RAPID-FIRE GUN,	138
LIEUTENANT J. L. PURCELL,	139
CHART OF CARDENAS BAY,	146
LIEUTENANT JOHN B. BERNADOU,	148
CONNING TOWER OF THE *WINSLOW*, SHOWING EFFECT OF SHOTS COMING THROUGH FROM OPPOSITE SIDE,	149
ENSIGN BAGLEY,	151
CAPTAIN CHARLES V. GRIDLEY,	157
CHART OF MANILA BAY,	162
PROTECTED CRUISER *OLYMPIA*,	165
ADMIRAL MONTOJO,	169
PROTECTED CRUISER *BALTIMORE*,	173
PROTECTED CRUISER *BOSTON*,	177
PROTECTED CRUISER *RALEIGH*,	180
GUN-BOAT *CONCORD*,	182
MANŒUVRING OF THE FLEET AT THE BOMBARDMENT OF SAN JUAN,	199
UNPROTECTED CRUISER *DETROIT*,	201

LIST OF ILLUSTRATIONS

	PAGE
Unprotected Cruiser *Montgomery*,	205
Sampson's Squadron in Nicholas Channel. (Drawn by L. A. Shafer from Diagram by John R. Spears),	208
Captain Charles E. Clark,	213
First-Class Battle-Ship *Oregon*,	217
Commodore Winfield S. Schley,	222
Chart of Cienfuegos,	223
Map of Cuba,	229
The *Mayflower* on the Blockade,	235
Captain C. W. Jungen,	237
Lieutenant Hobson,	243
The *Merrimac* in the Entrance to Santiago Harbor,	245
The Spanish Prisoners Exchanged for Hobson,	247
Hobson's *Merrimac* Crew in the American Lines,	251
Captain F. A. Cook,	254
Captain F. J. Higginson,	255
Auxiliary Cruiser *Yankee*,	257
Port Guantanamo, or Cumberland Harbor,	262
Picket Sentry on Guard Duty,	264
Dr. John Blair Gibbs,	265
Tents of Officers on the Beach,	266
Within the Trenches at Camp McCalla,	268
A Spanish Contact Mine Picked Up by the Propeller of the *Texas*,	272
Watching the Bombardment of Baiquiri,	277
Shot-Hole in Port Bow of the *Texas* Made by a Six-Inch Shell,	281
Shot-Hole Starboard Hammock Berthing, Midships in the *Texas*,	282
Lieutenant Victor Blue,	288
First-Class Battle-Ship *Massachusetts*,	292
Chart of Santiago Harbor,	295
Admiral Cervera,	297
First-Class Battle-Ship *Indiana*,	299

LIST OF ILLUSTRATIONS

	PAGE
RICHARD WAINWRIGHT,	302
CONVERTED YACHT *GLOUCESTER*,	303
THE BURNING OF THE SPANISH SHIPS,	305
INFANTA MARIA TERESA,	309
THE SISTER SHIPS *ALMIRANTE OQUENDO*, *INFANTA MARIA TERESA*, AND *VIZCAYA*,	313
THE BOW OF THE *ALMIRANTE OQUENDO*,	317
VIZCAYA AGROUND AT ASERRADEROS,	321
CAPTAIN JOHN PHILIP,	323
HEAVILY ARMORED CRUISER *CRISTOBAL COLON*,	325
THE BOW OF THE *VIZCAYA*,	331
RELIEF, HOSPITAL SHIP,	334
FIRST WARD—THE *RELIEF*,	335
SHOT-HOLE IN THE SMOKE-STACK OF THE *BROOKLYN*,	338
SHOT-HOLES IN THE BERTH-DECK OF THE *BROOKLYN*,	339
TWO-TURRET MONITOR, *MONADNOCK*,	347
THE *REINA MERCEDES* AS SHE LIES AT THE ENTRANCE TO SANTIAGO HARBOR,	351
A SIX-INCH GUN ON THE AFT-DECK OF THE AUXILIARY *HIST*,	354
COMMODORE JOHN C. WATSON,	356
ENSIGN CURTIN,	359
SUWANEE, *VIXEN*, AND *ST. LOUIS* AT SIBONEY,	361
PORT OF MANZANILLO,	363
CAPTAIN D. DELEHANTY,	364
FIRST-CLASS BATTLE-SHIP *ALABAMA*,	367
FIRST-CLASS BATTLE-SHIP *KEARSARGE*,	371
ELLIPTICAL TURRET OF THE FIRST-CLASS BATTLE-SHIP *ALABAMA*,	374
PLAN AND VERTICAL SECTION THROUGH ELLIPTICAL TURRET AND BARBETTE,	374
BOILERS OF THE *KEARSARGE*,	375
OUTLINE DIAGRAM OF A FLOATING STEEL FORT CALLED A BATTLE-SHIP,	376

LIST OF ILLUSTRATIONS

	PAGE
CAPTAIN CHARLES O'NEIL,	377
THE EVOLUTION OF THE SIX-INCH GUN,	379
DIAGRAM SHOWING THE ARMOR PROTECTION OF A BATTLE-SHIP,	380
KRUPPIZED ARMOR-PLATE SHOWING EFFECT OF A SIX-INCH PROJECTILE WEIGHING 100 POUNDS,	382
DECK PLAN OF THE *INDIANA, MASSACHUSETTS,* AND *OREGON,*	383
LOADING THE AMMUNITION-HOISTS FOR THIRTEEN-INCH GUNS ON THE *INDIANA,*	385
RAMMING HOME THE CHARGE IN A THIRTEEN-INCH GUN,	385
THE NEW FIRST-CLASS BATTLE-SHIP *MAINE,*	387
FITTING A SIX-POUNDER ON THE *MANGROVE,*	390
CHART SHOWING POSITIONS OF THE SHIPS OF ADMIRAL CERVERA'S SQUADRON, AND THOSE OF THE UNITED STATES FLEET IN THE BATTLE OF JULY 3, 1898, OFF SANTIAGO DE CUBA,	*End of Volume*

INTRODUCTION

THE principal object held in view, while writing this history, was to give, within convenient limits, an account in every way truthful of those events of our war with Spain in which our navy had a part. And it seems proper to say here, first of all, that among the many remarkable features of this war few are more cheering to the student of history than the promptness with which the Administration spread before him the material that he needed. And not only was the material furnished promptly; it was also given almost in full. The official reports of the commanders of our ships, as well as of our squadrons, have been made public almost as soon as received by the Navy Department. The reports have been in every case at once modest and yet detailful statements of what had been done. Further than that, and better than that, from the point of view of a student of history, so many despatches relating to such disputed matters as the conduct of the battle off Santiago have been printed, that no point of importance is now unsettled. It is possible to assert that this history has been taken, in all important matters, directly from official sources.

As to parts of the narrative not taken from official reports and despatches the principal source of information has been in the accounts written by naval officers for such periodicals as *Scribner's*, the *Century*, *Harper's*, the *Army and Navy Journal*, and the *Army and Navy Register*.

The people of the United States are greatly indebted to those officers who contributed, over their own signatures, to the general knowledge of what was done, and to the Navy Department, as well, for relaxing the rule that ordinarily prevents a naval man's appearing in print. I have also had a number of letters from and personal interviews with naval officers whose work I have described.

In addition to these sources of information I have had recourse in a few cases to what has been written by newspaper reporters. It is with extreme regret that I find a word of explanation regarding the accuracy of the newspaper reports necessary. A time ought to come, and so it will come, when every reporter's sense of honor will be so strong that it will be as difficult to find a misstatement in a daily paper as it is to find one now in a reputable monthly magazine. But that time is not yet here, and so I must say that I know every reporter whom I have quoted to be a trustworthy writer except one whom I do not know personally, the reporter of the London *Mail*, whose interview with Admiral Montojo is given; but I know the managing editor of the *Mail*, and his character warrants the use of that report in any history.

Perhaps it may not be amiss for me to add here, that a very interesting feature of the war was the presence of many newspaper despatch-boats in the operations around Cuba. No such work as they did was ever known before in the history of naval wars. And I know that the reporters so engaged were, with a few exceptions, unwearied and fearless in energy and enterprise, and were entirely sincere and faithful to the readers of the papers represented. I speak from actual knowledge in this matter, for I was myself one of the reporters during the earlier months of the conflict on the Cuban coast.

If any inaccuracies be found in this history, they are blunders and not due to a lack of trustworthy sources of information.

But to give a truthful narrative of the events of the war is not quite all that I have attempted here. It seemed necessary to review briefly the events in the history of Cuba that compelled us to interfere in the affairs of another nation. And this was the more necessary for the reason that we had been more or less involved in the trouble between Spain and her "ever faithful" island of Cuba. It has been no pleasant task to recount even briefly the facts regarding Spain's rule in Cuba, and still less so the bearing of the affairs of the *General Lloyd Aspinwall* and the *Virginius* on the conflict just ended. But unless I have labored in vain, the reader must see that these accounts could not be omitted. Perhaps while perusing them it will be seen that undue patience and forbearance in international dealings, as in dealings between men, sometimes come to be considered an evidence of weakness; that dignity and firmness, backed even by physical force, are absolutely necessary if we would preserve peace and do right, especially when dealing with those who are weak and greedy and shifty.

As to the facts in the cases of these two ships, they were taken from an account of the *Aspinwall*, written for *Scribner's Monthly* by one connected with the administration then in power, and from a message of the President (Ex. Doc., No. 30, 43d Cong., 1st Sess.) containing all the documents and much other matter relating to the *Virginius*.

Further than that I have given a short, but what I believe to be an adequate, account of the growth of our navy from the inception of the White Squadron. It is a matter that deserves attention for more reasons than one, but is needed here in order to help us comprehend the ability of our naval men. To describe the heterogeneous squadron with which Sampson went to San Juan, is to show his resourcefulness. The squadron of protected cruisers which Dewey took to Manila had a battle-ship task to accomplish in attacking ships and forts at once; but what it lacked in armor-plate was made up by the Harveyized grit of its commanding officer and crews.

On the whole here is a story the facts of which, however told, must stir the heart of every American who has red blood in his veins.

It was a war to bring peace where anarchy reigned. We sought the enemy in his own chosen arena. We met him man-fashion, and we literally swept him from the seas. Four of the finest armed cruisers and two of the best torpedo-destroyers in the world, with nearly a score of lesser war-ships were driven to the rocks or sunk out of sight, while hundreds of their crews were killed. And yet in all that work we lost one man killed, and less than a score wounded, while the damage done to our ships did not disable even so much as a single gun for one minute. Nor was our work in blockading and attacking shore batteries much less brilliant or much more destructive to us. There was never a war, afloat or ashore, like this.

J. R. S.

Rear-Admiral William T. Sampson.

OUR NAVY IN THE WAR WITH SPAIN

CHAPTER I

THE DEMAND FOR INTERVENTION

EFFORTS TO SUBJUGATE THE INSURGENT CUBANS THAT HAD DE-
GENERATED INTO A PITILESS WAR OF EXTERMINATION WHERE-
IN EVEN WOMEN AND CHILDREN WERE DELIBERATELY STARVED
TO DEATH—WHERE INTERVENTION WAS A DUTY AND NON-
INTERVENTION NOT ONLY CRUEL BUT DASTARDLY.

THE student who is looking for the origin of our war with Spain must go back as far as 1814, the very year in which the Spanish bestowed upon the island of Cuba the appellation of "the ever faithful." Spain had been overrun by the armies of Napoleon, and a Napoleon had been placed upon her throne, but Cuba had proved faithful to the Spanish régime, and when the Spanish line once more entered the Madrid palace there was as sincere rejoicing in Cuba as in any district of Spain. Cuba was at this time in an especially prosperous condition. The cultivation of sugar and tobacco had but recently been introduced. A valuable class of citizens had come to her—the industrious French who fled from the negro revolutionists of Santo Domingo. The tremendous crops raised on virgin soil by slave-labor were sold at enormous prices. The Spanish Government looked at the prosperity of the colonists with the eyes of greed only. "In spite of the high-sounding title of 'Faithful Cuba,' bestowed on her generous island sons, Spain subtly reverted to her old methods, and used their country as a conquered El Dorado, the quickly developed resources of which she was determined to turn to her selfish account, regardless of possible consequences. The Cubans, however, who had learned many things since the opening of the century, soon showed a distinct disinclination to submit to this process." Nor was it misrule alone that roused the antagonism of the Cubans, for though they were all of Spanish descent— and so far as the social leaders were concerned, of unmixed blood—they were treated as inferiors by the Spanish officials, who came out to wring fortunes from the island, and what was infinitely worse, the Cuban ladies were contemptuously called *pelareas*, or "croppies," a term originating in their fashion of wearing cropped or short hair.

The Spanish repaid Cuban loyalty not only with increased taxation, but they added personal insult and contempt to financial injury.

The Spanish system, first shown in its perfidy in 1814, reached a climax of cruelty under Governor-General Weyler, known as "the Butcher," who landed at Havana on February

10, 1896. The Cubans had been in revolt from time to time for half a century, the last outbreak having been started early in 1895. Weyler was appointed because he had in former years, in a subordinate capacity, made a reputation for pitiless rigor in the exercise of official powers in the island. He began his rule by proclaiming that all residents who did not actively aid him in extirpating the revolution were to be considered and treated as armed enemies, and that meant that they might be shot at the order of any officer of the army in command of any troop. No form of trial was needed. The officer's order was sufficient.

Governor-General Weyler.

In the long war ending in 1878 the Government had issued an order commanding all country residents to remain on their plantations at night, and to keep white flags flying above their buildings in token of their loyalty. People found beyond their landed limits might be shot, and buildings found with no white flag displayed were to be burned. Without waiting for this order to be promulgated throughout the country districts, the soldiers went forth to kill, pillage, and destroy. So it happened that thousands of innocent planters were murdered and robbed. But Weyler went still farther than that, for he compelled a few wealthy planters to take troops to their plantations, and there support them, while all other inhabitants, no matter how impoverished they might be, were compelled to concentrate themselves in the garrisoned towns. These people brought from the farms were called *reconcentrados*. A few—here and there a family—were able, after mortgaging their land, to raise enough money to buy food. The small landholders, the *Guajiros*, who held a few acres only, and lived from hand to mouth, together with the laborers or *peons*, were without any resource for obtaining even the commonest articles of food, save only as the rich gave them in charity.

In this way tens of thousands of helpless people were brought to the garrisoned towns, to sit down in idleness, leaving the fields to lie uncultivated and the supplies of vegetables to cease. In short, this was an order for the starvation of perhaps half the population.

For the men who came to town one may feel but little pity. It was often said that if they lacked the courage to go to the mountains and join the insurgent bands in the fight for independence they deserved no sympathy. That is an iron dictum, but if it be accepted, there yet remain the thousands of women and children who could not fight and who were not permitted to cultivate the soil—who were compelled to lie down and die.

Of the atrocities perpetrated by the Spanish soldiers in bringing these unfortunates to the towns—how unarmed men were shot for the pleasure of seeing them quiver and die, and how women were outraged—no adequate account has ever been given nor ever can be, nor ever ought to be. The foraging ants that ravage the tropics in search of insect prey are not as cruel as Weyler's soldiers were, for the ants instantly kill their victims, while Weyler's were reserved for the slow torture of starvation, where mothers were compelled to look upon dying children and children upon dying parents, helpless to avert the fate that awaited all. However much the numbers of the Cuban army were exaggerated in the public prints of the United States during 1896 and 1897, the stories of the suffering under Weyler were never half told, simply because no man was able to portray them as they were. Words failed.

Having garrisoned the important towns, built block-houses along the railroads, and two lines of tiny forts connected by barbed-wire tanglements (trochas) clear across the island, Weyler sat down to watch his victims die. The country that he controlled was what lay within range of his Mauser rifles, and not a yard more. The insurgents, though in small bands, and wretchedly armed, ranged the interior at will.

Of systematic effort to hunt the insurgents from their retreats, there was absolutely none, and the forays that were made at rare intervals were worse than useless for the intended purpose, for they resulted in little more than the devastation of the plantations visited, while every injury done to Cubans was sure to bring reprisals in some form. The Spaniards did manage to kill two or three leaders. José Marti and General Maceo became victims. But no head was made in wiping the insurrection away. The only thing accomplished was the all but utter prostration of every form of peaceful industry throughout the island, and the gradual extinction, by cruel starvation and murder, of such of the Cubans as came within the Spanish power.

The English author of "Cuba, Past and Present," who refers to us as "the easily excited Americans," on "the very verge of hysteria," in speaking of Weyler, says:

"His desperate struggle to stamp out the revolt seems to have driven him to frenzy. He might be Cæsar Borgia come to life again. He conceived it his duty to extinguish the civil war at any cost, and he used the self-same methods which made the fame (or shame) of Hernando Cortez. Since the days of Alva the horrors he perpetrated have rarely been equalled in human history."

That was in Cuba, an island, lying just ninety miles off our coast, and entirely "within the economic orbit of the United States." Its prostrate people appealed to us for help.

At that cry some who dreaded the influence of war, and the results of interfering with any matter beyond our own borders, replied that the Cubans were as cruel as their masters, which was true; that they were incapable of self-government, which seemed altogether probable; and that therefore we ought not to interfere. But others—characterize them as you will—replied:

"If what you say of the Cubans be true, then we must interfere if it be only to drive from the Americas the barbarous government that could produce such a people." And when these spoke the nation and the civilized world applauded.

"There must be a stage in misgovernment which will justify the interference of by-standing nations," wrote Mr. Anthony Trollope, while in Cuba fifty years ago. And to this may be added the words of John Ruskin in his essay on "War:"

"I tell you that the principle of non-intervention, as now preached among us, is as selfish and cruel as the worst frenzy of conquest, and differs from it only by being not only malignant but dastardly."

CHAPTER II

TEACHING SPAIN TO DESPISE US

WHEN OUR SENSE OF HONOR WAS SO LOW THAT AMERICAN SHIPS WERE SEIZED ON THE HIGH SEAS BY FOREIGN MEN-OF-WAR AND WE PERMITTED THE AGGRESSOR TO CHANGE THE REAL ISSUE—AMERICAN CITIZENS SHOT TO DEATH WITHOUT TRIAL AND AN AMERICAN CONSUL CONFINED TO HIS OFFICE BY AN ARMED GUARD—TWO STRIKING PICTURES OF SPANISH DIPLOMACY IN THE HISTORIES OF THE *ASCIVIALL* AND THE *VIRGINIUS*.

How we tried to restore order in Cuba before we resorted to armed intervention shall be told farther on. It is necessary to relate first two incidents in what is known as the ten-year war between the Spanish and the Cuban insurgents. Two American ships were seized by the Spaniards under circumstances that warranted war on our part, but we showed extreme forbearance in both cases, with the result that the Spaniards came to regard us with a hearty contempt. There is an old proverb which says, "when you clinch the devil you must use your claws." It applies here. If we had been firm in asserting our rights in 1869 and 1873 we should have had no war in 1898.

On the morning of January 21, 1869, the American steamer *Colonel Lloyd Aspinwall,* while on her way from Port-au-Prince to Havana, found herself within five miles of the Cuban coast in a deplorable condition. She had weathered a gale that had lasted for three days, but the seas had swashed across her decks, poured down her hatches, drowned her fires and choked her pumps. Only by extraordinary efforts in bailing had she been kept afloat. But the sea had gone down at last and heading away on her course, she was making fair progress, when at noon she was overhauled by the Spanish warship *Hernan Cortes,* and boarded by an armed force. The Cubans were at that time engaged in what is known as their "ten years' struggle for liberty," and the Spaniards patrolled the Cuban coast to head off filibustering expeditions. The *Cortes* was one of the patrol boats.

To the Spanish officer, Captain McCarty brought the ship's papers, but the officer said:

"I cannot examine them. My orders are to take you to Nuevitas."

Captain McCarty protested, saying that he was "the bearer of despatches of the utmost importance for the Government of the United States," and for the American Admiral (Poor) in command of the station, then in Havana, but to Nuevitas he was obliged to go with an armed force on board. There he was detained six days, with his papers sealed in a trunk by the Spanish officials, when he was ordered to proceed to Havana still under guard. This he refused to do unless his papers were returned to him, and the result of his refusal was that the Spanish steamer *San Francisco* towed him there.

Here he and all his crew were still held as close prisoners on board until February 13th— in all twenty-three days after the ship was seized, before he was allowed even to communicate with the American Consul. So it was not until she had been under Spanish guns for a month that our Government learned of the outrage.

Secretary of State Fish replied to the Consul's formal notice by telegraphing: "Report particulars, and if seized on the high seas demand immediate release." As she had been seized more than a marine league from shore, the demand was made. The Spaniards simply ignored it.

The seizure was by no means the first of its kind, though because of the fact of Government despatches being on board, it was the most aggravating. However, the State Department waited until February 26th, when the formal protest of Captain McCarty was received by mail, and then it made a demand on the Spanish Minister at Washington, Don Lopez Roberts, for reparation, adding to the demand these words:

"This Government trusts that your Government will, when the matter shall have been brought to its notice, of its own accord offer a suitable apology for the indignity." This official demand was made on March 5th. The Spanish minister waited a few days, and then unofficially informed the Secretary of State that the case was in the Prize Court at Havana! A demand for a reply to the previous demand was at once sent, whereat the Spanish Minister sent another unofficial note saying that the *Aspinwall* had been "seized on suspicion that she had been landing arms on the coast of Cuba."

Secretary of State Fish once more officially demanded her release, saying that even if she had landed arms

Sagasta.

there "you could not seize her for that unless you took her in Cuban waters."

Of this the Spanish minister took no notice, so far as the record shows, and Secretary Fish did nothing until April 6th, when he notified United States Minister Daniel Sickles, at Madrid, that "the President is not satisfied with this prolonged delay."

At that Sickles, on April 8th, called on Prime Minister Sagasta, who replied that the case was "undergoing examination in the prize court." To this Sickles replied that the United States could not recognize the jurisdiction of a prize court unless a state of war existed between the Spanish and the Cubans. If such a war did exist, the United States would be obliged to recognize the Cubans as belligerents, and this would soon be done. To this Sagasta replied that "the decision of the court will be given with all possible promptness."

And that was about all the satisfaction Sagasta would give him, though Sagasta did at last promise to release the steamer.

Meantime the *Aspinwall* was lying beside the Spanish flag-ship in Havana. She was under guard all the time and her crew were not permitted even to wet down her sides to keep the sun from starting the calking from her seams. After three weeks of this confinement the Spaniards brought a force on board to search her bunkers. The coal-handlers did not complete their search the first day, so that night they put an armed guard over the bunkers. At that Captain McCarty put his own crew to guard the Spanish guard and so prevent their sneaking arms into the bunkers during the night.

This fact is of importance, not alone as showing the Spanish character. It shows that McCarty believed his own Government would be likely to ignore the real principle of the case if arms were found on board. Whether she had arms in her bunkers or not had nothing to do with the main principle in the case, for the *Aspinwall* was an American ship and she had been seized on the high seas in time of peace. The Spaniards knew that they had no right to take her, but they were trying to establish a precedent, following which they might take ships wherever found when carrying arms to the insurgents in Cuba, and in their contempt for the Americans they thought they should succeed. As a matter of fact their feeling in this matter was well-nigh justified.

Having waited a week for Sagasta to fulfil his reluctant promise to release the steamer, Minister Sickles, on orders from Washington, called once more to learn why nothing was done. This was on April 14th. Sagasta replied that the local authorities at Havana had said that they "had no power to take the case out of court." At that Sickles declared emphatically that the United States Government considered the holding of the *Aspinwall* in a prize court an acknowledgment on the part of Spain that a state of war existed, and that belligerent rights would, therefore, be accorded the insurgents forthwith. Having said that,

Sickles was about to withdraw when Sagasta stopped him and said:

"The council of ministers decided yesterday to release the vessel forthwith on receiving from you a formal demand in writing for her surrender as an American vessel *bearing official despatches.*"

The written demand was made the same day, and it contained, shameful to relate, the words about her having official despatches on board. Spanish diplomacy succeeded in evading the real principle at issue. They released her on the ground that she carried those despatches. They did not concede that they had no right to seize an American ship on the high seas, and, more than that, they did not release her forthwith, as Sagasta promised to do, but waited thirteen days longer. The *Colonel Lloyd Aspinwall* was held with her crew as prisoners on board for ninety-eight days, all told, before the guard was withdrawn. Even then Admiral Poor, who, with the old *Severn* and the monitor *Saugus*, was in Havana, felt obliged to send the *Aspinwall* to Key West without waiting for badly needed repairs, lest the rampant volunteers of Havana destroy her under his guns.

Close in the wake of the *Aspinwall* case came that of the *Virginius*. The principles involved were much the same in both cases, but in the *Virginius* case American citizens were shot to death on the order of a Spanish military officer, and the Spaniards, with their agents and friends in this country, set up the claim that she was really a Spanish ship.

It appears that the *Virginius* was originally an English ship built to run the blockade during our civil war, that she was captured while engaged in her nefarious traffic, that she was sold as a prize in 1867, but reverted to the Government because she was not paid for, and that on August 20, 1870, she was sold to John F. Patterson for $9,800 cash. She was then lying at Washington. In September she was brought to New York and thoroughly overhauled and repaired.

On October 4, 1870, she cleared for Curaçao with a cargo of one hundred and seventy barrels of bread, two boxes of saddlery, and four boxes of clothing, the whole of the value of $1,430, and the next day while going down the beach below Sandy Hook she overhauled the tug *Virginia Seymour*, and took from her twenty Cubans, of whom the leaders were General M. Quesada, his secretary, Adolfo Varona, and Señors Eloy Camacho and Domingo Mora.

It is certain that Patterson had complied with the law to the satisfaction of our Government officials, and that the papers of the *Virginius* were in proper form, but Patterson had violated the law—he had purchased the ship for the

Cuban Junta, in New York, and turned her over to Quesada, a Cuban. And thereafter she remained under the control of Quesada, although she had various Americans, from time to time, serving as captain.

The *Virginius* reached Curaçao on October 15th. A few days later came the schooner *Billy Butts*, and next day after her arrival she and the *Virginius* went out to sea, where the *Butts* transferred some hundreds of cases of arms, ammunition, and equipments, with four brass howitzers, to the *Virginius*, after which the *Virginius* went to Puerto Cabello and entered into an agreement with Guzman Blanco, the Venezuelan leader, by which Quesada was to help Blanco in a revolution then in progress, in return for which Blanco was to aid the Cuban insurgents later on.

Under this agreement part of the arms and ammunition were landed for Blanco's use and a part placed on a gun-boat belonging to Blanco, after which the *Virginius* towed the gun-boat out to sea and stood by while it captured a small fleet of armed coasting schooners belonging to Blanco's enemies. The *Virginius* also towed the captured vessels to port.

When Blanco's triumph was assured the *Virginius* reshipped the arms, etc., and with a force of Cubans and Venezuelans sailed from Puerto Cabello, on June 14, 1871, and made a successful landing of the expedition at Boca de Cabello on the south coast of Cuba.

During this time her first captain had left her and the chief engineer had served as captain, with Eloy Camacho as navigator. The Spanish faction here claimed that Camacho was the captain, but this was not so. It is true, however, that Quesada's wishes were always followed.

The *Virginius* next went to Colon and remained there several months. There Francis Bowen took command, in April, 1872. At that time a band of fifty Cubans was in Colon awaiting opportunity to go to Cuba. The American man-o'-war *Kansas* was in the harbor, and so was the Spaniard *Pizarro*. On May 1st, the *Virginius* sailed for Carthagena under sealed orders, and by direction of the American consul the *Kansas* escorted her from port to prevent an apprehended attack from the *Pizarro*.

The fact that the *Kansas* did this is proof sufficient that the papers of the *Virginius* were all in proper form at this time. The *Kansas*, of course, would not have protected a pirate, nor would she have had anything to do with a Spanish merchantman.

Meantime, while at Aspinwall, the *Virginius* had run in debt, and Captain Bowen gave a bottomry bond for $10,000 to Mahl Brothers, merchants, to secure it. The fact that there was no communication with Patterson, the nominal owner, is considered good evidence that he had no financial interest in her. And that is to say the ship was continually handled in violation of the laws of the United States.

Eventually the ship reached Maracaibo (August 11, 1872), where a new crew, with Charles Smith, an American, as master, took charge, and then legal proceedings were begun on the bottomry bond for the sale of the ship, and she was sold at auction for $17,500.

Quesada's secretary, at this time, a man named Alfaro, bid her in in the name of a Caracas Englishman, and it was proposed that she hoist the British flag; but when it was learned from the British consul that a British man-o'-war was ready to seize her as a pirate in case that was done, Alfaro prevailed on the local authorities to nullify the sale, and she was kept under her original papers.

It appears from the testimony in the case that during all this time the American consuls, in the ports where she called, knew that the *Virginius* was being handled exclusively in the interests of the Cuban insurgents. Indeed, Captain Smith testified that the consul at Maracaibo said to him, "Why don't you get rid of that damned pirate? She is nothing but a pirate, and you will get caught, by and by, and they will hang you." But the fact is the forms of law were complied with, so far as her papers showed. The proof that her papers were kept in order is to be found also in the fact that when she returned to Colon in May, 1873, Captain Reid, of the *Kansas*, was still willing to protect her. Lieutenant Autran of the Spanish man-o'-war, *Pizarro*, wrote to Reid, insisting that the *Virginius* was liable to capture, on the ground that she belonged to Cuban insurgents, and had committed an act of hostility to Spain in landing armed forces on Cuban soil. He ended his letter by asking "whether the *Virginius* was entitled to fly the American flag?" and Reid replied that she was, and that he should protect her "at all hazards."

Autran at first said he would fight it out, but he changed his mind and merely requested that the *Virginius* be sent to New York, where the Spanish Government might proceed against her in our courts. Whether this request should have been granted or not does not appear from the papers (see H. of R., Ex. Doc. No. 30, 43d Cong., 1st Sess.). Certainly that would have saved much trouble, but the request brings out clearly the fact that Spain had a good remedy for every evil that she suffered through the deeds of the *Virginius*. Because the *Virginius* was flying the American flag and was protected by our man-o'-war, Spain had only to make a claim and prove the facts, to recover heavy damages from us. Further than that our courts would have punished every American guilty in the matter, that could be reached by them.

Spain did not act on that proper claim, but the career of the filibuster was rapidly drawing to an end. On July 5, 1873, loaded with arms and men for the Cubans, she sailed from Colon escorted by the *Kansas*, made a good landing and reached Kingston, Jamaica, in safety. There Captain Joseph Fry, an American citizen, took command, a number of Englishmen as well as Americans were shipped as members of the crew, war material and many men were taken on board, and on October 23, 1873, she sailed once more. She had cleared, in due form, at the American Consulate for Port Limon, Costa Rica; but she went to the Cuban coast, where she fell in with the Spanish gunboat *Tornado*. Turning her about, her crew fled, literally, for life, back toward Jamaica. For eight anxious hours they held their way, with hope steadily failing, and then they surrendered. That was at 10 o'clock at night on October 31, 1873. They were at that time eighteen miles from the east end of the British island.

The *Tornado* carried the *Virginius* to Santiago, where crew and passengers, one hundred and fifty-five in number, were placed in close confinement. On November 4th the Spaniards

Wall at Santiago where members of the crew of the *Virginius* were shot.

began slaughtering their prisoners. Four were shot to death on that day. On the 7th thirty-seven more were executed, including Captain Joseph Fry and eight other Americans, and sixteen British subjects, members of the crew. On the 8th, twelve more were shot.

It appears that the members of the crew who were shot were not even court-martialed, but were "ordered by the Captain of the Port to be executed on November 7, 1873, at 4 o'clock P.M." (See report of Vice-Consul Schmitt, p. 175, Ex. Doc. No. 30, 43d Cong., 1st Sess.)

Worse yet, American prisoners were not allowed to see the vice-consul until two hours before they were shot, the first telegraph dispatch which the consul sent to his superiors was held back for two days, the consul was insulted in a variety of ways while in the discharge of his duty; and, when the hour came for the slaughter of the prisoners, he was confined to his office by two armed guards who were placed at his door.

It was claimed by the Spanish sympathizers in the United States that the local authorities went ahead in their bloody work unauthorized by the Madrid government. The truth was, that the local authorities were in constant communication with Havana, the Havana newspapers were full of the facts, the editorials exulted in the slaughter, and the whole matter, news and editorial, was cabled to Madrid, where it appeared in the papers from day to day. It was not until the 13th that Madrid interfered, and the interference then was due solely to fear of what Great Britain would do.

A ship flying the American flag was seized on the high seas, carried into a Spanish port, and fifty-three of her people shot to death on the order of a Spanish military officer.

Although General Grant was then our President, the official news of the outrage on our flag did not seem to stir the Administration to any special activity. Indeed, because General Daniel Sickles, our Minister at Madrid, was emphatic in his demands he was recalled. A protocol was eventually signed, by which Spain was to be allowed to submit evidence that Cubans owned the *Virginius*. The outrage on the flag and the outrage on American citizenship in the slaughter of Americans among the crew were brushed aside, and the whole matter was eventually settled by the return of the ship and the payment, after years of waiting, of a few dollars per head to the relatives of the murdered men. It was freely charged at the time that the Spaniards used money in Washington to bring about this result. This charge was probably untrue, but quite as sorrowful were the appeals made in the newspapers opposed to war. For these said of our warships, "there is not among them a seagoing vessel fit to contend with the Spanish frigates." "We could raise men enough to rid the island (Cuba) of the volunteers and regulars in a few weeks, but how should we get at the volunteers and regulars?" "As we now stand, it is hard to say where the fighting would be after we went to war." So ran the appeals to fear; so strove the peace-at-any-price party to cultivate cowardice.

But enough of that. It has been worth while mentioning it at all only because to recall it is to help to save us from such shame in the future.

Further than that, a considerable squadron

of such ships as we had was gathered at Key West during the negotiations, and the condition of the ships when brought together was such as to compel public consideration of the needs of the navy. The *Virginius* affair was in a way, too, like that of the *Chesapeake* before the War of 1812. It served, though remotely, to prepare us for a war for a principle. Moreover, as our attitude in the *Chesapeake* affair did but degrade us in the eyes of the aggressor, so our management of the *Virginius* case increased the contempt of the Spanish people for whom they were pleased to call " the American pigs."

CHAPTER III

THE WHITE SQUADRON

MONEY GRUDGINGLY PROVIDED FOR A NEW NAVY—THE ADVISORY BOARD—A FRIGATE, TWO CORVETTES, AND A DESPATCH-BOAT—WHAT "JUNKETING" DID FOR THE NAVY—DISCOURAGING THE YOUNGER OFFICERS WHILE DEMANDING INCREASED SERVICE.

Almost a quarter of a century passed away before the anarchy in Cuba again roused our people to thoughts of war. It was, on the whole, a period of remarkable prosperity for us as a nation. What breadths of prairie lands and mountain valleys were settled! What deserts were reclaimed! What wondrous resources were developed! Indeed it was in this period that we achieved, at last, industrial independence of the world, and that, if we look at it rightly, was second only to the political independence we had obtained so long before by force of arms.

The bearing these statements have upon a history of the naval war with Spain shall be explained at once. It was because of our commercial greatness that the Spaniards believed us a nation of money-getters who would not fight lest we lose dollars, and so they were led to rush blindly into a war where disaster inevitably awaited them. Another view of the matter is not less instructive. The building of a new navy was the most important step taken in all those years for the achievement of industrial independence.

Moreover it was because of our industrial independence that we were able to bear the shock of war with scarce an added throb in the arteries of commerce. There was never a moment when anyone doubted our ability to pay in gold the expenses of the war, and the depreciation of even "wild-cat securities" was no greater when war came than is known in times of peace and over-expansion of credit.

But before entering upon the story of our navy in the war with Spain it is necessary to tell what kind of a navy we had when the war began, and how we got it. It will help us to understand how it was that swift destruction fell upon our enemies, while we escaped, if the expression may be allowed, with losses so insignificant as to excite universal wonder.

There was a time (1865) when the American navy, in ships as well as men, was the most powerful in the world, but it was neglected, and even treated by legislators as a means for dishonest gain, until it became the world's standard of inefficiency. Indeed it had deteriorated so far by 1873, only eight years after our civil war ended, that even Spain's navy was well-nigh a match for it. But a worse degradation awaited it. The need of improving it was made apparent by the *Virginius* affair, and yet the peril of the nation served only to invite the Secretary of the Navy to an act that was the most disgraceful in the history of the Department. He deliberately began to build new ships under the false pretence that he was repairing old ones. Physically the sea-power of our navy, if we may use Mahan's adaptation of Ruskin's term, reached its lowest ebb in 1873. We did in succeeding years add a few vessels to the force, but they were built under circumstances that destroyed self-respect, and they were in no point superior to other ships already in existence. As a whole the tide of the navy still ran ebb, leaving the mud-flats bare, and it was not until June 29, 1881, that anything was done for a real rehabilitation. On that date a board, called the Rodgers board because Rear Admiral John Rodgers headed it, was appointed to consider the state of the navy and report what action ought to be taken by Congress in the matter.

As a matter of fact but one vessel, the Ammen ram, was built out of all that this board recommended. But it is a significant fact that public opinion was prepared for the appointment of such a board by the writings of naval officers on naval matters before it came into existence, and, although the ships it recommended were not built, its statement that new ships were imperatively needed received respectful consideration. The Navy Department had been smirched, but the honor, integrity, and ability of the personnel of the navy had never been doubted for a moment. In eight years our force afloat descended from the highest place to the lowest, in spite of the remonstrances of the naval officers; but they were not wholly disheartened. They continued their appeals to the public, using the pen as vigorously and efficiently as they have always used gun and sword, and at the end of another period of eight years they turned the tide.

As a result of the Rodgers report, Congress, in the following year (1882) inserted this paragraph in the naval appropriation bill approved on August 5th:

"Any portion of said sum not required for the purposes aforesaid (in the general uses of the Bureau of Construction and Repair) may be applied toward the construction of two steam cruising vessels of war, which are hereby authorized, at a total cost, when fully completed, not to exceed the amount estimated by

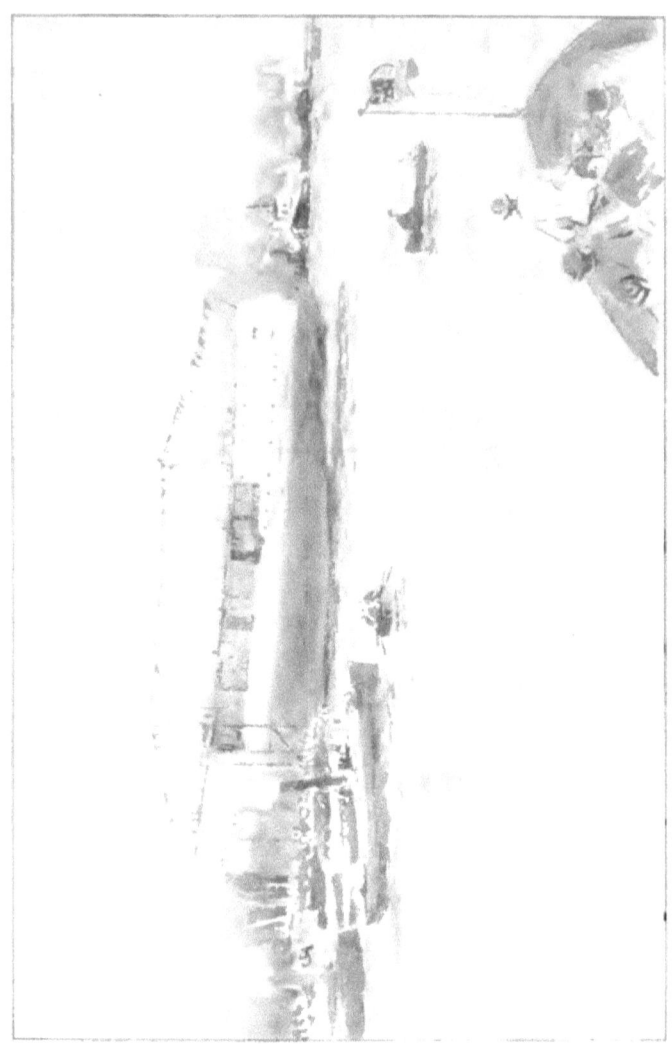

Launch of the United States Steamship *Raleigh*.

the late Naval Advisory Board for such vessels, the same to be constructed of steel, of domestic manufacture. . . . One of said vessels shall be of not less than 5,000, nor more than 6,000 tons displacement, and shall have the highest attainable speed. . . . One of said vessels shall be of not less than 4,300, nor more than 4,700 tons displacement."

It was also provided that the vessels should have full sail-power. The Secretary of the Navy was directed by the same act to appoint a naval advisory board of five naval officers "without reference to rank, and with reference only to character, experience, knowledge, and skill, and two persons of established reputation and standing, as experts in naval and marine construction, to be selected from civil life." Further than that the Secretary was directed to advertise for models and plans to be submitted by anyone, practically, and last of all was a paragraph saying that any sum left over from the appropriation for the Bureau of Steam Engineering might be applied to building engines for the ships so authorized.

In this grudging fashion—never in the history of our nation was a great work undertaken more grudgingly — we prepared to build the new navy.

Meantime Mr. William E. Chandler had become Secretary of the Navy. By his appointment Commodore R. W. Shufeldt, Chief Engineer Alexander Henderson, Commander J. A. Howell, Lieutenant Edward Very, and Naval Constructor F. L. Fernald, with Messrs. Henry Steers, ship architect, and Miers Coryell, Marine Engineer, were organized as the Advisory Board. Assistant Naval Constructor F. T. Bowles was detailed as Secretary, while Passed Assistant Engineer C. R. Roelker, and Assistant Engineer H. P. Norton, were ordered to give their services in the actual work of designing ships and machinery. Assistant Naval Constructor Richard Gatewood, of the Bureau of Construction and Repair, was also employed.

The work of preparing plans for a new navy worthy of the nation, that was given to these gentlemen, was a task the magnitude of which has never been properly appreciated. It was not alone that without real experience in modern war-ship building they were expected to turn out something superior to all that the unbroken activity of European nations had produced; they had to do their work under the carping criticism of a people ignorant of the subject in hand, grudging in the matter of granting funds, and strongly suspicious of the honesty of the administration that was to give out the contracts. The underhanded and dishonest work done in the building previously described, now came back to plague the men who were sincere and honest in their intent and actions. Not only did the acts of Robeson delay the beginning of a new navy by ten years; they clogged the work when it was begun, so that the progress made was exasperatingly slow for four years longer.

Having authority to do something the Advisory Board cast about to see what ought to be done first, and at once perceived that with the resources of the country it was rather a question of what they might do. Congress had authorized one cruiser of a size to compete with the best then afloat, and one of a more moderate size; but it was apparent that we did not have the men and facilities to construct a worthy ship of the largest size. We had allowed Europe to do "the experimenting for us," but we found that it was impossible after all for a nation to serve an apprenticeship by proxy. So the Advisory Board very properly recommended that instead of building the big and expensive cruiser, we try our 'prentice hand on something smaller and more nearly within our capacity.

The matter was taken to Congress, where the discussions were humiliating to one who has a pride in the navy; but by the act of March 3, 1883, authority was obtained for building three small cruisers and a clipper despatch-boat.

Under date of April 28, 1883, Secretary Chandler invited proposals for one cruiser of 4,500 tons, two of 3,000 tons each, and a despatch-boat of 1,500 tons.

Because these were to become the first of our new navy, as full a description of them as may be understood by a reader unversed in sea-craft should be given as a matter of record. The largest ship of the four has been described as a steam frigate. She was planned to have guns on two decks, the upper of which, called the spar deck, was to carry four eight-inch rifles; and the lower, or main deck, two five-inch and eight six-inch rifles. She was to be 325 feet long, 48.2 feet wide, and to draw 19 feet of water. Her engines were to develop 5,000 horse-power, which, with twin screws, should drive her fourteen knots per hour.

Nine athwartship bulkheads were provided to make water-tight compartments, to keep her afloat, though one or two were flooded. A double bottom was placed under the machinery. A protective deck of steel armor one inch and a half thick, and curved over her vitals, was to keep out shot; while the coal, nine feet thick when her bunkers were full, was to provide an additional protection. When finally built, she was named the *Chicago*. That was the very best ship we could hope to build then, although England had fourteen-knot battle-

Atlanta, Protected Cruiser. Dimensions, 271 x 42; draft, 21; displacement, 3,000. Speed, 15.6 knots. Main Battery, two eight-inch, six six-inch guns.

ships armed with ten-inch and twelve-inch modern rifles!

The *Atlanta* and the *Boston* were the names given to the two smaller boats, and they were called steam corvettes—or ships with all the guns on one deck. We were still held by the old style of rating ships. The plans gave ships 276 feet long, 42 wide, and drawing about 17 feet of water. But in these ships the old design of a single deck, unobstructed fore and aft, was abandoned. Nor did they provide either forecastle or poop as the Rodgers board had desired for ships of that size. Instead of all that a superstructure was planned amidships, which angled out to a barbette forward on the port side and another aft on the starboard. Each of these barbettes was to be provided with an eight-inch gun which, because of the position of the barbette and the shape of the superstructure was to have a wide sweep on both sides as well as over the ends of the ship. Besides these great guns three six-inch rifles were to be provided for each broadside, and one on each side could be used for fore or aft fire as well.

This plan, according to Admiral Simpson, " is an innovation that was very startling to the conservative mind; but the more familiar the idea becomes, the more apparent becomes the increased offensive power of the ship."

" It is not unfashionable now," says Bennett, "to criticise harshly that board for not knowing everything that experience has taught since, but its work speaks well enough in results for the thoroughness and the earnest endeavor of its members to do the best possible for the service in the beginning of its new life." As a matter of fact one of them was to speak for herself in actual battle. The *Boston* was at Manila.

It was provided that the ships must be made "of steel of domestic manufacture," the specifications as to quality meaning that it should be of the best known to the world at that time.

A considerable technical knowledge of steam-engines is needed to fully understand the re-

Dolphin, Despatch-Boat. Dimensions, 240 x 32; draft, 17; displacement, 1,486. Speed, 15.5 knots. Main Battery, two four-inch guns.

quirements for her machinery, but it may be worth while saying that the engines of the new cruisers consisted of small and large cylinders, the steam from the boiler passing through the small cylinders at full pressure, and then to the large at greatly reduced pressure—a system that, as since developed in the "triple," and the "quadruple expansion" types, has effected enormous savings in coal consumption, while increasing in wonderful fashion the power applied to driving the ships. The engines of the new cruisers were, on the whole, planned in the right line of development. Twin screws were also provided.

As to the despatch-boat, she was to be 240 feet long by 32 wide—a leaner model than the others—but there was nothing about her to especially distinguish her from a big yacht, and as a yacht for "junketing" parties she was hailed by the political opposition. In guns she was to carry but one six-inch rifle, backed by a few rapid-fire rifles, of an average of two-inch bore. She was named the *Dolphin*.

It is a curious fact that the prejudice excited by the tales of junketing prevented, in the years that followed, the construction of any other vessel than this for carrying despatches in time of war. The people could not be made to see that such vessels would be needed, and so when war came we found ourselves in a plight, where we had to buy all the available yachts in our waters, paying enormous prices, and finding them at best makeshifts. Only the skill of our officers saved them from being really ridiculous.

The bids sent in answer to this call are now chiefly interesting as showing the number of firms in the United States willing to undertake the work. Three firms on the Delaware River, two firms in New York City, one from Baltimore, one from Boston, and one from St. Louis answered the call.

Mr. John Roach, who owned a shipyard at Chester, Pa., the Morgan Iron Works in New York, and controlled steel-making works at Thurlow, Pa., had found by experiment that he could produce steel of the required quality

The White Squadron in Mid-ocean.

From a drawing by R. F. Zogbaum.

at a lower price than any of his competitors deemed possible, and he was therefore the lowest bidder. On the whole, the contracts were $315,000 below the next lowest bids, and $774,100 less than the estimates of the Advisory Board.

Contracts for the *Atlanta*, the *Boston*, and the *Dolphin* were signed on July 23, 1883, and for the *Chicago* on the 26th. It is worth mention, too, that following the completion of these contracts Mr. Roach was obliged to contract with three iron mills besides that one at Thurlow for the production of steel for the work he was to do, and it was with the signing of these contracts that the industry of steel making first obtained a permanent foothold in this country.

The year of 1883 is notable. For the interest of this history it is chiefly so because in that year the building of the White Squadron, as we afterward affectionately called our fleet, was actually begun. But it should not be forgotten that August 5, 1882, was the day on which the first act for the building of the new navy was signed by the President. On the whole we are entitled, as a nation, to all the satisfaction we feel in recalling those days of small beginnings. But for the sake of the future, the reader, who has heard so often in this year of 1898 that it was the man behind the gun who brought us honor, should consider the following extract from the report of the Secretary of the Navy for 1883:

"PERSONNEL OF THE NAVY.

"The Act of August 5, 1882, provided for a gradual reduction in the number of officers of the navy until a standard should be reached corresponding to the necessities of the service. This gradual reduction is now in progress, and should be allowed to continue."

In the very act that first provided for the building of war-ships fit to represent the American people, it was also provided that the younger officers of the navy—the very men in whom the country must of necessity trust when the new ships were completed—should have their hope of promotion and fair reward for honest service cut off.

CHAPTER IV

ARMORED CRUISERS AND BATTLE-SHIPS

BUILDING OF THE ILL-FATED *MAINE*—THE *NEW YORK* AS AN ERA MAKER—OUR BATTLE-SHIPS THAT HAD PART IN THE WAR WITH SPAIN WERE NOT WHOLLY FREE FROM MISTAKES—THE BEGINNING OF OUR INDUSTRIAL INDEPENDENCE.—THE HESSIAN PLANS FOR CRUISERS.

It has been worth while describing the early work on the White Squadron in considerable detail, if only for the reason that to consider it well is to save our honest pride from degenerating into vanity. That there is danger of national vanity will appear when the story of the war is reached, but we may refer to one fact by way of illustration—the fact that we are loud in boasting about our marksmanship, although in the only battle where shots and hits were counted, we scored but three times in a hundred shots.

Having made a beginning in the work of building a new navy we held our course without deviation, though the speed was very slow.

The exigencies of politics favored the work in curious fashion (as I have told in detail in Volume V. of "The History of Our Navy") and there was an abundance of money in the Treasury.

William C. Whitney, Secretary of the Navy.

A "Gun Foundry Board" appointed in 1882 made a report in 1883 that, a year later still, led Congress to appropriate a million dollars for building guns. Then a new Administration came that carried on the work with increasing vigor and success, although one singularly disheartening mistake was made. Secretary Whitney seems to have entirely overlooked the fact that we needed to develop naval architects, as well as ship-yard mechanics, and went abroad for plans for the new ships Congress authorized him to build. This is a most important matter. The employment of Hessian naval architects was at least as great an evil as the employment of Hessian crews to man the completed ships would have been. For it was not so much the new ship of the highest quality that we then needed as it was the ability to produce the best ship wholly from our own resources.

Fortunately the plans that were purchased abroad were in not one case perfect. The ships we built from them were the *Charleston*, the *Baltimore*, and the *Texas*, and these were all very good ships; but it was three years after we bought the plans of the *Texas* before they

Charleston, Protected Cruiser. Dimensions, 312.7 x 46.2 ; draft, 18.7 ; displacement, 3,730. Speed, 18.2 knots. Main Battery, two eight-inch, six six-inch slow-fire guns.

were altered into a shape where a practical ship could be made from them, and radical changes had to be made by our builders in the plans of the others before the ships could be completed.

However, Mr. Whitney amply atoned for this error by his tact in handling the rather niggardly appropriations given by Congress. He stopped the practice of buying steel forgings abroad. Forgings for our first eight-inch guns and the armor for the *Miantonomoh* were purchased in England. Whitney held back the contracts for steel until he had enough in hand to warrant a firm of steel-makers in this country erecting a plant to make the forgings here. On "the 1st day of June, 1887, contracts were entered into with the Bethlehem Iron Company of Bethlehem, Pa., one of the largest and most enterprising of American steel manufacturers, under which the United States were guaranteed that within two and one-half years from the date of the contract, this country would have within its borders a plant equal to, and probably the superior of any in the world for the production of armor and the forgings for high-power guns." So says the Secretary's report for 1888.

The contracts with John Roach in July, 1883, prepared the way for the steel plates needed for steel hulls and for the ingots for the smaller sizes of guns. The contracts with the Bethlehem Iron Works created the plant by which we were enabled to armor and fully arm the hulls that we were then already able to construct. Few dates of greater interest than these two are known to the history of the United States, for not only did the contracts eventually enable us to produce naval ships unsurpassed by any in the world—they gave us industrial independence.

Perhaps the most important ship of the new navy that was in hand in Whitney's time was the ill-fated *Maine*. She was the first new armored ship wholly of American design. She was built by the Government at the Brooklyn Navy-yard, as the *Texas* was built at Norfolk. It was argued that Government navy-yards

From a copyrighted photograph by E. Muller.

Maine, Second Class Battle-ship. Dimensions, 318 x 57; draft, 22.5; displacement, 6,682. Speed, 17.5 knots. Main Battery, four ten-inch, six six-inch guns.

should be fitted not only to repair, but to build ships. The important fact that the naval strength of a nation depended on the extent of the facilities for building ships was becoming known. The *Maine* was for a long time known as Armored Cruiser No. 1, because she was designed for considerable speed, with a coal capacity sufficient to last her on a long cruise.

She was 318 feet long and 57 wide, with a maximum draught of 22.5 feet. Her side armor was twelve inches thick, and she had two turrets, each eight inches thick, with barbettes, that is, solid steel breastworks or forts, built about their bases, that were twelve inches thick forward and ten aft. Her keel was laid on October 17, 1888, and she was launched on November 18, 1890.

For guns the *Maine* carried four ten-inch rifles in her turrets, and six six-inch guns in her broadside. She was also provided with four Whitehead torpedoes, which had come into use by the time she was launched. It was proposed that she carry small torpedo-boats—big launches that, as was supposed, might be of use at night, or even in time of battle—but the views of naval officers eventually changed as to the value of such small boats, and her torpedo-boats were abandoned.

By the time the *Maine* was commissioned she was designated as a second-class battle-ship, and placed on the list with the *Texas*, that carried a single twelve-inch gun where the *Maine* carried two tens.

The *Maine* was never appreciated by the nation for quite her real worth, because before she was in commission the larger and much more powerful *Indiana*, *Massachusetts*, and *Oregon* were contracted for and so far advanced that they overshadowed the smaller ship. Indeed, the *Indiana* was put in commission on November 20, 1895, but two months and three days after the flag was hoisted on the *Maine*. But the *Maine* was in every way an honor to the flag she bore. As an American naval product she should have appealed especially to the people, but her intrinsic merits, as well as the advance she showed in our knowledge and skill in ship-building, were notable.

Considered as an advance in war-ship building, the *Maine* carried twelve-inch armor where the Roach-built ships had an inclined deck one inch and a half thick. She carried ten-inch guns, to the others' eight-inch, and she could steam, in spite of her weight of guns and armor, at a speed of two knots faster than either the *Atlanta* or *Boston*. We can imagine, perhaps, what her efficiency was from the work the other second-class battle-ship, the *Texas*, did when the hour of trial came.

The next of the new navy to receive notice is the *New York*, a remarkable ship in a variety of ways, but especially so for the reason that she was an era maker in war-ships. The *New York* was authorized by the act of September 7, 1888, and that act was further noteworthy because we obtained from it the smaller cruisers *Olympia*, of 5,870 tons, the *Cincinnati* and *Raleigh* of 3,213 tons each, the *Detroit*, *Mar-

New York, Armored Cruiser. Dimensions, 380.5 x 65; draft, 26.7; displacement, 8,200. Speed, 21 knots. Main Battery, six eight-inch, twelve four-inch guns.

blehead, and *Montgomery* of 2,089 tons each, and the gun-boat *Bancroft* of 839 tons—on the whole a stirring squadron of fighting ships, such as we had not dreamed of five years earlier.

We had tried our 'prentice hands at armored-cruiser building in the *Maine,* but we were now to show the skill of the master in the construction of the *New York.* The contract was signed with the Cramps on August 28, 1890. A month later they laid her keel, and on December 2, 1891, she slid down the ways into the water. The picture of the beautiful spectacle served to illustrate many a periodical of the day and not a few printed since that time. She was 380.5 feet long by 65 wide, had a maximum draft of 26.7 feet, and displaced, when ready for service, 8,200 tons of water. She was driven by twin screws, and two sets of triple expansion engines were coupled to each shaft in such fashion that, when cruising, one of each set could be disconnected and the ship driven, with a small consumption of coal, by the other. The contract speed of the ship was to be twenty knots an hour, but the Government had adopted a policy long before of giving a premium for an excess of horse-power above contract amount, and in this case offered a premium of $50,000 for each quarter of a knot that might be obtained above the contract speed of twenty, exacting at the same time a penalty as great for falling below that speed.

Quite as interesting as this advance in steam enginery—interesting especially in view of the influence of the old marline-spike sailors of the navy—was the fact that this ship, a real cruiser, was unprovided with sails. She did, indeed, have two masts, but a new nomenclature had come into use. They were not masts for spreading sails. They were "military masts," and were used for carrying tiny cannon, once called "murdering guns," high up above the smoke of battle; and they were also convenient as perches for lookouts and the display of signals. The *Maine*, on the other hand, was supplied with large sail-power.

For offensive operations the *New York* was supplied with two eight-inch guns in a bow turret, two more in a turret aft, and one on each side protected only with a shield. To supplement these great guns were twelve of four-inch calibre, besides a host of the " murdering guns."

Now, because she was to be a real cruiser, it was not advisable to load her with heavy armor. On the other hand she was to be what may be called an all-around fighting machine and must carry some steel to keep out an enemy's projectiles. Accordingly a belt of steel four inches thick, to protect the water-line, was worked into her sides over a space ample to cover her machinery. To supplement this a steel deck, in the form of an arch, was built within the protective walls, beginning well below the waterline and rising up over all the machinery. This deck is six inches thick on the slope, and three inches thick on the flat top. A shot from an enemy to reach her machinery would have to pass through the four-inch belt on her sides and then penetrate the six-inch slope of the protective deck. And that could not be done by any shot, for the four-inch belt would explode the heaviest shot, and the arched deck is strong enough to stop the pieces. The turrets holding the big guns are five and a half inches thick, and each is protected with a ten-inch barbette.

On December 2, 1891, the *New York* was launched, and the 22d of the following May found her at sea on her official trial trip. If we consider its effect upon the navy and the nation, we shall look in vain for another day in all our history to compare with it, though the days of the famous race of the *Constitution* off the Jersey beach were somewhat like it. We had heard from time to time of the progress made in building her. We had read boastful descriptions of her plans, and we had learned, although we did not realize it, that in offensive and defensive powers she was extraordinary; but some were doubtful. Even among the officers detailed to watch the trial, there was not a little doubt as to her full success, but when they gathered in the engine-room and with eager eyes watched the swift beating of connecting rods and the smooth whirr of shafts, and in the midst of the perspiring heat of the air, found the bearings cool and frictionless, while indicator cards showed such power as they had never seen before, their fears faded away. For four hours they kept their watch on engine-room and taffrail log and clock, and then, when the time was done, the whole crew broke into cheers that could not be restrained, while a blue-shirted sailor clambered aloft to lash a broom to the masthead, for she had covered twenty-one sea miles per hour during the whole trial.

No such a ship as that had ever floated the gridiron flag — no such a ship of the class floated any flag. The shame that for twenty-five years had rested on our navy was wiped out.

And then came the battle-ship era.

It was on June 30, 1890, that an act to authorize the building of battle-ships became law. It provided for three, and there were no unnecessary restrictions to hamper the designers. There is a story, that may or may not be true, to the effect that when the bill was signed, Secretary Tracy sent for Lewis Nixon, then in the Constructors' Bureau, and, after telling him of the authority obtained, said:

"Now, sir, what you've to do is to design a ship that can lick anything afloat."

Benjamin F. Tracy, Secretary of the Navy.

The American theory in this matter was put in words by Commander McCalla, of the *Marblehead*, who, while preparing for the war with Spain, had sundry legends painted about the ship for the encouragement of the crew, among the number being this:

A Barbette before it is installed.

"The best protection against an enemy's fire is an effective fire of your own."

We planned our first battle-ships to carry guns on this theory, but we were still hampered by the idea that our ships must be strictly for coast defence. So we sacrificed both speed and coal capacity, and we put on armor that was at least thick enough.

Beginning with the guns, the designers gave to each ship four of thirteen-inch calibre, the largest size that could be handled effectively afloat, and quite the equal of any in foreign navies, although guns of sixteen-inch calibre are found there.

These guns were naturally located in two turrets placed amidships forward and aft. Around each turret was placed a barbette, and from this barbette steel walls were drawn diagonally out to the sides of the ship in such fashion that each turret stood at the apex of a wedge formed by these walls. Reaching the sides of the ship, these walls were united with the side armor in an obtuse angle, and on each of the four angles so formed a smaller turret was erected. So there were two big turrets above the keel and four on the rails. In each of the four smaller turrets were placed two eight-inch guns, while along the side armor walls were located four six-inch guns.

Little has been said so far about the so-called secondary battery, save to speak of them as "murdering guns." The secondary battery provided for these ships was in numbers, at least, the most remarkable ever sent afloat at that time.

Going next to the engine-room, we find 9,738 horse-power provided to drive a hull that displaced 10,288 tons, and the speed obtained was 15.547 knots per hour. The armor varied in thickness in proportion to the estimated needs. The side armor protecting the machinery was 18 inches thick; in the main turrets, 15, in the

One-pounder on a Battleship's Superstructure.

barbettes, about the main turrets, 17; the walls thence to the side armor, 8; the small turrets, 6; while the flat protective deck, laid fore and aft, was 2¾ inches thick. These three ships were named the *Indiana*, the *Massachusetts*, and the *Oregon*. The latter was built by the Union Iron Works of San Francisco, and the others by the Cramps of Philadelphia.

We know, now, that these ships are not the best that might have been built. It was a mistake to give them such a small coal capacity, for one thing. The turret-guns, when swung around on the broadside heel the ship over enough to expose her deck to a plunging fire from an enemy's fort. Moreover the eight-inch guns cannot be fired directly fore and aft, because of the effect of the gases on the crews of the big turrets. We did rather better in the *Iowa* that came after the *Oregon* class. We gave her twelve-inch guns, which are more easily managed than the thirteens, and we increased both power and coal capacity.

As to our great guns for arming these ships it is unfortunately the fact that we had made less progress, when our war came upon us, than Europe. In Europe the ordnance officials had

Columbia, Protected Commerce Destroyer. Dimensions 412 × 58, draft, 25, displacement 7,375. Speed 22.8 knots. Main Battery, one eight-inch, two six-inch bow-fire, eight rapid-fire four-inch guns.

Cruiser Columbia on Dry-dock, showing the arrangement of Triple Screws

produced a great variety of calibres which, because measured in centimetres, seem strange to us. Thus our enemies had for their heaviest guns afloat on their big cruisers a calibre of 11.02 inches (28 ctm.), and for their broadside guns a calibre of 5.51 inches (14 ctm.), with other sizes between and below on their smaller cruisers and gun-boats. We have adhered, and very properly so, it seems, to calibres of four, five, six, eight, ten, twelve, and thirteen inches, but when we had reached a muzzle velocity of 2,200 foot-seconds for our six-inch guns—2,200 foot-seconds for its best showing—we were obliged to rest for lack of appropriations, while England went on improving up to a velocity of 2,700 foot-seconds in some calibres. But that was not the worst of it either, for the breech-blocks and cartridges were improved so that they had rapid-fire guns in their broadside batteries of the five-and-a-half and six-inch calibres, while we had in service nothing better than five-inch. And in our broadside batteries, curiously enough, considering our traditions, we had four-inch and five-inch guns where the Europeans had five-and-a-half, six, and six-and-a-half inch guns.

Little more need be said here of ships and guns. With the *New York* and the *Brooklyn* (literally a greater *New York*) for our armored cruisers; with the *Columbia* and *Minneapolis*, built for commerce-destroyers and scouts; with a beautiful fleet of smaller cruisers and gun-boats; with a small but very efficient flotilla of torpedo-boats, and with six monitors of which five were begun in the days of false pretence, but were finished in honest fashion, we supposed, in the year 1897, that we had a sea-power that would insure peace. That we were mistaken—that we were not powerful enough to overawe a vain and foolish nation—is now well known to all.

CHAPTER V

TREACHEROUS DESTRUCTION OF THE *MAINE*

OUR EARLY EFFORTS TO REMOVE ANARCHY FROM CUBA—THE *MAINE* SENT TO HAVANA TO PROTECT AMERICANS—THE UNDISPUTED CONCLUSION OF THE COURT OF INQUIRY REGARDING THE LOSS OF THE *MAINE*.

WHAT we as a nation actually did in answer to the Cuban appeal for help was to strive during two long years to fulfil our treaty duties toward Spain. There were Cuban committees in all our coastwise cities who raised funds, and at intervals sent expeditions to aid the insurgents. There was no law under which our Government could prevent their raising money, but there was a law to stop filibustering expeditions, and in executing that law we spent thousands of dollars. We detailed naval as well as revenue ships to watch the filibusters. We did not stop all the expeditions, and the friends of Spain, ignoring the fact that with a force of more than a thousand ships we had been unable to prevent the work of blockade-runners during the Civil War, were quick to accuse us of neglecting our treaty duty. But the truth is we repressed the work of filibusters with such rigor that many of the friends of liberty cried "shame." To the English writer who called us "easily excited Americans," Uncle Sam might reply by paraphrasing the words of a much greater Englishman: "When I consider my opportunities, by God, I stand astounded at my own moderation."

But even the prolonged patience of conscious power had to come to an end when the atrocities of Weyler became fully known. The condition of Cuba was a matter for long consideration in the Cabinet of President McKinley in 1897, and the result was that Minister Stewart L. Woodford said in diplomatic but unmistakable language to the government of Spain:

"You must take Weyler out of Cuba or we will do it for you."

Let no mistake be made when interpreting that demand. It was not a seeking for a fight. It was an assertion that we would have peace not only within but about our borders. It was an assault, but it was the assault of the sanitary officials of an international board of health.

It was our first step in the name of humanity, and for the moment the Spaniards were willing to listen to an appeal to reason. Weyler was recalled on October 2, 1897, and he sailed from

Havana on the 30th. Captain-General Blanco succeeded him. At the same time they promised to give Cuba some such a government as that in Canada. While the island was to remain Spanish territory the people were to govern themselves. With any other civilized nation this proposed change in policy would have brought peace. But Spain could not keep her promise. She had instituted changes in the government of Cuba in former years—she had even given the island representation in the Spanish Congress—without affording any relief to the people of the island. Indeed matters had grown steadily worse instead of better. The promise of an autonomous government as carried out was a sham. A later promise to give relief to the *reconcentrados* was a more infamous sham, because it provided for permitting the starving people to go out to plant when they had neither tools nor seed. And when some did straggle out to gather the spontaneous products of the earth the Spanish soldiers, responsible only to local officers, shot many of them to death for the pleasure they had in inflicting suffering, and to enable their officers to report victories over bodies of insurgents!

In his first warning to the Madrid Government President McKinley set a date, December 1, 1897, by which time some manifest progress must be made in establishing order in Cuba, lacking which a message would be sent to Congress recommending intervention—with arms if necessary. The Spanish Government replied that the time allowed was insufficient, and the date was changed to March 1, 1898.

Meantime, the knowledge that our Government would interfere was spread over the world, and the Cuban tories of Havana with the Spanish rabble began to menace the Americans resident there. The newspapers were particularly virulent in their remarks about Americans, and cartoons were circulated among those who could not read, in order to incite ill-feeling toward us.

In short, there was a steady threat of war in the attitude of the Spanish toward our movements in the interests of peace in Cuba. McKinley and his Cabinet, among whom the active president of the Massachusetts Peace Society held the post of Secretary of the Navy, were determined that they would use every endeavor, consistent with the pacifying of Cuba, to maintain peace, but the threat of war could not be ignored. The North Atlantic Squadron was sent to the Florida Keys, early in January, for the winter's drill. The presence of our ships in such a place was a plain statement that we were in earnest in our demands for order in Cuba—that we were ready to support our demands with force. It was hoped and really be-

The Battle-ship *Maine* Entering the Harbor of Havana.

lieved that when Spain saw our readiness for war she would yield to the demands of reason, and give independence to the unconquered Cubans.

Having started in this line of action we were compelled to hold our course as long as Spain remained obdurate. Theodore Roosevelt, of New York, was then Assistant Secretary of the Navy. While Secretary of the Navy Long used his influence in the Cabinet for the preservation of peace, Assistant Secretary Roosevelt showed his extraordinary energy in preparing the navy for emergencies. But neither work for peace in the Cabinet, nor the drilling of the seamen at Key West could change the aspect of affairs in Cuba—especially in Havana, and at last, in order to provide a refuge for Americans there, in case of a mob attack, the second-class battleship *Maine*, Captain Charles D. Sigsbee, was, on January 25, 1898, ordered to Havana.

This was not only a move in self-defence,

Theodore Roosevelt, Assistant Secretary of the Navy.
From a copyrighted photograph by Rockwood.

and, therefore, clearly within our rights; it was, in a way, a move in the interests of peace. The presence of a war-ship for the protection of Americans would naturally serve as a warning to mobs and prevent attacks on Americans likely to lead to the rupture of peace between the nations. Moreover, before the *Maine* was sent, her mission was fully explained to the Spanish Government and every diplomatic caution to prevent offence was taken.

Hon. John D. Long, Secretary of the Navy.
From a photo by Purdy, Boston (copyright, 1898)

To show the real attitude of Spain during this time we may quote the letter of the Spanish Minister at Washington, Dupuy de Lome, to a Madrid editor, in which occurred these words regarding our President:

"Besides the natural and inevitable coarseness (*groseria*) with which he repeats all that the press and public opinion of Spain has said of Weyler, it shows once more what McKinley is: weak, and catering to the rabble, and, besides, a low politician."

When this was made public, the Minister

admitted he had written it, and resigned. Señor Luis Polo y Bernabe took his place, with many fine words, but the incident increased the Spaniard's hate for the American, and decreased the chance of Spanish yielding to the demand for peace.

As we look back upon the conditions of affairs in the two nations in those days, the contrast between the two peoples (not the officials) is instructive: the one was so vituperative, so ready in the use of adjectives expressive of contempt; the other so incredulous about the threat of war, and, withal, not a little amused by the antics of Spanish spokesmen. Our Government did, indeed, steadily prepare the navy for war, but it is significant of the mental attitude of our people that a bill for an increase of the army's efficiency failed to pass Congress. The Spanish sneeringly said we were absorbed in the pursuits of business, and they were right so far. They added that we would not, and could not, fight effectively, and the Bishop of Santiago de Cuba is said to have asserted that, with ten thousand men, he would land on our shores, march to Washington, and raise the holy emblems of his office along with the flag of Spain over what he supposed was an infidel capitol of an infidel people. He did, without doubt, believe what he said. The Spanish soldiers in Havana, to a man, believed it. They called us pigs, because that was more expressive of contempt, but they regarded us rather as they regarded a bull before the matador appears, sword in hand ; and picadores were not lacking among the Spanish officers in Havana.

Now, at this time many people in Havana— even commissioned army officers — believed

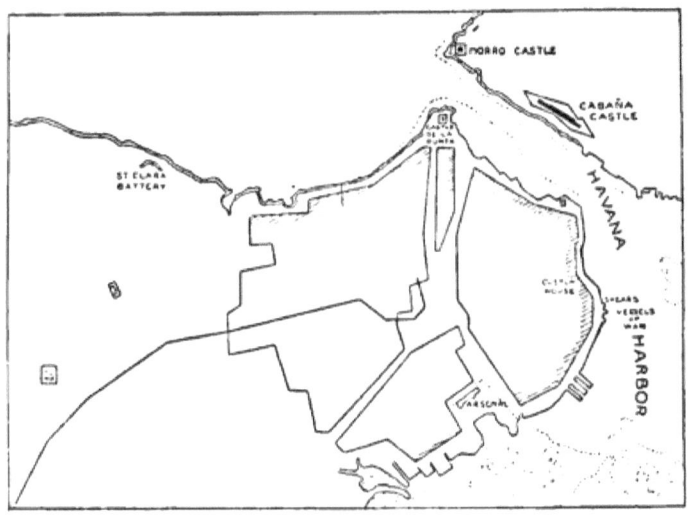

Chart of Havana Harbor.

that the *Maine* was our most powerful battleship, if not our only one, and there she lay moored to Buoy 4, where no man-o'-war had ever been moored, and but rarely a merchantship. There was a huge torpedo under her. It would be easy to explode it and thus seriously weaken the Yankee navy.

At 9.40 o'clock on the night of February

DESTRUCTION OF THE MAINE

15, 1898, the hull of the *Maine* quivered from a heavy shock, the bow rising high out of the water; a second shock was felt, "a low, heavy grumbling" was heard, followed instantly by a booming explosion; the forward decks opened, and a huge mass of flame was flung high in air. Then her electric lights went out and the hull settled down in the water, while officers and men came running up the after ladders, and the cries of men in distress were heard with the splashing of *débris* falling into the water about her. The water was at most but thirty feet deep, and when she had settled on the bottom her upper deck and superstructure were still above water. Here a fierce fire soon spread in the splintered woodwork, to light the hideous scene. Boats at the after end remained uninjured on the davits, and these were got afloat even before the ship was on the bottom.

Captain Sigsbee
From a photograph taken on the St. Paul.

The explosion was forward; the officers were

quartered aft, and so escaped its worst effects. With two exceptions they reached the upper deck and gathered about Captain Sigsbee, who was standing "cold as an iceberg" surveying the scene. But even as the last officer arrived—and their coming was the work of seconds only— the order "Abandon ship" was given, and the survivors on deck entered the boats and began the work of gathering up those who, though burned and broken, were still able to keep afloat after they had been blown into the sea. They even found one man in the water who had been asleep in his hammock under the deck with his shipmates when the explosion occurred, and had been thrown up through the bursting deck and out into the sea unhurt.

The Spanish war-ship, *Alphonso XII.*, was lying near by, and so was the American merchant ship, *City of Washington*. To these ships and to the piers the survivors were taken, and the wounded sent thence to the hospital.

Having taken care of all that survived, Captain Sigsbee wrote a brief dispatch to the Department, telling of the explosion and the plight of the survivors, and added these words:

"Public opinion should be suspended until further report."

When the reporter who carried this dispatch reached the shore, he found it thronged with Spaniards who were looking at the wreck and

The Wreck of the *Maine*.

indulging in the most extravagant expressions of joy. "Hurrah for Spain!" "Death to the Americans!" "To-morrow we shall have good fishing in the harbor!" (referring to the dead sailors) were only a few of the shouts heard there. In the drinking-places that were the resorts of the army officers, the men who were ordinarily satisfied with beer or table claret were opening champagne by the basket.

Next day an official count of the survivors was had. Captain Sigsbee found twenty-four officers (commissioned and warranted) and eighteen men uninjured, and fifty-nine men in the hospital. He reported the lost and missing at 253, among whom were Lieutenant Friend Jenkins, and Assistant Engineer Darwin R. Merritt. There was some discrepancy between the list of the crew as held by Paymaster Littlefield of the *Maine*, and that at the Navy Department, and there was for a time some doubt about the exact number lost. Then, too, some of the wounded died, but the total deaths were at last summed up at 267, including Lieutenant John J. Blandin, who, although apparently in fairly good health for some months after the explosion, developed disease of the spine and brain as a result of the shock, and died on July 16, 1898.

As we recall the days following the destruction of the *Maine*, the state of mind throughout the nation seems astounding—for the appeal for a suspension of judgment made by Captain Sigsbee was everywhere heeded. Immediate preparations for an examination of the wreck were made by the Government, however, not only to recover the bodies of the dead, but to learn all the facts likely to show the origin of the explosion. Divers from our own fleet were sent to Havana, and the services of professional wreckers in New York were secured. Rear Admiral Sicard, commanding the squadron at Key West, on February 17th, appointed, as a Court of Inquiry, Captain W. T. Sampson, of the *Iowa;* Captain French E. Chadwick, of the *New York;* Lieutenant Commander William P. Potter, Executive Officer of the *New York,* and Lieutenant Commander Adolph Marix, as Judge Advocate. To entirely avoid offence to the Spaniards no armed ship was sent to look after the wreck ; but on the 19th when the Spanish officials at Havana proposed a joint Spanish and American investigation into the loss of the *Maine,* the proposition was declined.

The sittings of the Sampson Court were held in secret, and the members were entirely faithful in refusing to divulge what they had learned and determined, until they made their official report, which was transmitted to Congress by the President on March 28th. The important findings in this report were :

" There were two explosions distinctly differ-

Chadwick. *Sampson.* *Potter.* *Marix.*
Court of Inquiry on the Destruction of the *Maine.*

ent in character, with a very short but distinct interval between them, and the forward part of the ship was lifted to a marked degree at the time of the first explosion. The first explosion was more in the nature of a report, like that of a gun, while the second explosion was more open, prolonged, and of greater volume. This second explosion was, in the opinion of the court, caused by the partial explosion of two or more of the forward magazines of the *Maine*.

"At frame 17. the outer shell of the ship, from a point 11 feet 6 inches from the middle line of the ship, and 6 feet above the keel when in its normal position, has been forced up so as to be now about 4 feet above the surface of the water; therefore about 34 feet above where it would be, had the ship sunk uninjured. The outside bottom plating is bent into a reversed V-shape, the after wing of which, about 15 feet broad and 30 feet in length, is doubled back upon itself, against the continuation of the same plating extending forward.

"At frame 18 the vertical keel is broken in two, and the flat keel bent into an angle similar to the angle formed by the outside bottom plating. This break is now about 6 feet below the surface of the water, and about 30 feet above its normal position.

"In the opinion of the Court, this effect

could have been produced only by the explosion of a mine situated under the bottom of the ship at about frame 18, and somewhat on the port side of the ship.

"The Court finds that the loss of the *Maine* was not in any respect due to fault or negligence on the part of any of the officers or members of the crew of said vessel.

"In the opinion of the Court the *Maine* was destroyed by the explosion of a submarine mine, which caused the partial explosion of two or more of her forward magazines."

The testimony taken by the Court was made public with the report. The result was that not only the people of the United States, but all fair-minded people throughout the world, were convinced beyond peradventure that the *Maine* and her men had been hurled to destruction by a deliberate act. They had chosen an hour, too, when the loss of life would be as great as possible, and yet so early that the spectacle might afford pleasure to a vast host of their compatriots.

Nevertheless, while our flags were still at half mast in memory of the dead a Wall Street financier, a representative peace-at-any-price man, telegraphed an appeal for peace, in which appeared this question:

"What is the loss of two hundred and fifty lives to a universal depreciation in values?"

CHAPTER VI

THE DAYS JUST BEFORE THE WAR

A DISPLAY OF POWER THAT WAS WITHOUT EFFECT BECAUSE OF SPANISH OBSTINACY—$50,000,000 FOR DEFENCE—A FLEET OF AUXILIARY WAR-SHIPS—HOW WE LEARNED THAT WE MUST DEPEND ON OUR OWN SHIP-YARDS—SAMPSON IN COMMAND—A COMBINATION THAT GAVE THE REST OF THE WORLD PAUSE.

A STORY told of "Fighting Bob" (Captain Robley D.) Evans, says that he was in the Navy Department one day, after the destruction of the *Maine*, and in the course of a conversation found opportunity to express his views as to what should have been done in the matter. He said:

"If I had been in Admiral Sicard's place I would have taken my entire squadron into Havana harbor the next morning, and then I would have said to them, 'Now, we'll investigate this matter, and let you know what we think about it at once.'"

"If you had done that you would have been recalled and severely reprimanded," said Secretary Long, somewhat warmly. The captain's eyes twinkled, as he replied:

"I don't doubt that, sir; but the people would have made me President at the next election." At that the Secretary is said to have winced a wee bit and turned the conversation to something else.

Whether true or not the story illustrates the feelings of the majority of the naval officers after the murder of the *Maine's* crew. They think, even now, that war would have been avoided by the course of action laid down by Captain Evans, but the people, as a whole, did really suspend judgment until the report of the Sampson Court; that is to say, if the Court had reported an internal explosion only, the people would have believed it implicitly. But the chief facts that proved Spanish treachery became known before the seal of secrecy was placed on the lips of all naval officers connected with the investigation. Ensign W. V. N. Powelson, an expert in naval architecture, saw that the bottom plates of the *Maine* were above water and he learned that her keel was just awash. He told these facts to a personal friend and so they got into print. There was but one conclusion from those facts. The smile faded from the faces of our people, who had been amused by Spanish braggadocio. The doubts disappeared from the minds of those who had

clung to the idea that the Spanish might have
been, to some extent, justified in their policy
in Cuba. There was still an idea that the Cubans,
knowing well the effect such an outrage
would have, might have placed the torpedo;
not a few of the Americans who have had
dealings with the insurgents believe they were
entirely capable of the atrocity; but, without
exception, every American who was in Havana,
and every other foreigner, for that matter, has
said that the Spanish patrol of the harbor was
entirely efficient, and that it was only by the
action of Spanish officials that a mine could have
been placed anywhere in the bay. In no considerable
degree did what we call "fake" news
or hysterical editorials influence the sober judgment
of the people regarding their duty toward
Spain. It was the spread of the real facts, the
growth of actual knowledge of what the Spaniards
in Cuba stood for and what they had done
there, that forced the conviction upon us that
we must drive them to the further side of the
sea. The conviction was literally forced upon
unwilling minds. The people who knew the
Cubans best, felt, and many of them said, that
the whole hybrid race was not worth one good
American life. While sitting on the hotel
veranda at Key West, distinctively a Cuban
settlement, a survivor of the *Maine* said:

"If we do have to fight Spain, the first thing

we'll do after we've licked her is to make her take Key West back," and the whole audience laughed heartily and approvingly. But when the laugh was ended it was agreed that the production of such a race on our borders was sufficient cause of war in itself. Further than that it was not the destruction of our battle-ship and the murder of our sailors, but it was the existence of a state of affairs where such an infamy was possible that compelled us to fight.

By the handling of our war-ships we had endeavored to educate the Spanish into a knowledge that we had material of war fit for a conflict, but because we showed remarkable self-restraint after the destruction of the *Maine* —showed the self-restraint of a determined race instead of the froth of an impulsive one— they were convinced that our stock-brokers would rule us in the interest of preserving values. So the Spanish Government thought to set us running by a menace—they demanded the recall of Consul-General Lee. It was a very diplomatic demand in its form, but it was understood for what it was intended, and it was promptly refused. This menace was made on Saturday, March 5th. It was refused the same day, and on the following Monday the President, with the leaders in Congress, determined on an act that, it was hoped, would convince Spain of the entire hopelessness of her course toward our people and the Cubans. On Tuesday, March 8th, a bill was introduced into both houses appropriating $50,000,000 for the defence of the nation. It was to be used by the President at his discretion, absolutely unhampered by any restriction. The bill passed unanimously and without debate.

Now, at that time the Treasury had an available cash balance of $224,541,637. To fully understand what the act of Congress meant we must recall the fact that Spain at that time had been unable to pay her troops in Cuba for many months and that she had been a beggar at the doors of European money-lenders—had secured loans only at such sacrifices as are made to pawn-brokers. We were giving, as we supposed, an effectual answer to Spanish assertions that we were full of greed for money and devoid of manhood, but the fact that we appropriated only about one-fifth of our available cash was considered by the Spanish, rather than the potential energy of the sum appropriated. The fact that we had appropriated but one-fifth indicated, to their minds, that we were just what they had supposed us to be. In proof of this may be quoted an article from the leading Spanish illustrated periodical—*La Illustracion*—regarding our navy. It asserted that our navy was "manned by hirelings who calculate, while they are fighting, what their value, in cents, should be worth to them;" that it was a "navy without traditions of any kind," and that the ships were all poor imitations of European vessels, that our "tests of armor and other work were unsatisfactory," and that "it will be nothing remarkable, if, in a short time, we see all these vessels go to the rubbish heap."

It was soon apparent that the chief object in view when the $50,000,000 was appropriated would not be attained, and we at once began using the money not for a defence fund, as it was called, but to prepare for an aggressive war.

The squadron at Key West at this time included the *New York*, Captain French E. Chadwick; *Iowa*, Captain William T. Sampson; *Texas*, Captain John W. Philip; *Massachusetts*, Captain Francis J. Higginson; *Indiana*, Captain Henry C. Taylor; *Marblehead*, Captain Bowman H. McCalla; *Montgomery*, Captain George A. Converse; *Nashville*, Captain Washburn Maynard; *Detroit*, Captain James H. Dayton; the *Fern* (transport), Captain William S. Cowles, and two or three torpedo-boats. To increase this force the monitors *Puritan*, *Amphitrite*, *Miantonomoh* and *Terror* were overhauled and ordered to Key West. The South American squadron under Captain Chester, which included the *Cincinnati*, the *Bancroft*, and the *Castine*, started north. Two curious gun-boats that had upper works like a battle-ship and were built for the China rivers, the *Wilmington* and the *Helena*, were turned from their destination to increase the growing fleet. The *Newport* had a survey-

Brooklyn, Armored Cruiser. Dimensions, 400.5 × 65, draft, 27, displacement, 9,215. Speed, 22 knots. Main Battery, eight eight-inch, twelve five-inch guns.

ing party on the Nicaragua Canal-route, but the survey was abandoned, and the officers and the ship ordered where they could be of service should war come.

By March 18th, the growth of hostile feelings in Spain impelled the formation of what was called a flying squadron at Hampton Roads, for the protection of our coast in case the Spanish cruisers should force the fighting. Captain W. S. Schley was placed in command there, with his flag on the *Brooklyn*. The *Massachusetts* and the *Texas* were sent from Key West, and to these were added the unequalled flyers *Minneapolis* and *Columbia*. That was a remarkable combination for a battle line, but it had its advantages in the way of a solid nucleus with the flyers for scouts.

Meantime the conferences that had been held from time to time during the winter, between the Navy Department officials and the manufacturers of war material began to have practical results. An order for $2,800,000 worth of projectiles was placed in one day (March 12th), for instance. Then Captain Frederick Rodgers, Lieutenant-Commander J. D. J. Kelley, Naval-Constructor J. G. Tawresey, Chief-Engineer Albert F. Dixon and Lieutenant Nathan Sargeant were appointed as a board to charter and buy merchant ships and yachts that might be converted into men-o'-war of some efficiency. The Navy Department had some years before begun gathering data regarding private vessels flying the American flag, with a view of such an emergency as was now at hand, and Congress had helped on this work by pro-

Copyright, 1898, by B. H. Hart.

Texas, Second Class Battle-ship. Dimensions, 318×57; draft, 24.5; displacement, 6,315. Speed, 17.8 knots. Main Battery: two twelve-inch six six-inch guns.

viding for the transfer of the two British-built liners, *New York* and *Paris*, to our flag, along with the construction of those companion flyers, the *St. Louis* and *St. Paul* in an American yard (the Cramp's). Here were four of the swiftest class of vessels in the world that could be chartered, ready for use, as soon as guns could be mounted on emplacements already prepared. This made an admirable beginning, but to them were added some dozens of smaller but very efficient boats, either purchased or chartered, of some of which we heard in actual battle, while a few vessels which the board rejected as worthless were sold to the Government in spite of the board, because their owners had influence. But while this altogether discreditable fact must be stated, in order that the shame of it may tend to prevent similar operations in future, it should be added that such dealings were far less numerous by count and, it is said by naval officers, less numerous in proportion to the whole number purchased, than appeared during the Civil War. Our patriotism was more apparent in this war, and our greed less.

Of auxiliary "cruisers and yachts," the naval list of July, 1898, contained thirty-eight; but that list is very misleading, as a reference to the squadron lists printed elsewhere in the list shows. In all, more than fifty vessels, ranging in size from yachts of little more than 100 tons up to the liners of 16,000 tons displacement, were added to the navy, placed in command of naval officers, armed with guns suitable for their strength, and sent sooner or later where actual service was to be expected. To these fighting and despatch-vessels were added later a ship fitted as a floating hospital, the *Solace;* another as a floating machine-shop, the *Vulcan;* and a third fitted to distil fresh water from the sea, the *Iris*—most useful and well fitted for the purpose, every one. We also made use of revenue-cutters and light-house supply-ships.

That guns were found for these auxiliary fighting-ships, with ammunition to feed them was due in part to the foresight of Congress in appropriating money several years before to provide guns for such an emergency, and to the activity and efficiency of the ordnance officers in charge of the gun-factory at Washington—Captain Charles O'Neil, assisted by Lieutenants Frank S. Fletcher, Albert M. Beecher, and Isaac K. Seymour.

And in connection with these converted merchantmen it should be said that the increased demand for seamen which came as they were commissioned was met to a large extent by the men of the naval militia, the citizen sailors, organized in various coastwise and lake towns for training as man-o'-war fighters. The skill as well as the cool bravery which these men showed afloat, as will be told farther on, made their officers proud of them.

In this way several hundred guns, thoroughly effective in a fight with unprotected ships (six-pounders and larger), were sent afloat in the hands of men who could see through the sights, while a handful of the swiftest yachts purchased, such as the *Mayflower*, with her speed of seventeen knots, were fitted with torpedo-tubes and named torpedo-boat destroyers. As compared with the real destroyers of which Spain made boast these looked rather ridiculous, for they were not only relatively slow but they towered in the air like tenement-houses. Nevertheless they served a useful purpose.

Another plan for strengthening our defences was in ordering some of the old single-turret monitors of the *Jason* class into service at various ports—seven in all being found fit for use. They carried big smooth-bore guns, a weapon not in favor, these days, but entirely efficient against unarmored cruisers or converted merchantmen should Spain show sufficient enterprise to send such vessels to hover off our ports.

The purchase and arming of merchant vessels went on exactly as our statesmen had foreseen, but one other and a very important resource in time of danger on which they had counted almost failed us. We had always hoped to buy war-ships abroad while yet diplomatic relations should be maintained, and we had stopped the building of ships rather sooner than we should have done but for this supposed resource. The time for purchase abroad was at hand when the $50,000,000 was appropriated, but with cash in our hands and liberality behind

New Orleans (ex *Amazonas*), Protected Cruiser (British built). Dimensions, 330 × 44; draft, 17; displacement, 3,600. Speed, 20 knots. Main Battery, six six-inch, four 4.7-inch guns.

the offers we were able to get just one effective ship—the *New Orleans*, formerly the *Amazonas*, built in England for Brazil. We did get the *Albany*, formerly the *Abreu*, but she was not completed and she could not be made ready before war was declared. We also got two torpedo-boats—one a good destroyer that did not reach us, and the other a sixty-foot harbor-defence mosquito.

We also got an 1,800-ton gun-boat, built in England in 1882 for Portugal. She was called *Diogenes*. Portugal did not complete the purchase, and her builders remodelled her on speculation and we got her—not at all a bad ship, but not a notable addition to the navy either. We named her the *Topeka*.

The two cruisers were purchased by Lieutenant John C. Colwell, the Naval *Attaché* in London. We sent Commander W. H. Brownson, whose reputation as a diplomat as well as a fighter is well established in the navy, to Europe to buy more, but there was nothing in the market, and we thereby learned that in future we must depend entirely on our own resources—a good lesson learned at a small price.

The purchase of the Brazilian cruisers was effected on March 14th. They are sister ships of the protected-cruiser class. There is a protective deck three inches thick on the slopes, and with full bunkers the coal gives some protection. Engines of 7,500 horse-power give a speed of twenty knots. The displacement is 3,600 tons, being somewhat larger than our own *Cincinnati* and *Raleigh*, with which they have been compared. In hull and machinery there is no great difference between them and our own designs, though they are about a knot swifter. But when we come to compare the guns, which are of the latest British make, we find a tremendous difference. For the British-built gun is fifty calibres long where ours are but forty; the projectile has a muzzle velocity of 2,780 feet per second to our 2,150, and its striking energy is 5,373 tons to our 3,204. The

Armstrong Gun on the *New Orleans*.

British projectile should pierce twenty-two inches of wrought iron to our fifteen. The British six-inch rifle is but little less powerful than our first eight-inch guns. The writer remembers that the naval officers at Key West used to talk about those guns in March with a degree of respect that was not appreciated by the unlearned, but after she arrived one look at the *New Orleans*, with her guns looking (for length) like old-time spars sticking from her sides, was enough to awaken awe as well as reverence.

While we were busy buying ships, Admiral

A Six-inch Gun on the *New Orleans*.

Sicard, at Key West, was engaged daily in preparing his men, as well as his ships, for war. Even before the $50,000,000 was appropriated, Assistant Secretary of the Navy Roosevelt had managed to get supplies of ammunition for target-practice, but once the big sum was in hand there was absolutely no stint on ammunition so expended. The importance of this matter cannot be exaggerated. Before war threatened, our allowance for naval target-practice was ridiculous; it was outrageously insufficient. The regulations for target-practice, issued on July 22, 1897, provided that each gun of a calibre of ten inches or greater should be fired once with a full service-charge, and eight times with a reduced charge every ——, well, now, in what period of time does the uninformed reader suppose? Every month, in order to make our man behind the gun the most skilful in the world? That would be a reasonable guess, but those *nine* shots were to serve for a *year's* target-practice! Imagine a trap-shooter keeping himself in training by firing nine shots a year! Even the guns of the rapid-fire batteries of four-inch and five-inch calibre, which we were to use in repelling a torpedo-boat destroyer later on, were to be fired but twenty-five times in a year. But Roosevelt changed all that. The pop and roar of target-practice made the welkin ring the whole day long where the ships of our squadron lay. The

Admiral Sicard, Commanding the North Atlantic Squadron Before the War.

largest guns were not fired often with full-service charges, more is the pity, but what is called sub-calibre practice—the firing of a one-pounder rifle fitted into the axis of the big bore, by which the eye of the gunner was fairly well trained—was kept going steadily.

Emphasis should be given to any statement regarding the work of Admiral Sicard before war began. We know now what "the man behind the gun" was able to do when the test came, and it should not be forgotten that it was Sicard who, to a great extent, trained the man. The training given our tars in the previous days of peace, though as good as that of other navies, was wholly inadequate if judged in the light of our naval traditions. And yet, during all those days of constant care and labor, the Admiral was suffering from a form of malaria due to the Gulf climate, and this at last overcame him so that he was obliged to give way. He was relieved from duty on March 24th, and Captain William T. Sampson, of the *Iowa*, who had served as chairman of the *Maine* Court of Inquiry, was placed in command of the squadron.

Selecting the man who had convinced the world of the treachery of the Spanish in the *Maine* affair was a wise bit of diplomacy—an expression of supreme confidence in that Court of Inquiry. But there was a still more important reason for giving him the command, and that was his manifest fitness, as appeared in his record in every post he had held since entering the service. He had shown conspicuous bravery at Charleston, in the Civil War, where he faced a fire so fierce that he sent all of his men to cover while he alone stood exposed to pilot the ship (the *Patapsco*), and throughout his service in various bureaus of the Naval Department, as well as in command at sea, he had made a reputation as one who could be depended on in any situation. As a writer on naval subjects he was unsurpassed for breadth and lucidity, and it is not unlikely that a paper read by him before the Naval Institute, in 1889, on "The Naval Defence of the Coast," was an important factor in the decision to select him. At any rate that paper established his reputation as a tactician. It is a notable fact that, although Sampson was fourth on the list of captains, and there were men of higher rank available, no protest was made when he was appointed. Captain Robley D. Evans took Sampson's place on the *Iowa*.

To sum up the work in connection with the navy, during the weeks of peace following the destruction of the *Maine*, it is apparent that we made every effort to strengthen our fleet and improve our men afloat—in short to prepare for war; and we were so successful that the best-informed officers of the navy who were gathered at Key West, were of the opinion that Spain would see the hopelessness of a conflict, and gracefully yield to overwhelming force. But the Spanish people were sincere in their belief that we were mere traders devoid of courage, as well as of every sense of honor. Moreover, they had hope in the jealous prejudice that our national prosperity

Captain Robley D. Evans, Commanding the *Iowa*.

had excited throughout the continent of Europe. They were confident that a combination of European powers would be formed, in which even England would join, to dictate to us what we should do in the Caribbean Sea, just as they had dictated what Turkey should do in the Mediterranean. And they were not without reason in this confidence, for, although the official documents have not been printed, we know that Germany and France were eager to join them against us, and that the one thing that prevented the combination was the generous declaration of the British Government that the moment the combination was consummated, the whole British fleet should be placed at our disposal. The Anglo-Saxon race was at last united for a moment, and in their presence the rest of the world instantly bowed in submission.

CHAPTER VII

THE WAR MESSAGE

SUMMARY OF REASONS FOR AMERICAN INTERVENTION IN CUBAN AFFAIRS—AGGRAVATING PROOF OF WORK OF SPANISH SPIES AND SPANISH INSINCERITY—DIPLOMATIC RELATIONS ENDED—THREATENING MOVEMENTS OF WAR-SHIPS.

Now although the civilized nations of Europe were unwilling to combine against England and the United States, nothing could prevent Spain's fighting to save Cuba. As has been recently pointed out by Captain F. E. Chadwick, the Spanish are always stubborn in defence. Even Spanish officials, who should have known better, believed they still might win, and those who were hopeless of success were compelled to lead on to war in obedience to the popular demand, lest a civil war come upon them through an uprising of the Carlists.

Spain had sent her beautiful 7,000 ton cruiser, the *Vizcaya*, to New York, to let us see what able ships floated her blood-and-gold banner. Later she sent a sister-ship, the *Oquendo*, to Havana, to cheer the hearts of her forces there. The two vessels lay there in the month of March, almost within hearing of the cheerful roar of our target practice at Key West.

As we strengthened our squadron there, Spain protested on the ground that we were threatening her and trying to overawe the government in Cuba for the benefit of the insurgents, which was true so far as the charge of threatening her was concerned. As we did not withdraw any of our force, but steadily increased it instead, Spain retaliated, so to speak, by sending out a squadron, under Admiral Cervera, to the Canary Islands, during the latter part of March. The make-up of this squadron was a matter of speculation, at the time; but it eventually included four of the big torpedo-boat destroyers like the *Furor*, three torpedo-boats, with a supply ship, the *City of Cadiz*, and the cruisers *Maria Teresa* and *Cristobal Colon*.

A report that the squadron had left the Canaries was received at Washington on April 2d. Meantime, reports had been flying about to the effect that the squadron was already in San Juan, Porto Rico. These reports tried the nerves of our naval officers not a little, for with seven efficient torpedo-boats in hand there was no telling what an able Spanish admiral might do. A direct request was made by a number of officers, who visited the President, for a blockade of San Juan to prevent the Spaniards entering there to refit, if they had not done so, and to hold them in if already there; but the President was not yet ready for war, and his conservatism was in the end justified.

Then it was learned that the Spanish squadron had gone to the Cape Verde Islands, where the *Vizcaya* and the *Oquendo* joined them, and thereafter the rumors regarding it were so numerous and contradictory as to be absolutely bewildering. Meantime, it must not be forgotten that our squadron in the far East, of which the *Olympia* carried the flag of Commodore Dewey, had been considering at Hong Kong an attack on Manila, while our battle-ship *Oregon* had sailed from San Francisco on March 19th, bound to Key West by the way of the Straits of Magellan.

The iteration and reiteration of the details of all the preparations for war stirred our people to a point where war and not peace was wanted. The battle-cry, "Remember the *Maine*" had been blazoned by the "jingoes," until the words danced before eyes that were loath to behold them. The evidence of Spanish atrocity and incapacity in Cuba was increased by the testimony of some of our own Congressmen, who went there to see for themselves. The demand that the President act on the report of the *Maine* Court of Inquiry grew rapidly under all this, but he was still slow to act—too slow to please a portion of our people. Nevertheless, a time came when action was inevitable. A message reciting the condition of affairs in Cuba and our interest therein, was prepared, and it was to have been sent to Congress on April 6th, with a request that the whole matter be acted upon at once. And this would have been done but for an appeal from Consul-General Lee, at Havana, for enough delay to enable him to get the Americans then in Cuba safely away. The Spanish population was growing so wild as to endanger the lives of all Americans, even that of General Lee himself, although he steadily refused to believe himself in danger, when it was patent to all other intelligent Americans there.

An exodus of Americans from Cuba followed. There were not many there—a few hundred in all, and most of these of Cuban birth—but on April 9th the exodus was completed. On that day, General Lee called at the palace to bid adieu, officially, to Captain-General Blanco. When he sent in his card, a porter came out and said Blanco was not well and could not receive callers.

At that time the transport *Fern*, the survey steamer *Bache*, and the Plant Line steamer *Olivette* plying between Tampa and Havana were in port. General Lee hauled down the flag over the Consulate, turned the consular affairs over to the British consul, and at 11 o'clock, on April 9th, boarded the *Fern*.

At about 5 o'clock that afternoon, the three steamers passed out of the harbor in a slow procession, with every passenger on deck looking with mixed amusement and regret toward the shore, where the Spaniards had swarmed to the water's edge and, frothing at the mouth in their frenzy, were hurling invectives at the ships and everyone on board.

When it was learned that General Lee had reached the United States, the President sent (April 11th) to Congress the long-looked-for message on the state of affairs in Cuba. It was about six thousand words in length. It began with the words, "Obedient to that precept of the Constitution which commands the President to give, from time to time, to the Congress information of the state of the Union, and to recommend to their consideration such measures as he shall judge necessary and expedient, it becomes my duty to address your body with regard to the grave crisis that has arisen in the relations of the United States with Spain." Thereafter he recounted the half-century of revolutions in Cuba, our efforts and expense in preventing the work of filibusters, the shocking results of Weyler's order of October 21, 1896, concentrating the rural population in the garrisoned towns, our contributions of food to the unfortunates, the deeds showing that the Spaniards were not making war on, but were exterminating the Cubans, our offers of friendly intervention and other peaceful acts to end the horrors, and the utter failure of Spain to heed us and to end them herself. The destruction of the *Maine* was treated only as one incident among many that proved the Spanish Government at once impotent and utterly vicious. It was undeniable that "the forcible intervention of the United States, as a neutral, to stop the war, according to the large dictates of humanity, and following many historical precedents, is justifiable on rational grounds."

"The grounds for such intervention may be briefly summarized as follows," said the message.

" First.—In the cause of humanity, and to put an end to the barbarities, starvation, and horrible miseries now existing there, and which the parties to the conflict are either unable or unwilling to stop or mitigate. It is no answer to say this is all in another country, belonging to another nation, and is, therefore, none of our business. It is specially our duty, for it is right at our door.

" Second.—We owe it to our citizens in Cuba to afford them that protection and indemnity for life which no government there can or will afford, and to that end to terminate the conditions that deprive them of legal protection.

"Third.— Right to intervene may be justified by the very serious injury to the commerce, trade, and business of our people, and by the wanton destruction of property and devastation of the island.

"Fourth (and which is of the most importance)—The present condition of affairs is a constant menace to our peace, and entails upon this Government an enormous expense. With such a conflict waged for years in an island so near us, and with which our people have such trade and business relations, when the lives and liberty of our citizens are in constant danger, and their property and themselves ruined, when our trading-vessels are liable to seizure, and are seized, at our very door by war-ships of a foreign nation ; the expeditions of filibustering that we are powerless to prevent altogether, and the irritating questions and entanglements thus arising—all these and others that I need not mention, with the resulting strained relations, are a constant menace to our peace and compel us to keep on a semi-war footing with a nation with which we are at peace."

In conclusion, "the only hope of relief and repose from a condition which can no longer be endured is the enforced pacification of Cuba. In the name of humanity, in the name of civilization, in behalf of endangered American interests, which give us the right and the duty to speak and to act, the war in Cuba must stop.

"In view of these facts and these considerations I ask the Congress to authorize and empower the President to take measures to secure a full and final termination of hostilities between the Government of Spain and the people of Cuba, and to secure in the island the establishment of a stable government capable of maintaining order and observing its international obligations, insuring peace and tranquillity, and the security of its citizens as well as our own; and to use the military and naval forces of the United States as may be necessary for these purposes. And in the interests of humanity, and to aid in preserving the lives of the starving people of the island, I recommend that the distribution of food and supplies be continued, and that an appropriation be made out of the public treasury to supplement the charity of our citizens."

On the very day that this message was sent to Congress, the Spanish Government notified McKinley that an armistice would be proclaimed at once in Cuba. The notice said that every preparation had been made for placing in operation the new autonomous government in a manner giving the widest liberty to Cubans.

It was characteristic of the Spanish Government to delay this notice until the President's message was, figuratively speaking, in the hands of the messenger bound to the Capitol. The delay showed conclusively that Spanish spies knew exactly what the President was doing, and, further, that the offer of the armistice was deliberately held back to the last moment in the hope that the offer would not be necessary.

It recalls forcefully the time when Minister Daniel Sickles demanded the release of the *Aspinwall*, and the evasions of Sagasta, who was then, as in this year, Prime Minister; and how, when Sickles turned to leave, saying the United States would at once recognize the Cuban insurgents as belligerents, Sagasta called him back to say that the Cabinet had, on the day before, decided to release the ship.

In fact, the Spanish offer of an armistice at this time, and under such circumstances, is a last proof of the utter insincerity of the Spanish Government in all the proposals it had made for the reformation of Cuban affairs.

The offer of an armistice did not stop the message. If it had any influence, it was simply to rouse further indignation. McKinley had asked for authority "to use the military and naval forces of the United States as may be necessary" to establish a stable government in Cuba. Various measures were proposed in answer to this request, and several days were consumed in discussing them ; but it was a time when the nation demanded patriots in place of politicians, and Congress, as a whole, answered the demand. There were just enough small men who persisted, as politicians, to emphasize the fact, manifest in our history since the adoption of our present Constitution, that when a real peril threatens us, our legislators, as representatives of the people, brush aside all petty affairs and considerations to face the emergency man-fashion. On April 18th all differences were compromised and a joint resolution passed that, after reciting briefly the evils that compelled action, declared :

"That the people of the island of Cuba are, and of right ought to be, free and independent.

"That it is the duty of the United States to demand, and the Government of the United States does hereby demand, that the Government of Spain at once relinquish its authority and government in the island of Cuba and withdraw its land and naval forces from Cuba and Cuban waters.

"That the President of the United States be, and he hereby is, directed and empowered to use the entire land and naval forces of the United States, and to call into the actual service of the United States the militia of the several States to such an extent as may be necessary to carry these resolutions into effect.

"That the United States hereby disclaims any disposition or intention to exercise sovereignty, jurisdiction, or control over said island, except for the pacification thereof, and asserts its determination, when that is accomplished, to leave the government and control of the island to its people." The vote in the House stood 310 to 6.

This act was signed by the President at 11.24 o'clock on Wednesday morning, April 20, 1898. Notice of this was sent to the Spanish Minister, Señor Polo y Bernabe, who requested and received his passports at once, and at 7.20 o'clock that night he left Washington. An ultimatum to Spain was despatched, but it was a mere formality. While McKinley was signing the joint resolution, Prime Minister Sagasta was making a speech to the Spanish Cortes, saying:

"To crown all, they have tried to throw against us a most infamous calumny, which fills all Spaniards with the holiest indignation against the villany of those who try to take away from us our indisputable sovereign rights over a cherished piece of Spanish territory. Acts, not words, are required. Let the present children of Spain answer in the same manner our fathers did when they were also wronged."

Our ultimatum reached Madrid by cable on the 20th, but the Spaniards refused to receive it. On the morning of the 21st our Minister there, Stewart L. Woodford, was informed that "the diplomatic relations which formerly existed between the two countries" were ended, and at 11.45 the affairs of our legation were turned over to Secretary Barclay, of the British Embassy. A few hours later Woodford and all the American officials were *en route* from the country, and although a formal declaration of war by our Congress and the Spanish Cortes was delayed a day or two, the first gun of the war was fired at 7.02 o'clock the next morning, Friday, April 22, 1898.

CHAPTER VIII

FIRST SHOT OF THE WAR

CAPTURE OF THE SPANISH MERCHANTMAN *BUENAVENTURA* BY THE GUN-BOAT *NASHVILLE*—HIS FLAG HOISTED IN HONOR OF THE FINE AMERICAN SQUADRON BETRAYED HIM—OFFICIAL PROCLAMATION OF THE BLOCKADE OF CUBAN PORTS.

THE honor of firing the first gun in the war with Spain belongs to our gun-boat—unsurpassed in her class—the *Nashville*, Captain Washburn Maynard in command. The circumstances in connection with the event were entirely unexpected in the squadron, but were interesting enough for record here, aside from the fact that they were connected with the first open act of hostility against the Spanish flag.

During the days between the President's message in connection with the report of the *Maine* Court and the signing of the Cuban joint resolutions, the men of the squadron assembled at Key West had been, as a whole, pessimists in all conversations regarding the possibility of war. If the truth be told, they wished that war might come. Doubtless there was an element of selfishness in the wish, but the writer, who talked with them every day, could not help seeing the broad view in which they regarded the matter. To repeat all they said would be to write an unanswerable essay on the moral superiority of some ambitions prominent in war-time over the ambition that

Nashville, Gun-boat. Dimensions, 220 x 38; draft, 11; displacement, 1,371. Speed, 16 knots. Main Battery, eight four-inch guns.

is most prominent in peace, with the unavoidable conclusion that the exercise of these superior ambitions is necessary to the life of the nation. But while they wished, they did not really hope for war. "One side or the other is pretty sure to back out" was the substance of the common remark.

The long veranda of the only hotel worth

FIRST SHOT OF THE WAR

mentioning in Key West was thronged with them on the afternoon of the eventful April 21st, when Minister Woodford was told to leave Madrid, and the talk was in the usual vein, although the doings in Congress during the two days just past were in a path leading straight to open war. The fact is, only meagre reports of even the most important events

Captain Maynard of the *Nashville*.

were received in Key West. Even Admiral Sampson (he had been appointed acting rear-admiral some days earlier) had good reason to complain of the neglect of the authorities in keeping him posted, for he often received his first news of important events through the bulletins sent to newspaper reporters from their Washington offices. But near the middle of the afternoon a long despatch came to Sampson, which shall be given farther on, and near the same hour (3 o'clock) three reporters of different papers were notified by their home offices that the squadron would sail for Cuba next morning.

The spread of this news through the crowd of officers was rapid and animating, and when the usual hour for going off to the ships came (5 o'clock) the pier at the naval station showed a degree of life and cheer that had not been known there since the *Virginius* affair.

The despatch that came to Admiral Sampson contained the definite order to sail, and along with it was the following proclamation, which the ship's printer struck off in circular form during the afternoon for distribution among the vessels of the squadron:

BLOCKADE OF CUBAN PORTS BY THE PRESIDENT OF THE UNITED STATES OF AMERICA.

A Proclamation.

Whereas, By a joint resolution passed by the Congress, and approved April 20, 1898, and communicated to the government of Spain, it was demanded that said government at once relinquish its authority and government in the Island of Cuba, and withdraw the land and naval forces from Cuba and Cuban waters, and the President of the United States was directed and empowered to use the land and naval forces of the United States and to call into the actual service of the United States the militia of the several States to such extent as might be necessary to carry said resolution into effect; and

Whereas, In carrying into effect said resolution the President of the United States deems it necessary to set on foot and maintain a blockade of the north coast of Cuba, including ports of said coast between Cardenas and Bahia Honda, and the port of Cienfuegos on the south coast of Cuba, aforesaid, in pursuance of the laws of the United States and the laws of nations applicable to such cases.

An efficient force will be posted so as to prevent the exit of vessels from the ports aforesaid. Any neutral vessel approaching any of said ports, or attempting to leave the same without notice or knowledge of the establishments of such blockade, will be duly warned by the commander of the blockading force, who will endorse on her register the fact, and the date of such warning, where such endorsement was made, and if the same vessel shall again attempt to enter any blockaded port, she will be captured and sent to the nearest convenient port for such proceedings against her and her cargo, as prizes, as may be deemed advisable. Neutral vessels lying in any of said ports at the time of the establishment of such blockade will be allowed thirty days to issue therefrom.

In witness whereof, I have hereunto set my hand and caused the Seal of the United States to be affixed.

(SEAL.) Done at the City of Washington, this 22d day of April, A.D. 1898, and of the independence of the United States the one hundred and twenty-second.

WILLIAM McKINLEY.

By the President.
JOHN SHERMAN,
Secretary of State.

But while this was evidence that war actually existed there was no stir on the fleet that night to betoken the events of the next day. The flags were hauled down at sunset; the anchor watches came on duty; the usual off-shore guard went out to patrol the sea beyond the flag-ship; the night was entirely calm as to the weather and without unusual event as to the shipping.

At daylight the *New York*, the *Iowa*, and the *Indiana* were lying at anchor off Sand Key light. The guard-boats *Detroit* and *Nashville* were steaming slowly to and fro several miles away to the south, while the *Castine*, *Newport*, *Machias* and a naval tug were lying inside the battle-ships. The scene was well-nigh devoid of life as the morning light first suffused the east, but in a few moments the smoke-stacks of the various ships, both at Sand Key and within the harbor, showed that the crews were firing up. In the growing day the guard-boats came in

Foote, Torpedo-boat. 160 x 16; draft, 5, displacement, 142. Speed, 24.5 knots. Battery, three eighteen-inch torpedo tubes, three one-pounder guns.

near the flag-ship where the torpedo-boat *Foote*, from the inner harbor, joined them, and the gun-boat *Helena* came to the end of the line of smaller boats.

A little later long lines of signal flags fluttered to the yard-arm on the foremast of the flag-ship, and in answer to these the ships all got up anchor, the smaller ships formed a line parallel with that of the armored ships, and the whole squadron headed slowly away toward Havana. The first turn of the propellers in aggressive action was made as the sun appeared. It was a solemn moment—everyone there knew that it was so, and yet few, indeed, seemed to realize the full importance of what was going on. The ships had been stripped for action for weeks, and they had been painted to the neutral tint of lead. There was no hustling at the guns nor any blare of trumpet even—there was no new sign of war save only as the signal flags on the *New York* gave orders to the other ships.

To add to the peacefulness of the scene, there were two or three merchant vessels at anchor in the roadstead, here and there a tiny fisherman from Key West went beating about, and a couple of yachts, employed as newspaper despatch-boats, were near at hand, while off on the western horizon was seen the smoke of a merchant steamer bound along the usual route through the Gulf Stream to the North Atlantic.

By 7 o'clock this steam merchantman had arrived so near to the squadron that lookouts with good glasses could see she was a black-hulled craft with two masts, and a single smoke-stack, while on her deck was a cargo of lumber that gave her a noticeable list to port. Our lookouts regarded her with idle curiosity, but the captain of the merchantman being filled with admiration for the "fine-looking lot of war-ships flying the American flag," determined to show his own colors, and sent a bare-footed sailor to hoist them to the little flag-staff above the taffrail and stand by to dip them in honor of the American flag-ship when passing the squadron.

Captain Chadwick of the New York.

As this sailor began bending his flag to the halyards, the lookout on our flag-ship suddenly became intensely interested, and a moment later as the colors floated up, spread wide by the gentle breeze, he removed the glass from his eye, and bending over his perch in the fighting top looked down expectantly to the bridge where Admiral Sampson, Captain Chadwick, and some other officers were standing. As he did so, an officer hailed him, saying.

"What flag is that?"

"It is Spanish, sir," he replied.

Two lines of signal flags rose quickly aloft

to the yard above his head, and while yet they were travelling to the yard, the helm of the *Nashville* was put hard over to port and she turned sharp off to cross the merchantman's bow. When barely a ship's length from the squadron line, Lieutenant Dillingham, her executive officer, ordered Gunner Patrick Mallia to fire a blank shot from the after gun (a four-inch rifle) on the port side of the ship. The puffing smoke, the splash of the wad a hundred yards away, and the roar of the discharge mystified the merchantman.

"What kind of a manœuvre are those warships going through that one should do that?" he said to himself, as he held on his way, but before his propeller had turned over a dozen times more the gun spurted flame and smoke again and this time something went screaming away across his bows, clipping wave-crests as it sped, until it finally tumbled and disappeared a half mile beyond his ship. There was no mistaking that. A solid shot had been fired across his bows, and he clawed the air in his haste to stop his engine and get his flag down. Running down close to the Spaniard the *Nashville* sent Ensign Thomas P. Magruder with a prize crew on board. They found that she was the *Buenaventura*, Captain Lazarraga, of Bilboa, Spain, bound from Pascagoula, Mississippi, to Rotterdam, with $20,000 worth of lumber—a ship of 1,741 tons, in very good order.

The *Nashville* escorted her into port, where thousands of people flocked to the water-front to see her and cheer her captors, while the

The First Prize of the War, *Buenaventura*, showing some of the Prize Crew on Deck.

cable carried reports of the event that were printed in newspaper extras throughout the nation within two or three hours after the first shot was fired.

The unaccustomed spectators of the morning's events off Key West, who had found themselves unable to realize fully the import of the movement of the squadron were roused to a full sense of what it meant by the sight of the *Nashville's* flashing guns, and the echoes of that shot, as they were carried by the cable around the world, told the most unwilling listener that war with Spain was actually begun.

CHAPTER IX

BRAVE WORK ALONG SHORE

CUTTING CABLES WITHIN NINETY FEET OF THE BEACH AT CIENFUEGOS UNDER THE FIRE OF 1,000 SPANISH SOLDIERS—WOUNDED WHO SUFFERED IN SILENCE LEST GROANS UNNERVE THEIR SHIPMATES—THE *WINSLOW* AT CARDENAS—A TORPEDO-BOAT SENT TO CUT A GUN-BOAT FROM THE PIERS OF A WELL-DEFENDED CITY—A TALE OF RARE HEROISM AND RESOURCEFULNESS—REMARKABLE TESTS OF COURAGE IN THE FACE OF SUPERIOR FORCES AFLOAT—RETURNING FIRE FROM THE SHORE—AT MATANZAS AND CABANAS.

IN proclaiming a blockade of the Cuban ports it was manifestly the belief of President McKinley that Spain had been waiting for us to make an actual display of force that would satisfy her honor so that she could then say she had held out until she had to face a vastly superior force. The extent of Spanish ignorance of our power—the fact that they really expected to conquer us, was, on the whole, inconceivable on this side of the water. Many naval officers, however, scouted what was denominated the "peaceful blockade." An immediate assault upon Havana was what they wanted. In fact, plans for an assault on Havana were made by Sampson and distributed among our ship commanders.

These plans would have been carried out, and with entire success, too, but for the fact that our army was insufficient in numbers. We had been dominated by the idea that a regular army of more than 25,000 men might subvert the liberty of the other sixty millions of the nation—that even that handful was aristocratic and dangerous! At any rate, our army legislation had been based on some such ideas. The truth is we did not have enough men to protect our forts from deterioration, let alone adequately defend them from foreign attack, and we had, therefore, to depend wholly on our navy for aggressive action, until we could recruit, equip, and train an army to hold such territory as our ships might capture. Meantime, the rainy season was at hand in Cuba —the season of fevers deadly to all unacclimated sojourners. Weyler, the former Captain-General, in an interview, expressed the belief, founded on hope, that we would effect a landing and that half our force would die of fever. In view of all of the conditions there was but one thing that we could do, and that was to blockade the coast and wait for the healthy season, with the chance, meantime, that the Spanish would send over the fleet that had so long threatened us from the islands off the African coast.

Leaving the *Nashville* to care for the *Buenaventura*, Admiral Sampson conducted his fleet across the narrow water to the coast of Cuba, that was sighted about 4 o'clock in the afternoon. The land-fall was made ten miles east of Havana. As the blue line of Cuban hills hardened into view, a steamer was seen heading to the east along shore, and the *New York* went in chase. In the course of an hour the stranger was captured, and found to be the merchant steamer *Pedro*, of Bilboa, Spain, bound from Havana to Sagua.

The next morning at about 10 o'clock, while the ships were stretching out in a line along the coast toward Matanzas, looking for the *Alfonso XII.*, that was due to arrive with 1,100 soldiers, a steamer was seen, coming from the east, by the *Marblehead*, *Cincinnati*, and *New York*, in the order named, and all three closed in on her. As they approached within range she began firing, but before we were ready to shoot at her, a keen-eyed lookout had seen that she was saluting our Admiral instead of firing hostile shots, and the *New York* substituted blank cartridges for those she had already prepared to use. It was an Italian man-of-war, bound to Havana.

Meantime our squadron had been divided

to cover ports having railroad communication with Havana, as follows :

Off Havana :—*New York, Iowa, Wilmington, Helena, Dolphin, Mayflower, Vesuvius, Ericsson, Porter*, and such auxiliaries as may be designated.

Off Mariel :—*Nashville, Castine*, and auxiliaries to be designated.

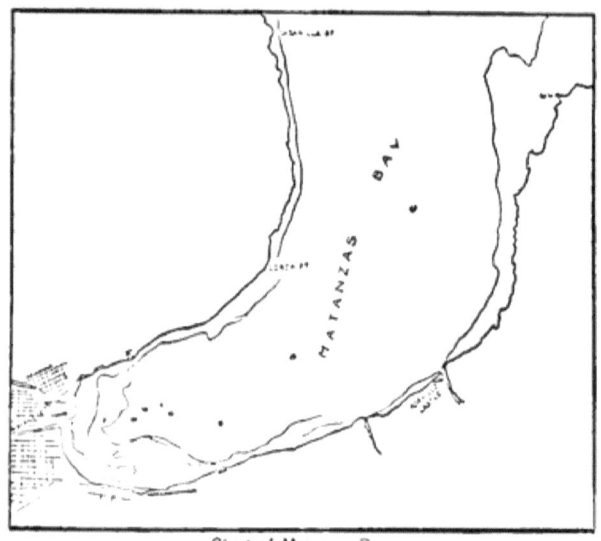

Chart of Matanzas Bay.

Off Matanzas:—*Amphitrite, Cincinnati, Dupont, Winslow*, and auxiliaries to be designated.

Cardenas :—*Newport, Machias, Foote, Cushing*, and auxiliaries to be designated.

Indiana, Marblehead, Detroit, and *Mangrove*, a separate division for special work, and to blockade Cienfuegos.

This list of blockaders must have special

consideration. They were to close Cuban ports for the time being against all comers, including merchant ships having a speed of perhaps fifteen knots, and yet there was the *Amphitrite*, with a speed at best of ten knots, and to her were added the *Puritan* and *Terror*, of a like speed. This is not to criticise the Admiral. He had to use the ships provided, and his disposition of them met the entire approval of all foreign critics who considered the matter. What is desired is to point out that we had to use our coast defence monitors for blockading foreign ports, because our naval policy had failed to provide for the emergency that was thrust upon us, and that what the navy eventually accomplished was done by the ability of men who were compelled to work with inadequate tools.

Not only did we use monitors and battleships on the blockade, we started in with four torpedo-boats. Only those who understand that a blockader should be able to live outside of the blockaded port for weeks without renewing its supplies of coal, can understand the absurdity of calling torpedo-boats efficient blockaders—torpedo-boats built solely for sprinting dashes by night, or through the smoke of battle, and wholly unable to carry coal or other supplies for blockade work.

Nor is that all. It was not only that we

were to seal the ports, we were to stand by for a fight with a Spanish squadron from over the sea that included four cruisers of twenty-knot speed, armored like battle-ships, armed with the best European guns, and aided by huge torpedo-boat destroyers.

The *Bancroft* and *Helena* on the Blockade. The Cuban shore can be seen in the distance.

However, this chapter is to tell something of what the blockaders did in the earlier days of the war. The *Helena*, Captain William T. Swinburne, was sent away to the west end of Cuba to intercept the steamer *Catalina*, bound from New Orleans to Havana with provisions. She fell in with the *Miguel Jover* instead, on April 24th, and found her loaded with cotton and staves. She was bound to Barcelona. The *Catalina* was captured by the *Detroit* the same morning to the westward of Havana. Meantime a number of small coasting schooners and sloops were taken. They were of no account as prizes, but the actions of the captured crews were instructive. These men, in most cases, had been enrolled in the Spanish naval reserve, and the papers in the vessels proved it. As their crews saw these proofs in our hands that they were naval men, they became instantly and utterly dejected. Their hopeless grief was so manifest that our officers who talked the language questioned them as to the cause, and in every case learned that they all expected to be shot to death. That prisoners of war might have their lives spared was something unbelievable to these Spanish naval reserves. Nor was it the ignorant schooner-men alone who were distressed in that fashion, for when a boat with a Spanish army lieutenant named Pedro Fernandez on board was taken, off Matanzas, a little later, the officer at once gave up all hope of life. Assurances that he was entirely safe did not quiet him, and it was not until he had had a good breakfast in the ward-room of the flag-ship and had been conducted about the vessel, that he might see her power and the discipline of her crew, and had seen the marines drilled on the quarter-deck, and, finally, was told that he was to be paroled and sent ashore, that he was fully convinced of the difference between our treatment of prisoners and that to which he had been accustomed. Those who know the volatile nature of his race may imagine how he then expressed his thanks and appreciation of the courtesies shown him.

To give in detail the incidents of the capture of the numerous vessels taken in the first two weeks of the war would weary the reader. The work of capturing the smaller vessels failed to incite any special interest in the squadron after the first day or so, but when the torpedo-boat *Foote* was fired on by the shore-batteries as she was scouting about the harbor of Matanzas, Admiral Sampson determined to reply, and the men heard the news with pleasure. It was a peaceful blockade in its way, but the squadron would resist fire from shore.

At noon on Wednesday, April 27th, the *New York*, the *Puritan*, and the *Cincinnati* steamed slowly into the harbor of Matanzas. The harbor is a bay of the form of a short-legged sock, with its mouth opening to the north and the foot pointing inland south of west. It is about three miles wide at the coast-line between Sabanilla Point, on the west, and Cape Maya, on the east, and perhaps five miles deep. It narrows to two miles between Point Gorda and the mouth of Cañamar River, where it turns to the west. The old fortress, Morrillo Castle, stands at the river-mouth, and new works had been erected at Point Gorda. New sand-batteries were also erected at Cape Maya and on the west side near Sabanilla.

Our squadron steamed in from the west, and as soon as it came within range, the Spaniards near Sabanilla Point opened fire. The fort over at Cape Maya joined in immediately, and their guns and projectiles made the welkin, but nothing else, ring. The *New York* returned the fire of the Sabanilla battery, the *Puritan* steamed over and bombarded the battery on Cape Maya, while the *Cincinnati* joined the *New York*. These were the first shots of the war fired at shore-batteries. The firing began, at a range of about three miles, at one o'clock. In twenty minutes the range was reduced to one mile and a half, and the batteries on both sides were silenced. The last twelve-inch shot from the *Puritan* was seen to strike and explode right in a puff of smoke where the Spaniards had just fired a gun, and the next instant that gun rose end over and end out of the cloud. Both batteries were silenced, but the extent of the damage done on shore is not now known. Our ships were not touched.

Because our squadron withdrew, the Spaniards claimed a great victory, and on the night following they held public meetings in Matanzas to raise money for improving the forts. The speeches, as reported next day in the Havana *La Lucha*, were full of patriotism. One gray-haired citizen declared he had previously secured passage for Spain, but "as soon as I learned that the port was blockaded, I cancelled my engagement, knowing honor demanded remaining to repel the insolent invaders of our cherished rights." The subscriptions to the defence fund, which were taken up following that speech, aggregated almost $2,500 in silver.

This subscription deserves mentioning in connection with one at Havana, that was also strengthened by the appearance of our warships. They started out to raise money there to build a four-million-dollar battle-ship as a small token of their loyalty, and with the aid of a benefit performance at the leading theatre succeeded in raising, it is said, $7,850. The relation between the sentiments expressed by the loyalists and the amounts subscribed is instructive.

The next incident of the blockade to be recorded is interesting for what followed, as well as in itself. The *Marblehead* and the *Nashville* were on the Cienfuegos blockade when, on April 29th, the *Argonata*, a Spanish steamer in the coasting trade, came along. She had slipped past the blockaders off Havana at night, but she was nabbed by the *Nashville*. There were a lot of passengers on board, including a colonel of the Third Spanish Cavalry, who was a relative of Weyler's; his first lieutenant, surgeon-major, seven other lieutenants, and ten privates. The soldiers were held as prisoners of war, while the women and children, with other noncombatants, were sent ashore near the mouth of the harbor.

This done, the *Argonata* was sent to Key West under Ensign H. C. Kuenzli, while the *Nashville* steamed around to the rendezvous of the Havana portion of the blockaders to report to Admiral Sampson.

As it happened the *Nashville* was unable to find the flag-ship at the usual rendezvous east of Havana, because Sampson had gone to Key West, unknown to the other ships. Captain Maynard went cruising to and fro looking for the *New York* for some time in vain, and then had the luck to see a stranger instead. The *Nashville* was heading to the east at 7 o'clock when the lookout reported a steamer's smoke a little on the starboard bow. It was not a clear morning, and some time elapsed before the stranger could be seen distinctly, but all at once, as if she were emerging from a fog bank, the lookouts saw that she was a war-ship with white sides and a yellowish smoke-stack. No flag could be seen, but it was certain that here was a cruiser of at least twice the weight of guns and twice as many men as the gun-boat *Nashville* carried, and what was more, she was heading straight toward Havana. There could be but one opinion regarding her. She must be a Spaniard bound to run the blockade.

As she was still well beyond range, there was ample time for the little *Nashville* to turn and run back to get help from one of the vessels off Havana, but not a soul on her thought of doing any such thing. A signal flag at the fore, indicating that the *Nashville* was looking for the Admiral, came down on the run; they hoisted the Stars and Stripes in its stead, while the call for quarters rang through the ship. Within three minutes from the moment that the stranger was seen to be a war-ship the *Nashville's* men were at their guns with their necks craned toward the other ship, while one gunner was so eager for the work that he caressed his weapon like a sweetheart as he leaned from the port to look ahead.

After all, it was no enemy, but a very good friend instead—the British cruiser *Talbot*, that displaces 5,600 tons to the *Nashville's* 1,371—a ship more than four times the size of ours, and carrying a battery many times more powerful.

It was a characteristic incident in the history of the blockade. The tug *Osceola*, armed with one six-pounder and a machine gun (called a lead-squirt), was on the coast of Cuba under command of Lieutenant J. L. Purcell, about the middle of May, convoying the transport *Florida*, with some Cubans on board. Suddenly the thick smoke of a coming cruiser was seen, and a little later a ship of "a type I'd never heard of," as Purcell said, appeared. He could only conclude that she was Spanish, and ordering the *Florida* to run, Purcell said: "I will go back and head her off that you may have time to escape." And he went back — actually went back to "head off" the *New Orleans!* And on another occasion the converted yacht *Scorpion*, commanded by Lieutenant-Commander Adolph Marix, and armed with four five-inch guns, ran up to the *Talbot*, as the *Nashville* had done, determined to make a fight had she proved to be Spanish.

A Colt Rapid-Fire Gun (lead squirt)

Maynard, Marix, and Purcell were average samples of the men behind the guns on the blockade.

Matanzas was bombarded on April 27th. Two days later the *New York* ran along the coast west of Havana. She stopped for a few minutes off the little port of Mariel, where two small block-houses could be seen, both well manned with Spanish soldiers. Finer targets for gun practice were never seen in Cuba, but when our men wanted to try, the admiral refused permission because it would make a useless slaughter—a killing of men where no object was to be attained by it. But when opposite the next port, Cabáñas, a few miles west, a troop of Spanish coast-guards opened fire from the brush with their carbines, they got some four-inch shells in return that scattered them in a panic.

Meantime, on the night of April 25th, an incident had occurred off Havana that, although it was of serious interest in a way, created a smile as wide as the stretched-out blockading squadron was long. The Spanish liner *Panama* had sailed from New York for Havana just before the first act of war, and every blockader was on the lookout for her, because she was carrying a cargo of food badly needed by the Spanish soldiers in Havana. Moreover she

Lieutenant J. L. Purcell.

was armed with several fourteen-pounders, after the manner of the Spanish Naval Reserve, while she was credited with a speed of from thirteen to fifteen knots.

Now, of all the ships on guard at Havana, the least efficient in speed and guns was the lighthouse supply ship *Mangrove*. The very qualities that made her admirable as a supply ship were against her as a blockader. She was very fat and comfortable, with a top speed of eight knots. But she had been selected as a good boat for cutting cables, and she had two six-pounders on her bows. Having put to sea in a hurry, her crew had not been supplied with small arms, save only as Lieutenant-Commander W. H. Everett, her captain, and his lieutenants carried swords.

Nevertheless, at 8 o'clock on the night of April 25th, when the lights of the *Panama* loomed out of the darkness, Captain Everett swung the *Mangrove* across her bow, and with a couple of shots brought her to. Then he borrowed a revolver, the private property of one of her crew, with which to arm Ensign Dayton, whom he sent as boarding officer.

It is not uninteresting to note here, as illustrating how the hopes of prize-money faded, that the *Panama* was supposed to be worth some hundreds of thousands of dollars when she was captured. When she was sold she brought $41,000, and this had to be divided with the *Indiana*, that came to supply a prize-crew after the *Mangrove* had held the Spaniard. As a matter of fact, the great majority of our naval officers would be glad to have the dividing of prize-money abolished in order to substitute some system of rewards like the giving of medals, or special rank, for notable services. They are of the "strange people," mentioned by Ruskin, "who have other loves than those of wealth and other interests than those of commerce."

On the whole the story of the blockade during the first two weeks was, from a navy man's point of view, fairly interesting, even though there was nothing like a real naval battle. We had shut off the commerce of the island and had given the Spaniards a couple of tastes of Yankee shells. We had also cut out the cable leading from Havana to Key West, as a first step toward isolating Captain-General Blanco from Madrid. As a next step in this last work it was proposed to cut the three cables leading from Cienfuegos to Santiago de Cuba and thence to Jamaica and Hayti. The *Marblehead*, Captain B. H. McCalla, had been on the Cienfuegos blockading station for three weeks, while the *Nashville*, Captain Maynard, and the revenue cutter *Windom*, Captain S. E. McGuire, had come to assist, when on the 10th of

May it was decided to cut the cables. The cable landing had been located by the little cable-house on the beach. Because of the shoal water inshore it was necessary to go in with several ordinary cutters (row boats) and two steam-launches to do the work, but the ships stood by to cover the party as well as might be.

Lieutenant C. M. Winslow was placed in command, with Lieutenant E. A. Anderson to assist, and volunteers were called for among the men, because of the great danger attending the work. At the call the entire force of all the ships volunteered, and selection had to be made from men who crowded and bulldozed each other in their anxiety to get to the front.

After the beach with the thick brush back of it had been well shelled, the boats all ran in until within about two hundred feet of the sand, where the two launches stopped, and the row-boats went on until ninety feet from shore, where they were covered as well as possible by one-pounders on the launches.

The Spanish had fled from the fire of the ships, but they came back when that was stopped—came at the end, a thousand strong, to low earthworks concealed in the brush, and armed with machine guns and one-pounders. Our launches opened fire on them, while our men in the cutters began fishing for the cables lying on the sand in the shoal waters. But it was slow work getting hold of the cables, and slower still getting them up across the cutters where pieces could be chopped from them, and the Spaniards were gaining courage every minute.

The fire from shore began at long range, but the range was decreased, and the rapidity increased as our work progressed. For a time their fire was wild, but by the time we had taken a length from one of the cables they had obtained the range. Finally one of the men at the oars was struck, but he held his place, and no one knew it until he fell in a faint. Then his mates saw a great pool of blood just under his thwart. He had been sitting there in silence bleeding to death, rather than risk alarming his mates by saying he was hurt.

A few moments later another fell in like fashion, and then another and another. Not a man cried out, nor did any one even so much as wince, save as the blows of the shot made them shiver for an instant. Even when Herman W. Kuehneister, a marine, was shot through the jaw in a way to mutilate the lower part of his face frightfully, he did not so much as groan.

For two hours and a half the men grappled and tugged and cut, under the fire of the Spaniards, who were lying behind breastworks and concealed in the brush. Our ships were powerless to defend, because our men were within thirty yards of the beach, and the guns of the launches were inadequate to the work. The Spaniards were rapidly increasing in numbers, and at the last it was estimated that a thousand of them were furiously pumping their Mausers at our boats. The water about the cutters was splashed as in a tropical rain-storm, and Lieutenant Winslow, having cut two of the cables, reluctantly left the third, and took his men out of range.

Then the *Windom* went in to avenge our losses. The Spaniards fled to a nearby lighthouse for shelter, but found it a hot corner. A four-inch shell toppled it over, and sent them in a wild cross-country race.

The official report gave our loss as one killed—Patrick Regan—with two—H. W. Kuchneister and Ernest Suntzenich, mortally wounded, and six others, H. Henrickson, John J. Doran, John Davis, Robert Valz, William Levery, and Lieutenant Winslow were hurt more or less. Only one of the wounded died, however, and there were two others very slightly wounded.

Winslow is a son of the Winslow who commanded the *Kearsarge* when she sank the *Alabama.*

That was the first time in this war that our

men were under a fire that drew blood. It was the first time that any man in the expedition had ever been under an enemy's fire, good or bad. The commander's report very truthfully said that they behaved with "the utmost coolness and intrepidity." Veterans never behaved better.

That was off Cienfuegos during the forenoon of May 11, 1898. In the afternoon of the same day our men, with equal coolness, faced bloodier disaster at Cardenas.

The *Machias*, under Commander John F. Merry, the *Wilmington*, under Commander Chapman C. Todd, the torpedo-boat *Winslow*, under Lieutenant John B. Bernadou, with the revenue cutter *Hudson*, under Lieutenant F. H. Newcomb, had been guarding the coast from Matanzas to Cardenas for some time, the rendezvous being off the mouth of Cardenas Bay. They had learned that three small Spanish gun-boats were lying at the piers in Cardenas, and the one question most considered by our crews, was how to get those vessels out for a fight.

Under the circumstances the question was not easily answered. Cardenas Bay is simply a great shoal-water lagoon, say twenty-five miles long and six broad, that is shut off from the sea by a long peninsula on the west, and innumerable islands in an irregular chain. The main channel has but ten and one-half feet of water in it at one place, and but fifteen feet in several miles of its course. So long as the Spaniards remained at the piers they were

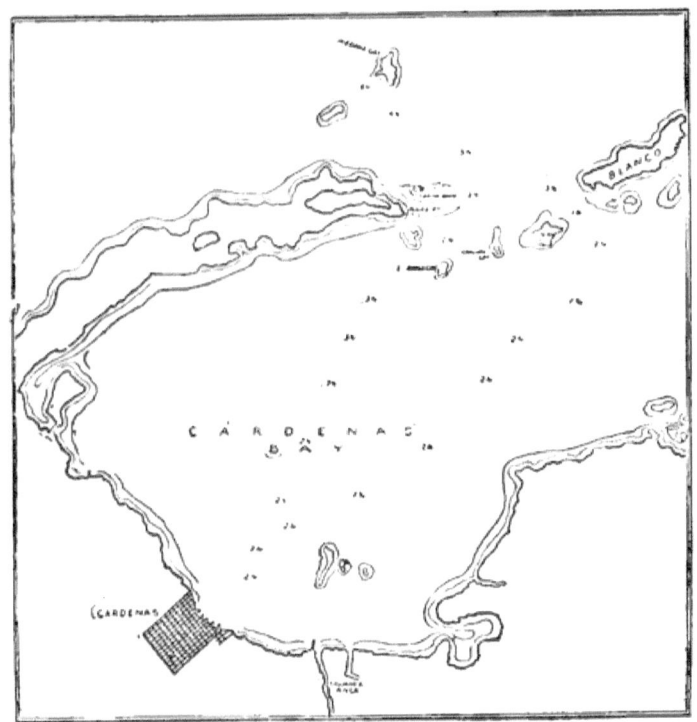

Chart of Cardenas Bay.

fairly safe, because of the greater draught of the American boats and the intricacies of the channel, which was also mined.

However, the torpedo-boat *Foote* had been used with success to draw the fire of shore batteries at Matanzas, and Commander Merry, as senior officer, on May 9th, sent the *Winslow* into Cardenas Bay to see what effect her presence would have on the gun-boats there.

Dashing across the shoals until within a mile or so of the town, Captain Bernadou opened fire with his little one-pounders. The *Machias* followed to the chain of islands where the water shoals, and there awaited developments. The fire of the *Winslow's* one-pounders, it may be said in anticipation of what is to be told of torpedo-boats farther on, was not especially effective against either the gun-boats or a shore battery near the town, while her torpedoes were entirely useless against the shore battery. However, she did exasperate the crew of a gun-boat until it steamed out in chase of her. Retreating slowly, the *Winslow* enticed the gun-boat out until within long range of the *Machias*. The men of the *Machias* were so eager that they couldn't wait longer, and the first round having landed a six-pound shell on the Spaniard, it made its best speed back to the piers. A channel mine was exploded near the *Winslow*, but no damage was done.

On the morning of the 11th, a channel not often used was sounded out, and at 1 o'clock in the afternoon, the *Wilmington*, the *Winslow* and the *Hudson* passed this and steered up the bay toward the city, the *Winslow* leading because of her shoal draught. On arriving within a mile and a half of the piers the *Wilmington* stopped, and Commander Todd ordered Bernadou to run in and cut out one of the Spanish gun-boats.

Lieutenant John B. Bernadou of the *Winslow*.

To fully understand the peril that the *Winslow* was to face it should be remembered that she was built of plates that a Mauser rifle can penetrate; that the afternoon was bright and clear; that she had to run toward the sun, with the sun's rays in the eyes of her men; that the distance she was to run was a mile and a half, that she was to cut out a gun-boat armed with larger guns than hers and defended not only by its crew, but by the crews of two other gun-boats, not to mention the land forces, and that her prey was tied up at the piers of a city of thick-walled houses behind which the sharp-shooters would have perfect protection.

Nevertheless, Bernadou and his men cheerfully drove the *Winslow* ahead for half a mile or more without incident, and then found their vessel steering between lines of little red buoys that were bobbing on the waves. The buoys seemed to be there to mark a channel, the men thought, but in a moment their mistake was apparent, for a masked battery to the east of the city opened fire with an accuracy that

The Conning-tower of the *Winslow*, Showing Effect of Shots Coming through from Opposite Side.
From a photo loaned by Collier's Weekly.

showed the buoys had been placed there to mark the range.

The first shot struck but a few yards away and the second, a three-inch shell, crashed through the *Winslow's* bow, completely wrecking the steering-gear and leaving her helpless.

A moment later the Spanish gun-boat at the pier began firing, and the *Winslow's* crew turned loose their three little one-pounders in reply. Then came a shot that knocked a big splinter of steel from the *Winslow's* deck. It buried itself in Bernadou's groin, making a serious wound, but Bernadou bound a towel around it, and shoved a one-pound shell into the towel as a tourniquet. That checked the flow of blood, and he ran aft to get the hand steering-gear at work. Before he could get there a shot had wrecked that, too, and as he stopped to consider what to do next a man from below reported one boiler pierced and one engine wrecked. The cloud of steam from the forward hatch confirmed the report, and there the *Winslow* lay helpless under the hottest cannon fire from the Spanish known to the whole history of the war.

It was then that the resourcefulness of the Yankee naval man became apparent for the first time in this war. The boiler was spouting scalding steam, but the men there cut off its connections. An engine cylinder was smashed, but it was at once disconnected, and with one boiler and a part of an engine in order, the engineers reported ready for service, and Bernadou ordered them to go ahead. Any movement would change the range at which the Spaniards must aim. Having no steering-gear to control her the *Winslow* gradually turned to one side, seeing which Bernadou stationed his assistant, Ensign Worth Bagley, at the hatch above the engines and began working the vessel forward and back. While Bagley stood there passing orders some of the coal-passers from the disabled boiler and other noncombatants gathered about him to gaze in idle curiosity at the Spanish batteries on shore — batteries that were by this time catching steel hail from the four-inch rifles of the *Wilmington*, not to mention smaller projectiles. The thought that they were in serious danger never entered the head of one of that group.

Ensign Bagley, Killed on the *Winslow*.

But though the Spaniards were at last under a deadly fire they were still working their guns, and the *Winslow* had not yet run clear of the red buoys. A Spanish shell came on board the *Winslow* right in the midst of the idle group, and striking a hose-reel, exploded. Bagley staggered forward to the signal mast, clutched at it vainly and sank down, dead, with his arms around it. Another man, crying, "Save me! Save me!" tumbled overboard, but was caught and hauled back. A half-dozen more were knocked about the narrow deck.

And then came the *Hudson* to the rescue. She was a mere tug in size and model, and the fire of the Spaniards became, for the moment, more furious as they saw that they had made another accurate shot, but Captain Newcomb brought his vessel within reach, and Lieutenant H. Scott threw a tow-line to the *Winslow*. When it was fast the *Hudson* started away as deliberately as if she had hold of a lighter in New York Bay. The line parted, cut by a shot, it is supposed, but Newcomb made fast again, this time alongside the disabled craft, and towed her clear, while the *Wilmington* shot the Spanish gun-boats and battery to pieces, and fired the town with her shells.

What losses were sustained ashore have never been definitely reported. Our own included Ensign Worth Bagley, John Barberes, oiler, G. Deneefe and George B. Meek, firemen, and E. B. Tunnell, cook, killed. The wounded were Lieutenant J. B. Bernadou, and William Patterson and Daniel McKeoun, seamen. The *Winslow* went to Key West under her own steam, and was repaired in a few weeks.

Bernadou was back in command after a brief sojourn in the hospital. It is a remarkable fact that nearly one-third the lives lost afloat in the war with Spain were destroyed by that one shell at Cardenas, while the lives lost in the two fights on that "bloody 11th"—six—exceeded all other naval losses afloat or ashore throughout the war, excepting those of the marines at Guantanamo, who also lost six.

Stirring as were the incidents of that fight at Cardenas one very significant fact—perhaps the most significant of the story—remains to be told. Bernadou, who was so cool and resourceful, has been conspicuous in the service as a student. As a linguist, he has translated a number of foreign naval papers for the use of our service. He has been an original contributor also to our naval literature, and at the same time has held a leading place as an expert in the manufacture of smokeless powder. It may surprise some to find what rule-o'-thumb sailors call "scientists" making such a record in battle, but the whole story of this war is full of such records. In fact, culture has made our officers at once physically braver and mentally more resourceful instead of enervating them.

CHAPTER X

DEWEY AT MANILA

GOOD WORK OF THE *BALTIMORE'S* MEN AIDED BY THE BRITISH IN HONG KONG—PRECAUTIONS ON THE WAY TO MANILA—A NIGHT ATTACK ON OUR SQUADRON—THE SCENE AT DAWN—WHEN MONTOJO BECAME DESPERATE—WRETCHED USE OF MINES AND TORPEDO-BOATS—A STRIKING EXHIBIT OF THE REPOSE OF CONSCIOUS POWER—CHRISTENING OF THE BABY BATTLE-SHIP —SPANISH VIEWS OF THE CONFLICT.

WE began our preparations for war in the hope that no more than a demonstration on the coast of Cuba would be needed to secure peace for that unfortunate island, but we were quickly driven by Spanish resistance into a conflict that flamed on opposite sides of the earth. Looking ahead to the growing war-cloud, the Navy Department had ordered the *Baltimore*, near the middle of April, to leave Yokohama and join Commodore George Dewey at Hong Kong, with a view of sending the entire Asiatic squadron (except the antiquated *Monocacy*) thence to Manila. The *Baltimore* was commanded by Captain Nehemiah M. Dyer and Lieutenant-Commander

Gottfried Blocklinger was his executive officer. The ship reached Hong Kong on that Friday morning (April 22d) when Sampson led his squadron from Key West, and the echo of the *Nashville's* gun in capturing the *Buenaventura* was heard in Commodore Dewey's cabin on the *Olympia* in Hong Kong harbor. The capture of the merchant ship was an act of war that would travel like a tidal wave to break in blood on the beach at far Manila. There was need of the *Baltimore* for instant service, and here she was in Hong Kong, but unfortunately foul-bottomed and short of coal and other supplies.

To the dry-dock, therefore, Dewey sent her, and her captain and executive officer were the men for the hour; moreover, she was in a British port. Rarely in the history of navies has such swift work been done. At the end of forty-eight hours she had been docked, cleaned, painted, and floated again, and every needed article taken on board. That was accomplished by Sunday, April 24th, and it was remarkably lucky so, for on that day the Spanish Government issued its formal decree, declaring that war existed with the United States, and in consequence of the notice thereof which was telegraphed to neutral governments, the Governor of Hong Kong, as the representative of Her Majesty's Government, was obliged to notify the belligerent Dewey to leave the harbor.

Under the rule, Dewey was allowed twenty-four hours in which to leave, but at 2 o'clock that afternoon the war-ships *Boston*, Captain Frank Wildes; the *Concord*, Captain Asa Walker, and the *Petrel*, Captain Edward P. Wood, sailed away. With them went the revenue cutter, *Hugh McCulloch*, Captain Daniel B. Hodgsdon (of the revenue service), which was assigned to despatch-boat service, and two transports, the *Nanshau* and *Zafiro*, which had recently been secured by Commodore Dewey with 3,600 tons of coal, and six months' supplies for the squadron between them.

At 10 o'clock on Monday the flag-ship *Olympia*, Captain Charles V. Gridley, followed by the *Baltimore* and the *Raleigh*, Captain Joseph B. Coghlan, sailed away also. Of the temper of the people our squadron left in Hong Kong, Gunner Joel C. Evans, of the *Boston* wrote (see *Century* for August, 1898) : "When we were leaving port for Manila the captain of the *Immortalité* (British) shouted to Captain Wildes : 'You will surely win. I have seen too much of your target practice to doubt it.'" Evans adds, "I believe the Russian, German, and French naval officers thought Spain would conquer."

Uniting his forces at Mirs Bay, in Chinese

territory, thirty miles from Hong Kong, Commodore Dewey started for Manila on Wednesday, April 27th, at 2 o'clock in the afternoon—the day on which Sampson bombarded Matanzas—the *Olympia* leading, with her band playing "El Capitan," and the *Baltimore*, *Raleigh*, *Petrel*, *Concord*, and *Boston* in line astern, and the other ships in a line parallel and to starboard. To the impatient crews the

The late Captain Charles V. Gridley of the Flagship *Olympia*.

speed maintained—eight knots—was nerve-trying, but Dewey knew that the Spanish at Manila had been notified of his start on the day he left Hong Kong, and that any time saved by high speed would not be worth the expense in coal, and it was not until Saturday, April 30th, that the coast of the big island of Luzon, on which Manila stands, was reached.

It appears now that Dewey had timed his squadron to arrive off Point Bolinao in the morning, for the reason that, according to reports at Hong Kong, the Spanish Admiral, Montojo, was to come out to destroy the American squadron on the open sea. Dewey was in search of the Spanish squadron, and by making his landfall on the coast of Luzon in the morning he would have a whole day for running down the coast, and so be in no danger of leaving the Spaniard concealed in some place behind him. The wisdom of so doing is apparent, even to a landsman who examines the chart of the island, for there are several hiding-places on the coast, Subig Bay, thirty miles north of Manila Bay, being especially adapted for what may be called a nautical ambush.

Some preparations for a battle were made before leaving Hong Kong. The ships were painted lead color, for one thing, and some of the boats were swathed in canvas, and nettings were stretched to stop splinters. Moreover, the ammunition-tubes were armored, as far as possible, by winding chain cables around them. On the way over, the men, with few exceptions, had their hair cut close to their heads, both for the sake of coolness in a hot climate and to facilitate the work of the surgeon in dressing probable scalp wounds. Now that they were on the coast the crew went to work with axes on the woodwork of the ships. Cabin partitions were cut away, and with doors, trunks, chests, curios—everything that could throw a splinter when struck by a shot—was cast overboard, until the sea was strewn for miles with the *débris* of beautiful and useful woodwork.

Meantime, on finding the north coast clear, the *Boston* and the *Concord* were sent ahead at full speed to examine Subig Bay, and before they were out of sight the *Baltimore* was sent to support them in case the Spaniards should be there, but at 5 o'clock our entire squadron was in the bay and no enemy had been seen.

Now, it was well known to Commodore Dewey that a telegraph station stood on Point Bolinao and that his presence on the coast had been known by the Spanish at Manila ever since his arrival. In order to fully appreciate what was done next it is necessary to consider the lay of the land in connection with this fact that the Spanish were not to be taken unawares.

A look at the chart shows that Luzon Island lies north and south, as to its length, and that Manila Bay is roughly a four-sided body of water projecting inland from the southwest corner of the island. The mouth of the bay is about six miles wide. One mile off shore from the north point lies Corregidor Island, and the water between this island and the south point is perhaps five miles wide. Now, Corregidor Island is a considerable body of land and, moreover, it rises six hundred feet above the sea. On its crest a battery of eight-inch modern Krupp guns had been erected, while the south point of the bay was guarded by a similar battery erected on El Fraile Island, which lies perhaps a half mile from the beach. If well handled these guns might sink the best battle-ship afloat, the guns on Corregidor being especially well placed to deliver a plunging fire. Nor was that all, for reports said that the Spaniards had filled the channel with fields of torpedoes.

Somewhere behind these formidable works lay the Spanish squadron, its officers waiting with guns loaded, no doubt, for the Yankees to come—the Yankees whose protected decks ranged from four and three-quarter inches thick on the *Olympia*, down to three-quarters of an inch on the *Concord*. It was a battle-ship job to hunt that Spanish squadron, and Dewey had not one armored ship, properly so called, to aid him, but he had a plenty of Harveyized grit in his own heart and among his crews, and he thought that might serve instead of battle-ships.

Calling his captains on board the flag-ship in Subig Bay, he gave them their orders, and then, at 6 o'clock, led the way down the coast at a speed that would bring him into the mouth of the wide channel of Manila Bay at midnight precisely. The other ships followed each other, with a hooded light on the taffrail of each for a guide to the one behind, the revenue cutter and the transports bringing up the rear of the war-ship line.

In perfect silence the squadron drifted along through the night in a course almost due south until well below Corregidor Island, and then turned to the east and north, straight into the bay. The heights of the Spanish island loomed like a mountain in the night, but not a sign of alarm was seen there as the squadron turned into the bay until the firemen on the revenue cutter, just as she was turning, were obliged to stoke her fires. At that a blaze of flame and a shower of sparks arose from her funnel, for she was using the inflammable Japanese coal, and the sentries on the island saw the flare. A moment later they sent a rocket worming its way into the sky.

An answering rocket arose from El Fraile instantly, while signal lights flashed for miles along the south shore of the bay. Then the quick flash of a great gun was seen on El Fraile, and a big shell with a roaring scream came hunting our ships. Instantly the *Boston* returned the fire with an eight-inch shell, "just to tell them they had seen us, surely," as Gunner Evans said, while the *Concord* fired two of her six-inch guns, and the *McCulloch*, which carried a few six-pounders, fired four times.

That ended the firing on both sides, although the taffrail-lights must still have been within plain view of the forts. Thereafter the ships slowly worked their way up the bay, with most of the men sleeping beside their guns until day broke, when all hands were once more called to duty, and hard bread, cold meat, and coffee were served to them as a morning "snack."

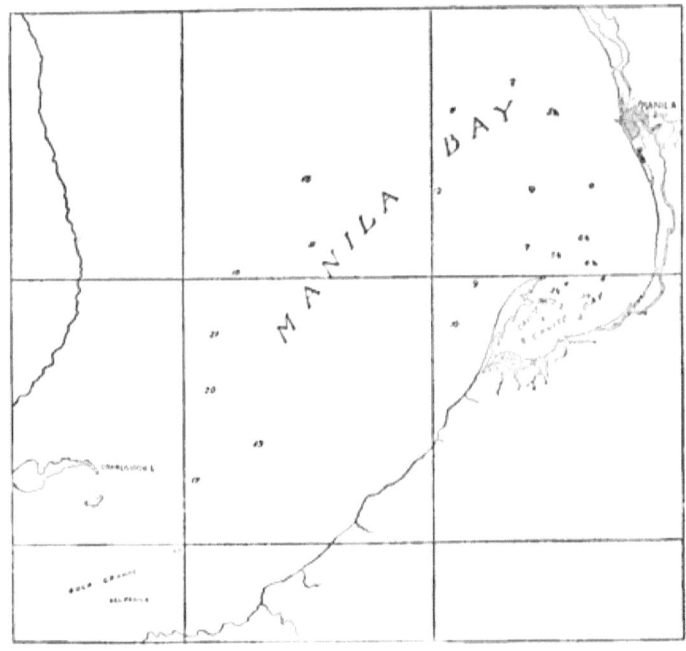

Chart of Manila Bay.

The squadron at break of day lay seven miles due west from Manila city (see chart), and perhaps an equal distance northwest of the little sandy hook, marked Cavite—a sandy hook which partly encloses a small bight in the coast where were lying the ships of the Spanish Admiral stretched out in a line that began behind the hook and led away toward Manila city for nearly a mile.

Not a Spanish ship had steam up—why should a Spanish admiral doubt the ability of the men in the forts down the bay to stop any Yankee squadron? Moreover, there were the forts on Cavite Point with their beautiful Krupp rifles to aid the Spanish ships, as well as guard the naval arsenal behind them, while over to the east, seven miles away, on the outskirts of Manila, were still other forts with Krupp guns, and the Yankee squadron must needs get within their range if a fight were really intended. The Yankees had passed the forts below, without doubt, but——

It was Sunday morning, May 1, 1898. At 5.15 o'clock precisely the Spaniards opened fire with a big gun in a Manila city fort. Our sailors saw a huge puff of smoke and then a big projectile dropped into the water a mile or so from the flag-ship *Olympia*. At this time Commodore Dewey was standing on the *Olympia's* bridge, while Fleet-Captain Benjamin P. Lamberton, Flag-Lieutenant Thomas M. Brumby, Executive Officer Corwin P. Rees, and the Navigator-Lieutenant C. G. Calkins were with him. Captain Gridley was obliged to go into the armored conning tower, lest a chance shell sweep the bridge and leave the ship without an officer of high rank. The men had already cleared away the dishes used in their light repast and had returned to their guns. The air was motionless and the sea a perfect level. The rose light of dawn had suffused the eastern sky, but a faint haze in the dead air curtained off the Spaniards in the little harbor at Cavite, so that they were wholly invisible. But Dewey knew they were there (ten fighting ships besides transports and two torpedo-boats), and hoisting the old flag to fore and main peaks and the spanker-gaff or taffrail staff of every ship, he left the transports with the *McCulloch* in the middle of the bay, headed the *Olympia* off toward the northerly end of the bay, swung her around in a wide arc toward Manila on the east, and with his fighting squadron following him with the precision of a tow on the great lakes, he steamed straight at his anchored prey. A signal at the yard-arm read, "Fire as convenient."

While yet he was several miles away the Spanish squadron appeared with colors up, and the fierce little gunners in the Cavite forts began to fire their big guns. The Spanish ships soon joined in, but Dewey held on his way into that hail of steel without reply, while his crews at their guns, "with set teeth and the smile that one sees so often on the faces of

men in the prize ring," awaited the word in silence.

At last, when a little more than two miles away from forts and anchored squadron, the *Olympia* swerved to the right (west), so as to pass the Spaniards broadside to broadside, and then, turning to the captain of the ship, Dewey said, quietly:

"When you are ready, you may fire, Gridley," and Gridley passed the order to the eager gunners in the *Olympia's* forward turret. The two long eight-inch rifles there were already trained on the Spanish flag-ship, and as the order was heard they made quick reply. Two darting flashes in the midst of a rolling cloud of smoke were seen, and with a shivering roar the projectiles were hurled at the doomed Spaniards.

"Almost instantly—it seemed like an echo—came the sound of the guns of the other ships" of the Yankee squadron. It was at exactly 5.35 o'clock that the first guns on the *Olympia* were fired. Our ships were slowed down as they approached the Spaniards to give our gunners a better chance. The headway was just about right to carry the guns of the leader clear of the smoke they made, and seeing this, and that the Yankees were now well within range, the Spaniards worked their guns with redoubled fury. To the crews of the transports it seemed that "never did spectators watch a more desperate game." The water on every side of our ships was cut and slashed into foam and spray, while the guns at Manila reached out to fill the air about the transports, as well as the fighting ships, with screaming shot.

Passing the anchored squadron at a range of a mile and a half, Dewey led his ships in front of the forts on Cavite Point, and then turning slowly about, went back at them with the fresh batteries to starboard. He had given the Spaniards such punishment as they had never dreamed of, but they were fighting with the desperation of cornered cats, and their fire seemed undiminished.

Indeed, as our squadron drew near once more, a huge mine-field was exploded a thousand yards or so in advance of the *Olympia*, and then, when it was seen that the mine had failed to do its work, the beautiful white flag-ship *Reina Christina* slipped her cable and came steaming out to meet the *Olympia*, rail against rail. Here, if ever, was uncircumspect valor—the clawing dash of the cat at the unrelenting bull-dog—but the guns of almost our entire squadron were turned upon her, and no flesh and blood could face the hell of bursting steel that was hurled upon her. Her sides were crushed in, her men melted away from their guns, and turning her about, Admiral Montojo headed her back toward the shelter of the bay. But just as she turned her stern fairly toward our squadron one of the clear-eyed gunners in the *Olympia's* forward turret let drive his eight-inch rifle. It was a shot like that fired by Commodore Macdonough at the flag-ship of the enemy on Lake Champlain, for it raked the *Reina Christina* from stern to bow, killing and wounding sixty men (her captain was among the killed), and start-

Admiral Montojo.

ed a fire in her splintered woodwork that could not be extinguished. She had come out to overwhelm our *Olympia*, and within ten minutes was sent drifting back, a flaming wreck from which every man able to do so was fleeing for life.

But though he had lost his best ship, Admiral Montojo would not yet surrender. Lowering a boat in the midst of the battle, like Commodore Perry on Lake Erie, he rowed away with his flag "through fire and smoke" to the *Isla de Cuba*. Reaching this vessel in safety, he signalled to two small torpedo-boats to go out and do the work in which he had failed.

A moment later the black sneaks came flying at full speed, straight for the *Olympia*. Her large guns were turned upon them the moment they appeared, but without effect, for their speed was too great for such unwieldy weapons, and while yet our men were reloading the great guns, the torpedo-boats had arrived at a range of 800 yards.

But there their careers ended. The lean secondary batteries—the murderous rapid-fire six-pounders—took up the fight, "the surface of the ocean burst into foam under the hail of shot" about the doomed boats, and then a cloud of white smoke or steam arose suddenly from the leader, and in an instant she sank out of sight. Whether her boiler was pierced or her torpedo exploded will never be known, for all hands on board of her perished.

And when she sank her mate turned about and fled to the beach, where it was afterward found riddled, and splashed with blood.

Steaming on to the east, our squadron turned back to pass the Spaniards a third time. They found the *Don Antonio de Ulloa* in flames near the burning Spanish flag-ship, but her crew were still firing their guns. Her captain had nailed the blood and gold flag to the mast, and she sank under the renewed fire of our ships, with her colors flying, and her guns working till the sissing water entered their hot muzzles.

Stripped naked to the waist, bare-headed and

bare-footed, and with the perspiration streaking their smoke-grimed bodies, our men were working the guns with regularity and precision, while the enemy fought back in a frenzy. The Yankees laughed and cheered. The Spaniards sputtered and screamed. The *Castillo* was now spurting flames from every hatch. The Lombardic griffin was closing its claws about the poisonous dragon.

Five times in all our ships steamed across the Spanish front. The tropical sun had come up in a cloudless sky to heat the dead air over the sea. For two hours our men with tense nerves had worked in the choking smoke about their guns, and in the magazines and the stoke-holes where the temperature varied from 116° up to more than 150°. Even the brawniest of Yankee sailors could not stand that work for many hours and keep his work up to the highest quality. The Commodore, with his iron frame, was still fresh and fit, but he remembered his men. Why should he exhaust them utterly? He would stretch out and rest for a time, while the dragon writhed broken and pierced in the clutch of his claws.

The signal to cease firing fluttered aloft on the *Olympia*, and then she led the way out beyond the range of the big guns and stopped. The crews from below came upon deck, gasping for air in some cases, but with one glance at the burning wrecks off Cavite Point they forgot their trouble, and with their hands in the air, or clasping one another about the neck, they found breath to cheer and shout for the old flag above them. And then when they quieted down because their voices were failing them utterly, the boatswains' whistles screamed a welcome call to breakfast.

As Dewey retired the Spanish governor of the island made haste to telegraph to Madrid: "Our fleet engaged the enemy in a brilliant combat, protected by the Cavite and Manila forts. They obliged the enemy with heavy loss to manœuvre repeatedly."

The firing that was continued from the forts long after Dewey was out of range was characteristic of the race as that despatch was, but their *vivas* as they saw our ships retire were choked with tears when they turned to look at their squadron.

It was at 7.45 o'clock that the *Olympia* led the line of battle off to a resting-place, and for three hours the men stretched out on deck, eating another bit of cold comfort, talking of what they had seen and done, and in many cases sleeping comfortably to make up for what they had lost the night before. At 10.45 the Commodore concluded that it was time to finish the morning's work, and sent the *Baltimore* in to renew the fight.

Baltimore, Protected Cruiser. Dimensions, 327.5 x 49; draft, 24; displacement, 4,413. Speed, 20 knots. Main battery, four eight-inch, six six-inch guns.

A refreshing breeze had come by this time, and with a lengthening cloud of smoke pouring from her funnels, the *Baltimore* ploughed through the dancing waves toward Cavite Point, making a magnificent picture in the eyes of the men on the other ships. So dense, indeed, was her aërial wake that she disappeared from their view, but in a few minutes (it was at 11.16 o'clock) the ringing reports of her guns told the story of her arrival within range. Then the *Olympia* and the *Concord* went in to help her. After a little time the *Boston*, the *Raleigh*, and the *Petrel* came to take their places, and the two divisions thus formed in our squadron alternated in the attack. Nor was this the only change made in the tactics. In the morning the ships in one long line had steamed to and fro across the enemy's front, but now the ships ran in until a mile and a half from the forts, stopped, took the range carefully and then opened a fire so deadly that almost every shot struck home. The morning's fight had been directed chiefly at the Spanish ships, but now the Commodore was determined to reduce the fort. At the range taken even our six-pounders were available—not that they could penetrate a sand fort, but they could hurl their vicious projectiles through the embrasures and drive the Spaniards from the guns there, while our big projectiles came to dismount the guns and destroy the works on every side.

However, the remaining vessels of the Spanish squadron were by no means ignored. Their flag-ship had been already destroyed, and the hulks of three others were blazing as the second part of the battle began; but the smaller vessels — especially the gun-boats — were still making a fight, hopeless though it must have seemed to their crews. They had one slight advantage in this, that the water about Cavite Point was too shoal for our cruisers, and seeing this, Captain Wood, of the little gun-boat *Petrel*, steamed boldly in where our cruisers could not go. He carried but four six-inch guns, two on a side, and they were of the old slow-firing style at that, but he proved the Roman dictum, that a short sword would serve when close to the enemy. The *Petrel* was named the Baby Battle-ship for her effective work in Cavite harbor.

Ship after ship was set on fire or driven ashore by her close-range fire. In one case a Spaniard hauled down his flag, and a boat was sent from the *Petrel* to bring the vessel out of the little harbor. But before the boat had covered a third of the distance, the treacherous devils opened fire on it. Exasperated by the infamy, the boat's crew returned on board and a fire was directed at that vessel that sank her with all on board.

Boston, Protected Cruiser. Dimensions, 271 x 42; draft, 21; displacement, 3,000. Speed, 15.6 knots. Main battery, two eight-inch, six six-inch guns.

A few minutes after 12 o'clock the *Boston* got so far in shore that her stern dragged into the bottom of the bay, and for a time it held her fast; but while steadied by the mud, Gunner Evans declares (see *Century* for August) that her forward eight-inch gun dismounted three guns in the Spanish fort, and those three were the only ones left in commission when she grounded.

For an hour and a half—from 11.16 A.M. until 12.30 P.M. (see Dewey's report)—the Spaniards sustained the slaughter afloat and ashore, and then their blood and gold banner gave place to one of white. The signal "cease firing" was spread on the *Olympia*, and as the smoke of battle drifted off down the bay, our squadron made the welkin ring with their cheers of victory. The *Olympia* and one or two others had drawn off before that event, leaving the *Petrel* to complete the work in the harbor, and the *Boston* to that outside.

"The Spanish lost the following vessels: Sunk, *Reina Christina, Castillo, Don Antonio de Ulloa;* burned, *Don Juan de Austria, Isla de Luzon, Isla de Cuba, General Lezo, Marquis del Duero, El Correo, Velasco,* and *Isla de Mindanao* (transport); captured, *Rapido* and *Hercules* (tugs), and several small launches," says Dewey's report. And to this he adds: "I beg to state to the department that I doubt if any commander-in-chief was ever served by more loyal, efficient, and gallant captains than those of the squadron now under my command. Captain Frank Wildes, commanding the *Boston*, volunteered to remain in command of his vessel, although his relief arrived before leaving

From a copyrighted photograph by J. S. Johnston, New York.

Raleigh, Protected Cruiser. Dimensions, 300 x 42; draft, 20; displacement, 3,213. Speed, 19 knots. Main battery, one six-inch, ten five-inch guns.

Hong Kong. Assistant-Surgeon Kindelberger, of the *Olympia*, and Gunner J. C. Evans, of the *Boston*, also volunteered to remain after orders detaching them had arrived. The conduct of my personal staff was excellent. Commander B. P. Lamberton, chief of staff, was a volunteer for that position, and gave me most efficient aid. Lieutenant Brumby, Flag-Lieutenant, and Ensign E. P. Scott, aide, performed their duties as signal officers in a highly creditable manner. Caldwell, Flag-Secretary, volunteered for and was assigned to a subdivision of a five-inch battery. Mr. J. L. Stickney, formerly an officer in the United States Navy, and now correspondent for the New York *Herald*, volunteered for duty as my aide, and rendered valuable service. I desire specially to mention the coolness of Lieutenant C. G. Calkins, the navigator of the *Olympia*, who came under my personal observation, being on the bridge with me throughout the entire action, and giving the ranges to the guns with an accuracy that was proven by the excellence of the firing."

To compare our squadron with that of the Spaniards only is entirely unfair to our sailors, for the Spanish squadron, though inferior to ours, was protected by the great guns of the Cavite forts and those of the forts at Manila which were just seven miles away. Some of the guns were eight-inch and some ten-inch Krupps having a muzzle energy according to Brassey's "Annual," of 14,050 tons—a gun that is about twice as powerful as the best on Dewey's ships, the eight-inch guns of the *Olympia* having a muzzle energy of 7,498 tons. The exact number of the guns in the Spanish forts has not been given in any of the reports from our squadron, nor has any good description of them appeared in the numerous works on Manila. But if we recall what one eight-inch shell did for the *Reina Christina*, and that Dewey's ships were within range of the shore batteries for about five hours of fighting, it becomes plain

Concord, Gun-boat. Dimensions 230 x 36 ; draft 16.7 ; displacement, 1,710. Speed, 16.7 knots. Main battery six six-inch guns.

that even one eight-inch gun at Cavite, *if well served*, would have destroyed our entire squadron. A single well-directed ten-inch shell would have destroyed the best ship under Dewey's command. But we know there were "several modern guns of a larger calibre than any on our ships," at Cavite alone, and that our ships were within easy range of these guns during the entire fight. It is certain that in weight and physical power of guns there was no superiority on our side, while the Spaniards had the advantage in the solid platform of their fort guns.

However, here is a table giving the list of the Spanish ships, with the number of men and guns, as reported by Brassey's "Annual," an unbiassed British work printed before the war:

THE SPANISH SQUADRON.

Vessel.	Class.	Tons.	Length in Feet	Complement.	Armament.
Reina Maria Christina.	Steel cruiser.	3,970	280	370	Six 6.2-inch (Hontoria), two 2.7-inch, three 2.2-inch quick-firing, two 1.5-inch, six 3-pounders, two muzzle-loaders.
Castillo.	Wooden cruiser.	3,342	246	300	Four 5.9-inch (Krupp), two 4.7-inch, two 3.3-inch, four 2.0-inch, eight quick-firing, two muzzle-loaders.
Don Antonio de Ulloa.	Cruiser	1,130	210	130	Four 4.7-inch (Hontoria), two 2.7-inch, two quick-firing, five muzzle-loaders.
Don Juan de Austria.	Cruiser	1,130	210	130	Four 4.7-inch (Hontoria), three 2.2-inch quick-firing, two 1.5-inch, five muzzle-loaders.
Velasco.	Cruiser	1,152	210	173	Three 5.9-inch (Armstrong), two 2.7-inch (Hontoria), two muzzle-loaders.
Isla de Luzon.	Gun-boat	1,030	200	160	Four 4.7-inch (Hontoria), four 6-pounder quick-firing, two 3-pounders, two muzzle-loaders.
Isla de Cuba.	Gun-boat	1,030	200	160	Four 4.7-inch (Hontoria), four 6-pounder quick-firing, two 3-pounders, two muzzle-loaders.
General Lezo.	Gun-vessel	524	157	97	Two 4.7-inch (Hontoria), one 3.5-inch, two quick-firing, one muzzle-loader.
Elcano	Gun-vessel	524	157	116	Three 4.7-inch (Hontoria), two quick-firing, two muzzle-loaders.
Marquis del Duero.	Despatch-vessel.	500	157	98	One 6.2-inch muzzle-loader (Palliser), two 4.7-inch smooth-bore, one muzzle-loader.
Isla del Mindanao.	Auxiliary cruiser.	4,195	376.5	......	Unreported.

The following in the same detail is

THE AMERICAN SQUADRON.

Vessel.	Class.	Tons.	Length in Feet	Complement.	Armament.
Olympia...	Protected cruiser.	5,870	340	450	Ten 5-inch rapid-fire, four 8-inch breech-loaders, fourteen 6-pounders and seven 1-pounder rapid-fire, four Gatlings, one field-gun.
Baltimore..	Protected cruiser.	4,413	327	386	Four 8-inch breech-loaders, six 6-inch breech-loaders, four 6-pounders, two 3-pounders, two 1-pounder rapid-fire, four 37-mm. Hotchkiss, two Colts, one field-gun.
Raleigh....	Protected cruiser.	3,213	300	313	Ten 5-inch rapid-fire, one 6-inch breech-loader, eight 6-pounders, four 1-pounder rapid-fire, two Gatlings, one field-gun.
Boston......	Protected cruiser.	3,000	271	278	Six 6-inch breech-loaders, two 8-inch breech loaders, two 6-pounders, two 3-pounders, two 1-pounder rapid-fire, two 47-mm., two 37-mm. Hotchkiss, two Gatlings.
Concord....	Gun-boat...	1,710	230	194	Six 6-inch breech-loaders, two 6-pounders, two 3-pounder rapid-fire, two 37-mm. Hotchkiss, two Gatlings.
Petrel......	Gun-boat .	892	176	122	Four 6-inch breech-loaders, two 3-pounders, one 1-pounder rapid-fire, two 37-mm. Hotchkiss, two Gatlings.

"Reports show that at the end of the engagement less than half the ammunition in the magazines of the ships had been discharged, and Admiral Dewey's command was in condition to participate in another battle after it had finished with the Spanish force in Manila Bay," says the *Army and Navy Journal*.

"The *Baltimore*, according to the report of her commanding officer, expended only 73 eight-inch shells, and the *Boston* only 48 of the same calibre, making an average of 20 projectiles for each gun. A larger number of six-inch shells were fired, the *Baltimore* discharging 175, the *Boston* 162, and the *Raleigh* 53. The *Raleigh* discharged 341 five-inch shells; 410 six-pounders were fired by the *Baltimore*, 220 by the *Boston*, and 137 by the *Raleigh*. The *Baltimore* fired 169 three-pounders, and the *Boston* 420, and the *Raleigh* 100."

Admiral Montojo had gone out of the bay some time before our squadron arrived, intending, he said, to meet Dewey on the open sea, but he must have taken a second look at the table of guns on board our ships and have considered that maybe the reports, current in Spanish periodicals, about the Yankees being incapable of fighting were somewhat exaggerated. Anyway, he returned to the protection of the boasted forts at Cavite, but only to find them impotent to save his squadron, though armed with "several" guns of the best European make and of larger calibre than ours.

The Spanish official account of the battle says:

"The Americans fired most rapidly. There came upon us numberless projectiles, as the three cruisers at the head of the line devoted themselves almost entirely to fight the *Christina*, my flag-ship. A short time after the action commenced one shell exploded in the forecastle and put out of action all those who served the four rapid-fire cannon, making splinters of the forward mast, which wounded the helmsman on the bridge. In the meantime another shell exploded in the orlop, setting fire to the crew's bags, which they were fortunately able to control. The enemy shortened the distance between us, and rectifying his aim, covered us with a rain of rapid-fire projectiles.

"At half-past seven one shell destroyed completely the steering-gear, another exploded on the poop, and put out of action nine men. Another destroyed the mizzen-mast head, bringing down the flag and my ensign. A fresh shell exploded in the officers' cabin, covering the hospital with blood, destroying the wounded who were being treated there. Another exploded in the ammunition-room astern, filling the quarters with smoke and preventing the working of the hand steering-gear. As it was impossible to control the fire, I had to flood the magazine when the cartridges were beginning to explode.

"Amidships, several shells of smaller calibre went through the smoke-stack, and one of the large ones penetrated the fire-room, putting out of action one master-gunner and twelve men serving the guns. Another rendered useless the starboard bow gun. While the fire astern increased, fire was started forward by another shell which went through the hull and exploded on the deck.

"The broadside guns being undamaged, continued firing until there were only one gunner and one seaman remaining unhurt for firing them.

"The inefficiency of the vessels which composed my little squadron, the lack of all classes of the personnel, especially master-gunners, and seamen-gunners, the inaptitude of some of the provisional machinists, the scarcity of rapid-fire cannon, the strong crews of the enemy, and the unprotected character of the greater part of our vessels, all contributed to make more decided the sacrifice which we made for our country.

"Our casualties, including those of the arsenal, amounted to three hundred and eighteen men killed and wounded."

Admiral Montojo, in an interview with a reporter of the London *Mail* soon after the battle, said:

"The *Reina Christina* and *Don Juan de Austria*, as you know, were old cruisers; the *Castillo* was a wooden cruiser, but was unable to steam, owing to the breaking down of her engines. The *Don Antonio de Ulloa* and the *Velasco* were helpless, and were undergoing repairs off the arsenal. The *Olympia, Baltimore, Raleigh*, and *Boston* engaged my flag-ship in turn about 5.30, attracted by my flag. I recognized the necessity of getting under way and slipped both anchors, ordering the other ships to follow my example. Although we recognized the hopelessness of fighting the American ships, we were busy returning their fire. The *Reina Christina* was hit repeatedly.

"Shortly after 6.30 I observed fire on my ship forward, and our steering-gear was damaged, rendering the vessel unmanageable. We were subjected to a terrific hail of shell and shot. The engines were struck and we estimated we had seventy hits about our hull and superstructure. The boilers were not hit, but the pipe to the condenser was destroyed. A few moments later I observed that the after part of the ship was on fire. A shell from an American ship had penetrated and burst with deadly effect, killing many of our men. My flag-lieutenant said to me:

"'The ship is in flames. It is impossible to stay on the *Christina* any longer.'

"He signalled to the gun-boat *Isla de Cuba*, and I and my staff were transferred to her and my flag was hoisted. Before leaving the *Christina* my flag was hauled down. My flag-ship was now one mass of flames. I ordered away all boats I could to save the crew. Many of the men jumped overboard without clothing and succeeded in reaching shore, several hundred yards away. Only a few men were drowned, the majority being picked up by the boats.

"Before jumping overboard Captain Cadarse's son, a lieutenant on board the *Christina*, saw his father alive on deck, but others say that as the Captain was about to leave, a shell burst over the ship and killed him. We estimate that fifty-two men were killed on board the *Christina* and about one hundred and fifty wounded. The chaplain was killed, and the assistant physician, the chief engineer, and three officers were wounded. The boatswain and chief gunner were both killed. In the *Castillo* only about fifteen men were killed, but there were many wounded, both on the *Castillo* and the *Don Juan de Austria*, on which thirteen men were killed. Altogether, so far as we know at present, four hundred men were killed and wounded on our ships.

"As soon as I transferred myself from the *Reina Christina* to the *Isla de Cuba* all the American shots were directed upon the *Isla de Cuba*, following my flag. We sought shelter behind the pier at Cavite, and, recognizing the futility of fighting more, I prepared to disembark, and gave orders for the evacuation of the remainder of the ships. The *Castillo* had been on fire from end to end for some time, and was, of course, already abandoned. The *Ulloa* was also burning. My last signal to the captains of all vessels was 'Scuttle and abandon your ships.'"

Admiral Montojo was wounded in the left leg by an iron splinter, and his son, a lieutenant, was wounded in the hand by a shell splinter. The Admiral said he directed the fight from the bridge of the *Reina Christina*, which was not protected.

A letter from Past-Assistant Engineer E. L. Beach, of the *Baltimore*, published in the New York *Sun*, says:

"Every shot fired from our fleet was most deliberately, coolly, and pitilessly aimed. The Spaniards fired an enormous number of times, but with apparently the most impracticable aim. Shells dropped all around our ship; we were in action for over four hours; hundreds of shot and shell fell close to us. Only five or six pierced us and they did no damage.

"The damage done by our ships was frightful. I have visited all of the sunken Spanish ships, and, had I not seen the effects of American marksmanship, I would hardly give credit to reports of it. One smoke-stack of the *Castillo*, a 3,300-ton Spanish ship, was struck eight times, and the shells through the hull were so many and so close that it is impossible that a Spaniard could have lived on her deck. The other large ship, the *Reina Christina*, was perforated in the same way. We did not employ much tactics, because there wasn't much need for them. There were the enemy, and we went for them bullheadedly and made them exceedingly sick."

That is to say, the Spaniards were wiped out, while in our squadron, the shell that did the most distressful damage exploded in the private room of Ensign John S. Doddridge on the *Boston* and ruined its looks.

While a few shot from the Spanish ships struck ours, not one from the forts did so, and the whole damage our vessels received was utterly insignificant. Three shots hulled the *Olympia*, but did no damage beyond cracking a plate or two.

Dewey's report on this matter says: "I am happy to report that the damage done to the squadron under my command was inconsiderable. Several of the vessels were struck and even penetrated, but the damage was of the slightest, and the squadron is in as good condition now as before the battle."

Admiral Montojo's statement regarding the loss of life on the Spanish side was given in detail some days later. The Spanish then reported that they had 78 killed on the ships and 23 on shore, a total of 101, while 235 were wounded afloat, and 45 in the fort—a total of 280. This gives 381 killed and wounded. On our side eight men were slightly wounded. They were all on the *Baltimore*, and were hurt by a 4.7-inch shot that came in on the gun-deck. The men were struck by the *débris* of a box of fixed ammunition that was exploded by this shell. They were: Lieutenant Frank W. Kellogg, and Ensign Noble E. Irwin, with M. J. Buddinger, R. L. Barlow, R. P. Covert, W. O'Keefe, R. Ricciardelli, and E. Snellgrove, of the crew. In addition to these, Boatswain's Mate Heaney, of the *Olympia*, had his fingers crushed by the recoil of a gun. Mention might be made, too, of the fact that the man at the wheel on the *Boston* had one cheek skinned by a flake of dried paint that was knocked from the ship's fore-mast by a shell that did not explode. It is said that when this shell came howling at the ship, everybody on the bridge except Captain Wildes involuntarily dodged. The Captain was using a palm-leaf fan and smoking a cigar at the time. He stopped waving the fan for a moment as the shell struck the mast, grinned at the junior officers, said, "We were lucky, gentlemen," and then once more began to wave the palm-leaf.

In considering this battle the engine-room must not be forgotten. In the old days the men behind the guns were also obliged to look after the motive power as well—after the sails. In these days the motive power is below the deck, and a host of men must stay there in a temperature running from 125° up to 160°, and keep the wheels turning. And their work is even harder in advance of the battle than it is during the actual combat, for the whole complication of machinery must be adjusted to a pitch that will show the right timbre, no matter what rude call may come from the man on the bridge. That Dewey's ships were manœuvred at will without break or mistake, was due to the fact that able engineers stood at the throttles. The list in Dewey's fleet was: *Olympia*, James Entwistle; *Baltimore*, John D. Ford; *Raleigh*, Frank H. Bailey; *Boston*, Richard Juch; *Concord*, George B. Ransom, all chief engineers, and *Petrel*, Past-Assistant Engineer Reynold T. Hall.

And then there was Paymaster John R. Martin, of the *Boston*, who, having no place at a gun, and no wounded to carry to the surgeon, lighted a spirit-lamp, and made coffee which he carried to those who were working hardest. His mental attitude was typical of that of the entire crew.

Many a year had passed since an American naval officer had had command in a battle between squadrons of ships. It has happened that on the occasions in our history where we have engaged an enemy with a squadron the commanding officer has been, with few exceptions, without previous experience in such a position. Dewey had been under fire as a lieutenant in the Mississippi Valley, and he won distinction at Port Hudson and Donelsonville—but Manila Bay was the first scene of his work as a commanding officer in a squadron battle. His success recalls the famous message of Perry on Lake Erie.

In recognition of Dewey's achievement, Secretary of the Navy Long cabled: "The President, in the name of the American people, thanks you and your officers and men for your splendid achievement and overwhelming victories. In recognition he has appointed you Acting-Admiral and will recommend a vote of thanks to you by Congress as a foundation for further promotion."

The name of Admiral Dewey was on the lips of the whole people within a day, and within a week the show-windows of every town blossomed with his portrait. The people saw and appreciated their hero—a most significant fact in the eyes of one who loves his country. For who shall estimate the influence of the hearty healthful cheer that swept across the nation when the story of Manila was told.

Many comments on the battle of Manila have been written by naval men. Of them all none is so valuable as those which point out the fact that while the Spaniards were utterly reckless of danger, the Americans showed cool courage; where the Spaniards fought in a frenzy of rage, the Americans made and maintained the attack with deliberate and relentless determination. The difference is in the blood, and the hope of the world lies in the racial distinction that was there manifested.

CHAPTER XI

SAMPSON'S FIRST SEARCH FOR CERVERA

A SQUADRON WITH THE SPEED OF A TON-OF-COAL BARGES SENT IN A CHASE OF TWENTY-KNOT SPANISH CRUISERS—THE BOMBARDMENT OF SAN JUAN DE PORTO RICO—WORK OF INEXPERIENCED MEN THAT SHOWED THEIR METTLE — ANOTHER VAIN CRUISE TO NICHOLAS CHANNEL.

THE important business that had called Admiral Sampson to Key West, as mentioned in a preceding chapter, was nothing less than a search for the mystifying Spanish squadron that had been lying at the Cape Verde Islands for some time before the war actually began. Not only was it a mysterious squadron in its movements; to a large part of our alongshore population it was positively fearsome.

And there was good reason, when the makeup of the squadron only is considered, for vigilance if not for alarm in our more weakly fortified harbors. The Spanish Admiral had at command three sister ships of a displacement each of 7,000 tons, each protected by a twelve-inch armor belt, besides a three-inch protective deck, and each armed with two eleven-inch guns, ten 5.5-inch guns, and the usual bristling host called the secondary battery. They were named the *Almirante Oquendo*, the *Infanta Maria Teresa*, and the *Vizcaya*. To them was added the *Cristobal Colon* of about the same size, that was supposed to carry two ten-inch guns, ten six-inch, and six 4.7-inch. She did not have the ten-inch guns on board when the fight came, but her other guns were all of the quick-fire variety (as were the broadside guns of the other ships) and they made a most formidable battery. Moreover, every one of these ships was rated at twenty knots per hour.

To aid these formidable cruisers there were supposed to be four of the latest style of torpedo-boat destroyers, each with a speed of thirty knots, and each carrying twelve-pounder rapid-fire guns; and while yet they were at Cape Verde there were also several ordinary good torpedo-boats.

On April 29th this squadron sailed for American waters and our Government learned the fact. Where they would make a landfall was a question, for the whole United States coast was in a way open to attack. Nevertheless, the ever-important matter of coal and water would have to be considered by Admiral Cervera, and our strategists could guess that when the Spaniards reached this side these two supplies would have to be obtained, and that a Spanish port would therefore be sought. On the whole, it was believed that San Juan on the north coast of Porto Rico would be the rendezvous of the Spaniards, and that they would arrive there soon after May 1st.

On this theory Admiral Sampson was ordered to take the best of his ships and go to San Juan to intercept the Spaniards before they got into port, if possible; if not, then he was to Deweyize them as they lay behind the Morro Castle, that guarded the entrance to the bay.

At 7.30 o'clock on the night of May 4th the flag-ship *New York*, the battle-ships *Iowa* and *Indiana*, the monitors *Amphitrite* and *Terror*, the cruisers *Detroit* and *Montgomery*, the torpedo-boat *Porter*, the armed-tug *Wompatuck*, and the transport *Niagara*, gathered off Cardenas on the north coast of Cuba, bound for San Juan de Porto Rico.

When the purpose in view is considered, the composition of this squadron was most remarkable—in fact it was absurd. This is not to criticise the Admiral; he had to take what the nation had provided and the Navy Department would let him have. We had, indeed, the battle-ships *Massachusetts* and *Texas* in commission, but at the behest of such people as those New Yorkers who moved their silverware to their country residences lest the Spaniards come and loot it, the Department had sent those two brave fighters to Hampton Roads for a coast-guard under the title of "Flying Squadron."

So Sampson had need to be content with the *Amphitrite* and *Terror* instead. With eight-knot monitors he was to go in search of four heavily armed and well-armored cruisers, having a speed of twenty knots per hour. True, he had the *New York* of twenty-one knots, and two battle-ships equal to fifteen and seventeen knots, but neither of these, of course, could be permitted to run faster than the eight-knot monitors. An eight-knot squadron was going in chase of a squadron of twenty knots! And Cervera was actually coming with three destroyers, while Sampson had the one torpedo-boat only.

Well, the seventeen-knot *Iowa* took the *Amphitrite* in tow, and the twenty-one-knot *New York* took the *Terror* in tow, and Sunday morning, the 8th, found the squadron off Cape Haytien, Hayti. Here, most fortunately, a dead calm prevailed, and the monitors were able to lie alongside the *Niagara*, and together refill their coal-bunkers, while the *Porter* lay outside of one of the monitors, and filled hers across the monitor's deck.

The coaling was completed on Monday, May

9th, and thereafter the squadron, with the monitors in tow, went on with the chase of Cervera until 5 o'clock on the afternoon of the 11th, being then less than fifty miles from San Juan. Admiral Sampson shifted his flag to the *Iowa*. He hoped and believed that the Spanish squadron was in San Juan, and he was going to force the battle from the deck of our latest battle-ship, with " Fighting Bob" Evans at his elbow.

Thereafter, for ten hours the ships washed along toward the port. At 3 A.M. on Thursday morning, May 12th, the flickering electric lights of the city came into view with the lamp in the lighthouse tower shining above them.

Then the *Detroit* steamed on to a post a thousand yards in advance of the flag-ship *Iowa*; she had a man over each rail swinging the lead to sound out the channel. The tug *Wompatuck* ran out to the west of the *Detroit* towing a small boat with a red flag which was to be anchored in ten fathoms of water off Cabras Island for a buoy to guide the squadron. And then came the fighting line, the *Porter* close under the shelter of the big *Iowa*, and the *Indiana*, the *New York*, the *Amphitrite*, and the *Terror* strung out at convenient intervals, and the *Montgomery* off the starboard quarter of the *Terror*, ready for a dash in on the westerly side of the harbor's mouth should the Spaniards appear.

It was a most impressive spectacle as the squadron seemingly drifted through the gloom

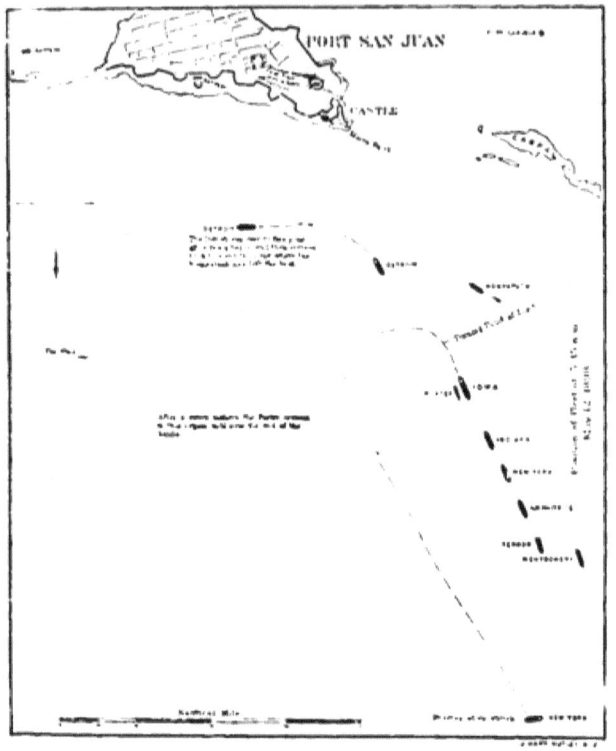

Manœuvring of the Fleet at the Bombardment of San Juan.

toward the city, and one who was there knows how the tiger feels as it creeps toward its sleeping prey.

In the first flush of dawn, that soon came on apace, the city appeared out of the shades as a yellow-walled checker of houses spread over a low ridge lying parallel with the sea. At the east the ridge fell away into a sandy beach that lost itself in a swamp. Along the front of this ridge the trade-wind rollers broke in splashing masses against a precipitous wall—a wall that at the west rose into a bluff sixty feet high, and there, dark and frowning, stood the Morro Castle, at once a fortress and a hopeless prison. The channel to the harbor ran under this bluff. Over to the west lay Cabras Island and Fort Canuelo, on a smaller island, while back of all, terrace on terrace, rose the hills and mountains of the interior.

While yet the night was over the waters, the crews were called to a breakfast of cold meat, bread, and coffee. Then the galley fires were extinguished, and at 5 o'clock precisely the men went to quarters, and loosened and loaded the guns for action, while a few walked to and fro scattering sand on the decks so that they might have a good foothold even though they became flooded with blood.

Then a signal fluttered to the yard of the *Iowa* and a moment later the Stars and Stripes appeared at every mast-head and at every other available point on all the ships. Even the Admiral's flag came down to be hoisted to a smokestack in order that Old Glory might float at the *Iowa's* truck.

From a copyrighted photograph by J. S. Johnston, New York.

Detroit, Unprotected Cruiser. Dimensions, 257 × 37; draft, 17; displacement, 2,089. Speed, 18.7 knots. Main battery, ten five-inch guns.

A little later the *Detroit* turned from the line on which she had steered and headed off to the east—parallel with the splashing breakers. The *Wompatuck* anchored her stake-boat 1,100 yards from the fort, and then, at 5.17 o'clock, at a range of 1,400 yards, a lean six-pounder on the starboard side of the *Iowa's* superstructure called to the sleeping garrison of the old Morro. A moment later the eight-inch guns in the *Iowa's* forward turret on the same side awoke the echoes.

Instantly the alert gunners on the *Detroit* took up the orchestral strain, and then came the thunder of the *Iowa's* twelve-inch guns, with the whirring roar of their shells, the distinct thud when the shells struck and the dull sounds when they exploded, all mingled with the sharp reports of the smaller rifles on the *Detroit*.

Turning slowly around, the *Iowa* headed out to sea, giving place to the other ships in the line in their turn, each firing at will as she arrived opposite the stake-boat. For six minutes there was no reply ashore, and then an old smooth-bore on the parapet of the Morro hurled a big round shell that exploded in the air within a quarter of a mile of our flag-ship, to the amusement of the sailors. After that a couple of modern guns in a new sand fort on the crest east of the Morro began to reply, while another small battery east of that, and perhaps half a dozen guns at the extreme east end of the city joined in. These were six-inch and eight-inch guns of the best make, and the eager cry of their projectiles was just what our men needed to train their nerves for a battle with the enemy's ships to come weeks later.

But there were no war-ships at San Juan, as our men had hoped. Three times our squadron ran in and shelled the forts of the city. In the first round the marksmanship displayed by the big guns' crews was deplorable, for the shells, as a rule, struck in the rocks at the foot of the cliff. But they got the range after that and knocked such clouds of dust from the old stone fort as obscured wide breadths of the city. Meantime, the smaller guns, especially those of the *Detroit*, had spattered the Morro with a rain of steel, driving all the gunners there to the bomb-proofs. As the armored ships turned out to sea in the first round, the *Detroit* headed over to the west parallel with the shore. She was within easy range of Mauser bullets, as well as of the old smooth-bores ashore, and the smooth-bores were effective against an unarmored ship like her. The Spaniards, thinking the others were fleeing, became furious in their efforts to sink her. The spectacle was enough to turn the heart sick, but her crew—well, Captain James H. Dayton stood on the end of the bridge as she turned under that fire, and with

Montgomery, Unprotected Cruiser. Dimensions, 257 × 37; draft, 17; displacement, 2,089. Speed, 18.7 knots. Main battery, ten five-inch guns.

his revolver shot at a floating sardine-can that a servant had thrown over the rail. He hit it five times, too, before it sank. And he was in coolness a fair sample of his crew.

The orders issued the night before said of the *Montgomery*: "If Fort Canuelo fires, she is to silence it." Fort Canuelo fired, to the joy of Captain George A. Converse and his crew. Running into a point on the west side of the channel corresponding with that of the *Detroit* on the east side, the *Montgomery* opened on the fort. It was a well-placed fort and its guns should have driven everything but our battle-ships under the sea, but its gunners, unable to face the *Montgomery*, fled under cover like prairie dogs.

The squadron was before the town for two hours. It was plain that a position could be taken just west of the Morro, out of range of the modern guns along the sea-front, where the city would be wholly at the mercy of our guns. The Spanish afterward admitted that they would have surrendered within an hour had we taken that position, although the real damage done by our shells was inconsiderable. But to take the town was useless so long as we had no men to land to hold it. As a matter of fact not one of our ships was fully manned, let alone providing a permanent landing party.

The marksmanship of the Spanish gunners was worse than at Manila. There was a zone about two miles from their forts, where the majority of their shell fell. In crossing this zone the *New York* and the *Iowa* were struck by a shell each. Frank Widemark was killed on the *New York*, and Samuel Feltman, Michael Murphy, Michael Sprown, and William Rapp were wounded. They were all near the eight-inch gun on the port side. On the *Iowa* G. Merkle, R. C. Hill, and John Mitchell were wounded. A man on the *Amphitrite* died of the heat in the stoke-hole. No damage was done to any of our ships.

Montgomery. New Orleans. Cincinnati.
 Panther. towing . . . . . Amphitrite. Wasp.
  Rogers. New York. Foote.

Sampson's Squadron in
Drawn by L. A. Shafer from

Detroit.   Mayflower.   Annapolis. Newport.
    Indiana.   Kanapaha.   Puritan.   Mianto-   Machias. Wilming-
                                  Vesuvius.   nomoh.   Associated   ton.
                                                           Press Boat.

Nicholas Channel.
diagram by John R. Spears.

"Cervera's fleet was not there; it was already two weeks out from the Cape Verdes; our squadron could move at very slow speed on account of the monitors; we were 1,000 miles from Havana, which had to be covered; the Flying Squadron, as far as we knew, was still north; we had no land force with which to hold the place, and no time to spare to await one if we were to look after Cervera—all those considerations made immediate movement westward imperative." So says Captain F. E. Chadwick, who was Sampson's chief-of-staff, as well as Captain of the *New York*, in a review of the navy's work written for *Scribner's* for November, 1898.

Back to Key West they went with the speed of a tow of coal barges. It was humiliating—nerve-destroying—but once Key West was reached (May 18th), the Flying Squadron was found there—at least the *Brooklyn*, *Massachusetts*, and *Texas* were there, and the *St. Paul*, auxiliary cruiser, under Sigsbee from the *Maine*, was with them. Here were ships for a squadron fit to search for Cervera, but a new complication had arisen. Cervera had actually reached American waters. He had coaled at Curaçoa, and gone north toward Cuba.

The *St. Paul* was at once sent away to scout on the south coast of Cuba, while Schley, with the *Brooklyn*, *Massachusetts*, and *Texas*, was ordered to Cienfuegos on the south coast. The *Iowa* was sent a day later to join him there, for Sampson was convinced that Cervera would go either to Cienfuegos or come by the east end of Cuba to race through the blockade and enter Havana. Schley sailed on May 19th.

Having sent Schley south, Sampson himself took the *New York*, the *Indiana*, the monitors *Puritan*, *Miantonomoh*, and *Amphitrite*, with the cruisers *Cincinnati*, *Detroit*, *Montgomery*, and a host of gun-boats and auxiliaries, and cruised away to Nicholas Channel on the north coast. It was on Saturday, May 21st, that he started east once more. In Nicholas Channel he awaited the enemy.

But this cruise, like the other, was in vain. The Spaniards had proved once more the adage that the timid slink more dangers than brave men run. On May 19th Cervera had entered Santiago harbor with his four beautiful cruisers and two destroyers, the third destroyer that he had brought over the sea having gone to San Juan, Porto Rico.

What was done when this fact was learned shall all be told in another chapter, save only that Sampson returned at once to Key West. When there a most welcome sight met his eyes, for the *Oregon*, all the way from San Francisco, had come (May 26th) to lend a hand in the work that was now to be done.

CHAPTER XII

THE *OREGON'S* FAMOUS RUN

A RACE AGAINST TIME 14,700 MILES LONG WITH NEVER A BREAK OR A LOSS OF A TURN OF HER WHEELS—MEN WHO WORKED FOR TWENTY-FOUR HOURS AT A STRETCH MORE THAN ONCE IN THAT CRUISE—A BOILER-MAKER IN A LIVE FURNACE—SHOTS THAT GAVE LIFE TO FAINTING FIREMEN—ALONGSHORE SIGNAL SERVICE.

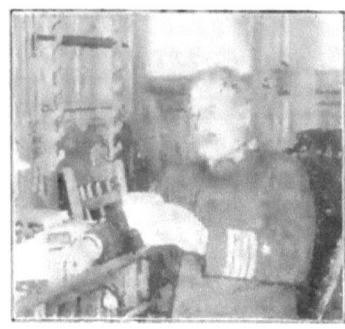

Captain Charles E. Clark.

THE run of the *Oregon*, Captain Charles E. Clark, from San Francisco was so remarkable (nothing approaching it being known to the history of battleships), that a few details must be given to show of what kind of mettle our engineers are made. Here was a ship that, with her bunkers full of coal, actually displaced over 12,000 tons. Leaving San Francisco on March 19th, she ran to Callao, over 4,000 miles, in sixteen days, and she had 600 tons of coal still on board when she arrived. A few trifling leaks developed about her boiler-tubes, but they were repaired without decreasing the speed of the ship. At Callao the machinery was entirely overhauled—cleaned and adjusted. While this was in progress the bunkers were refilled under the eyes of two cadet engineers, "who took twenty-four hours' watch at a time." The engineers were at work on the machinery for the same length of time without rest.

Meantime, "it was evident that war with Spain was inevitable," and "to guard against any treachery on the part of Spanish sympathizers," sentries were doubled and armed to shoot, while steam-launches were manned with armed crews and kept patrolling about the ship all night.

In the Straits of Magellan an increased speed was maintained, because a Spanish torpedo-boat that had been in Montevideo was expected to appear from behind one of the many capes in the narrow waters; while the men stood at the rapid-fire guns to give her a hot welcome.

At Sandy Point, the Chilian settlement of the Strait, the machinery was again overhauled and more coal taken. Of the work here, Captain Clark wrote: "The spirit on board this ship can best be described by referring to instances such as the engineer-officers voluntarily doubling their watches when high speed was to be made, the attempt of men to return to the fire-room after being carried out of it insensible, and the fact that most of the crew preferred to leave their hammocks in the nettings" (*i.e.*, go without sleep), "until they could get the ship coaled and ready to sail from Sandy Point."

At Rio Janeiro they heard (on May 4th) that war had been begun, and of the work of Dewey at Manila. At Bahia, on May 8th, they put on their war paint, sailing the next day, and on the 18th they took on 240 tons of coal at Barbadoes. They were off Jupiter Inlet, Florida, on May 24th. Here, Captain Clark communicated with Washington. The Secretary of the Navy told him that if any repairs were needed to go to Norfolk, but if the ship was in order to go on to Key West. Two days later they cast anchor off Sand Key light at Key West.

The *Oregon* was built at the Union Iron Works, San Francisco. That she should have stood the strain of a race 14,700 miles long without a break, shows that not one dishonest stroke was given her in the building. That neither bearings nor boiler-tubes went wrong in all that strain was due to the watchful care and ability of Chief Engineer Robert W. Milligan, and his assistants. We used to hear, in the days of our naval decadence, the sneers of men who called themselves (and who were) practical men—sneers regarding the ability of our naval engineers. It was admitted that our engineers had "book-learning," but denied that they were practically efficient. But that was long ago, and it is mentioned here only to give a back-ground to the splendid achievements of the engineers of the *Oregon*. A run of 14,700 miles with never a break—that tells the story.

An explanation of the fact that the *Oregon*, though well out from the Florida shore, while in Jupiter Inlet, was able to communicate immediately with the Navy Department—was able to send reports and receive orders, is interesting. A "coast signal service" was organized under Captain John R. Bartlett, U.S.N., beginning on March 15th. Eighteen stations, manned by 310 men, all told, were established. Each had a 90-foot mast with a 40-foot yard, and a full set of day and night signals. These were connected with 1,443 life-saving stations, 850 lighthouses, and 33 weather bureau stations, by means of telegraph lines, and it was arranged so that the entire system could be placed in communication with Washington within half an hour—something that was repeatedly done in practice trials. The movements of our own vessels were thus observed while an effective lookout for the enemy was maintained.

From a copyrighted photograph by C. C. Langill, New York.

Oregon, First-class Battle-ship. Dimensions, 348 x 69; draft, 27; displacement, 10,288. Speed, 16.79 knots. Main Battery, four thirteen-inch, eight eight-inch, and four six-inch guns.

To further display the sort of spirit shown by our engine-room force, an incident in one of the minor alongshore actions, in which the *Castine* had part, must be related. In the midst of the work, while at full speed, and under forced draft, "a fierce hissing noise was heard inside one of the furnaces. A socket-bolt in a back connection at the farthest interior extremity of the furnace had become loose, springing a leak. The steam was pouring in upon the fire, threatening in a few minutes to put it out and stop the progress of the vessel, if it did not cause a terrific explosion. All in the boiler-room knew that unless this hole was stopped disaster was at hand. One of the boiler-makers, named Huntley, ordered the forced draft turned off and the fires banked (*i.e.*, wholly covered over with coal). Taking a plank, he threw it in on top of the wet, black coal with which the fire had been banked," and then, in spite of the spurting steam from the broken joint, and the glowing hot furnace-roof above him, and the gases of the smothered fire beneath, he climbed in along that plank to the rear of the furnace and repaired the leak. "For three minutes he remained inside" in that hell hole, but when his friends drew him out fainting, he had accomplished the work.

One more tale of the men who worked where the heat was never below 125° shall be told. It was related of Milligan, of the *Oregon*, by Captain Clark, and it occurred during the most famous race of the war, to be described farther on. "The officers kept asking permission to fire," said Captain Clark, "so I told them to send one shot after the vessel. Just after the report of the shot the chief engineer, who had joined in shovelling coal in the engine-room, came up to me as black as anything could be, and begged that another shot be fired. He said his men were fainting down below under the heat and terrific strain, but if they could hear a few shots he was sure they would keep their strength."

CHAPTER XIII

SCHLEY'S CRUISE TO SANTIAGO

REASONS FOR HIS DELAY AT CIENFUEGOS—STOPPED TWENTY MILES FROM HIS DESTINATION AND THEN STARTED BACK TO KEY WEST—BREAK ON THE COLLIER—DASH OF THE *MARBLEHEAD*—WHEN SCHLEY SAW CERVERA'S SHIPS AT ANCHOR WITHIN EASY RANGE—A "RECONNAISSANCE" AT A RANGE OF FROM FOUR TO FIVE MILES—A BLOCKADING SQUADRON TEN MILES FROM PORT—ACTS OF AUXILIARY CRUISERS DESCRIBED.

As already stated, Schley with his squadron sailed from Key West bound for the south coast of Cuba in search of Cervera on May 19th, the very day, as it happened, that Cervera entered Santiago. His flag-ship was the *Brooklyn*, and he took with him the *Massachusetts*, the *Texas*, and the auxiliary *Scorpion*. His sailing order, written by Sampson, contained this paragraph:

"It is unnecessary for me to say that you should establish a blockade at Cienfuegos with the least possible delay, and that it should be maintained as close as possible."

On the next day (May 20th), the *Iowa*, the *Castine*, and the collier *Merrimac*, followed

Schley under orders to join him at Cienfuegos. Then at 3 o'clock on the morning of May

Commodore Winfield S. Schley.

21st, Sampson sent the *Marblehead* to carry a further order (No. 8 in the official report), of which the important part read:

"Spanish squadron probably at Santiago de Cuba, four ships and three torpedo-boat destroyers. If you are satisfied that they are not at Cienfuegos, proceed with all despatch, but cautiously, to Santiago de Cuba, and if the enemy is there, blockade him in port."

It was after sending this order that Sampson went to the coast of Cuba, gathered his big squadron, and went to the Nicholas Channel. But before leaving the vicinity of Havana he sent the auxiliary *Hawk* away to Schley with a duplicate of order No. 8, and with these additional instructions:

"It is thought the enclosed instructions will reach you by 2 A.M., May 23d. This will enable you to leave before daylight (regarded very important) so that your direction may not be noticed, and be at Santiago A.M. May 24th. It is thought that the Spanish

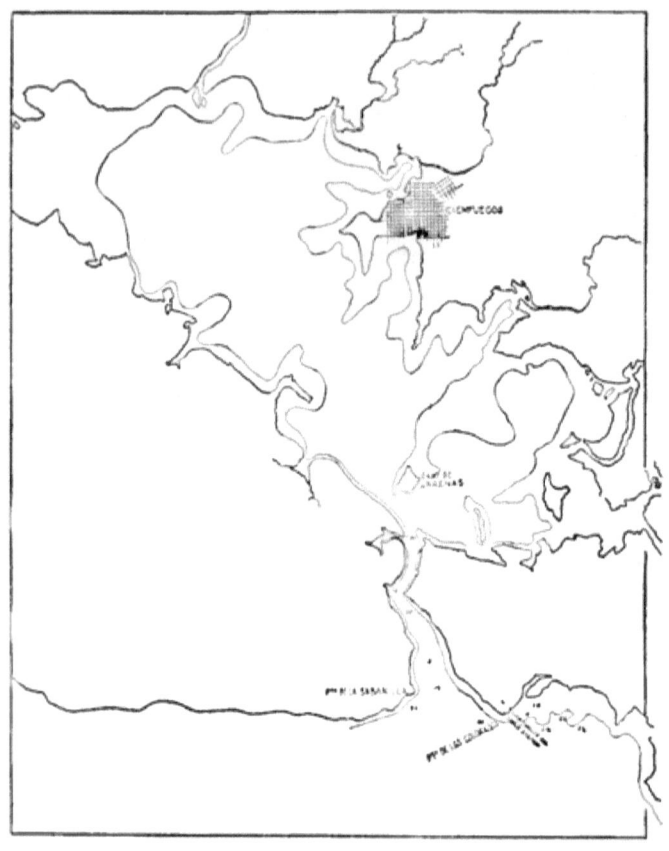

Chart of Cienfuegos.

squadron would probably be still at Santiago, as they must have some repairs to make and coal to take."

It is important to observe that order No. 8

did not definitely tell Schley to go on to Santiago unless he was "satisfied they are not at Cienfuegos," but it is plain from these additional instructions, sent by the *Hawk*, that Sampson meant to have him go to Santiago immediately.

Schley arrived off Cienfuegos late at night on the 21st. At daylight the next morning and again at 8 o'clock he steamed within a mile and a half of the light-house, without drawing fire, and then the *Scorpion* was sent away to Santiago to learn what the big scouts, supposed to be there, had seen. When closest to land a reporter on the *Texas* (T. M. Dieuaide, of *The Evening Sun*, New York, who is known by the writer hereof as a trustworthy man) looked over the harbor from the lookout-perch and saw "a gray smoke-stack and the masts of two schooners." He saw no other ships. "Most of the officers of the squadron," says Dieuaide, "were firmly convinced that the Spanish ships were not inside. Commodore Schley was firmly convinced that they were."

During this day (May 22d) the *Iowa* and the torpedo-boat *Dupont* joined Schley.

On May 23d, Schley wrote to Sampson saying, definitely, "the *Castine, Merrimac*, and *Hawk* arrived this morning." That was in a paragraph numbered 4. He then says (paragraph 1): "In reply to your letter, No. 8, I would state that I am by no means satisfied that the Spanish squadron is not at Cienfuegos. The large amount of smoke seen in the harbor would indicate the presence of a number of vessels, and under such circumstances it would seem to be extremely unwise to chase up a probability at Santiago de Cuba reported via Havana, no doubt as a ruse.

"2. I shall therefore remain off this port."

Another letter of the same date reports the coming of the British steamer *Adula*, en route to Cienfuegos, ostensibly to get British refugees. Her captain told Schley he had heard at Jamaica that Cervera had left Santiago on May 20th. Commenting on this report, Schley says:

"Now, on Saturday, May 21st, when about forty miles southwest of this port, I heard, from the bridge of this vessel, firing of guns toward Cienfuegos, which I interpreted as a welcome to the Spanish fleet."

On the morning of the 24th, the *Marblehead*, *Eagle*, and *Vixen* joined Schley. The lookouts of the squadron had seen three fires on a hill west of the port every night and three horses on the beach beneath the hill every day. McCalla, of the *Marblehead*, knew them to be a signal made by the insurgents, and he went to see them in person. He reported to Schley that they were trustworthy and that they said positively that Cervera's ships were not in the harbor.

Schley, in the afternoon of that day (May 24th), determined to obey the spirit of his instructions received by way of the *Hawk* on the 23d, and go on to Santiago. He left Cienfuegos soon after 6 o'clock.

It illustrates the spirit of his men to tell that the *Dupont*, which had bumped a hole in her bottom on a coral reef, and had started for Key West for repairs, came back at full speed to beg permission to go along as soon as she read the signals ordering the squadron to Santiago. A plug would keep out the water well enough if a fight with Cervera was in prospect.

The weather during the run of four hundred miles east was bad. At noon on May 26th the lookouts were able to see the Morro at the mouth of Santiago harbor, but at 5 o'clock in the afternoon Schley's squadron was still twenty miles away and the Morro could only be made out by means of glasses in the military tops. Before dark the scouts *Minneapolis*, *St. Paul*, and *Yale* joined Schley. Not one of these ships had seen Cervera's fleet, but Captain Wise of the *Yale* said to Captain Philip of the *Texas*:

"I firmly believe Cervera is in Santiago harbor." He had expressed his belief to Schley before that, no doubt, although there is no explicit report of his having done so. But Sigsbee, of the *St. Paul*, reported that he had captured the British cargo-ship *Restormel* as she was entering the harbor with a cargo of coal. The captain of the *Restormel* said he had been ordered to go to San Juan de Porto Rico with the coal, but if Cervera was not there he was to go on to Martinique, and in case Cervera had left Martinique he was to go thence to Santiago. It was in obeying these orders that he was entering Santiago. Dieuaide says that in the opinion of most of the officers of the fleet this confirmed the reports that Cervera was in Santiago.

Nevertheless Schley's squadron remained where it was until after dark, and then, to once more quote Dieuaide, "occurred the most remarkable thing of the naval campaign. Almost without exception every man in the squadron expected that the next move would be a dash toward the harbor entrance to draw the fire of the forts, perhaps the ships—who knew? But while everybody waited under the greatest nervous tension that can be imagined, the Ardois signal lights on the *Brooklyn* began to twinkle. Three thousand men watched that signal with almost bated breath. Slowly the red and white lights unfolded the message, while everybody spelled it out letter by letter. And this was it :

"'D-e-s-t-i-n-a-t-i-o-n K-e-y W-e-s-t a-s s-o-o-n a-s C-o-l-l-i-e-r i-s r-e-a-d-y v-i-a s-o-u-t-h s-i-d-e C-u-b-a a-n-d Y-u-c-a-t-a-n C-h-a-n-n-e-l. S-p-e-e-d n-i-n-e k-n-o-t-s.'"

The *Iowa* was lying within hail of the *Texas* and Captain Evans shouted to Captain Philip:

"Say, Jack, what the devil does it mean?"

"Beats me," replied Philip. "What do you think?"

"Damned if I know," Evans said; "but I know one thing—I'm the most disgusted man afloat."

Let it be repeated that the squadron was at that time twenty miles from the Morro of Santiago and it had not been any nearer nor had any effort been made to learn whether Cervera was within or not. At 9.15 o'clock that night the squadron did actually start back for Key West. The break on the collier was a bad one, but in his determination to get back to Key West Schley ordered the *St. Paul* to take her in tow. The *St. Paul* did so, and the squadron started, but the tow lines parted four times in succession. Then Schley ordered the break repaired so that she could go on under her own steam, but before the repairing was completed, the *Harvard* came from San Antonio, Jamaica, with orders for Schley to remain blockading Santiago no matter what happened.

Schley had telegraphed the Navy Department that he was going to Key West for coal. While off Cienfuegos he had complained in his despatches about the difficulty of transferring coal from the collier to his ships on the open

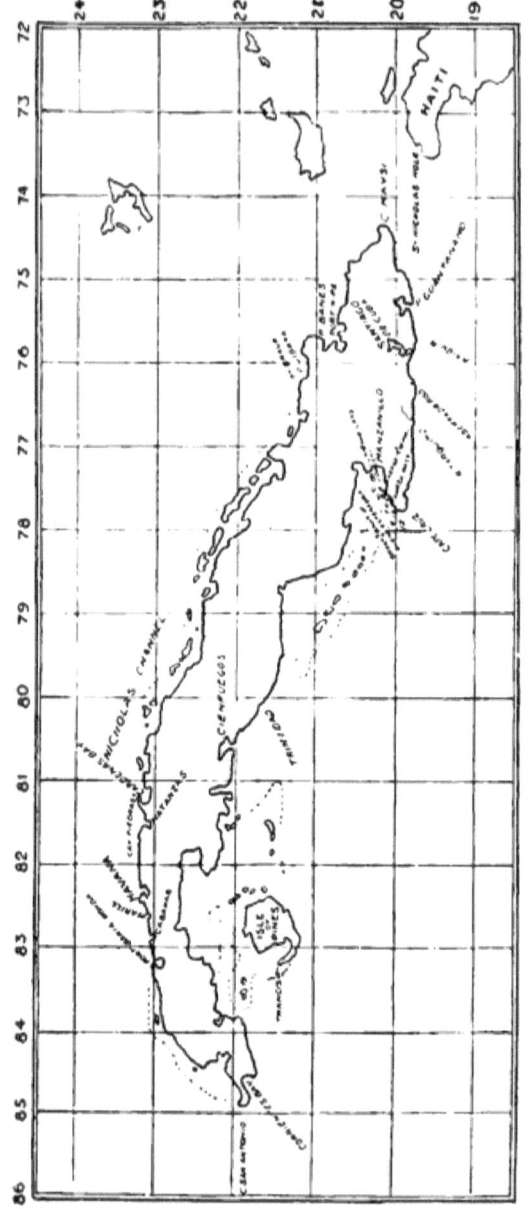

Map of Cuba.

sea. His despatch of May 24th had this to say on the subject in connection with his orders to blockade Santiago :

"I shall proceed to-morrow (25th) off Santiago, being embarrassed, however, by the *Texas* short of coal supply, and her inability to coal in the open sea. I shall not be able to remain off that port (Santiago) on account of general short coal supply of squadron. So will proceed to the vicinity of St. Nicholas Mole, where the water is smooth, and I can coal *Texas* and other ships [with] what may remain in collier."

But now, instead of going to the near-by port at St. Nicholas Mole, as he had said he would do, he was leaving Santiago and the enemy's squadron, and going to Key West. A Washington despatch says that Schley's announcement of the determination to return to Key West "created consternation" in the Navy Department.

Orders to remain were received by Schley on the morning of May 27th. The squadron was held idle where it lay when the *Merrimac* broke the tow line, but at 10.20 o'clock that night, the *Texas*, under orders from Schley, began coaling from the *Merrimac* and at 11 o'clock next day (May 28th) she had taken two hundred and sixty-seven tons ! The *Merrimac* had four thousand tons of coal on board.

In the afternoon of the 28th the squadron

steamed within fifteen miles of Santiago, and then stopped while the *Marblehead* was sent scouting past the mouth of the harbor. It is asserted that in the performance of this duty the *Marblehead*, an unarmored cruiser, ran within less than a mile of the old Morro on the high point on the east side of the bay, and saw distinctly the majority of the Spanish squadron, the *Colon* lying between La Socapa battery and the Morro, while others were strung along up the bay at the usual anchorage intervals. Not one of these ships had steam at a working pressure, and it is possible, though not probable, that the fires were entirely extinguished in some of them.

The *Marblehead* made her run past the harbor on the 28th. At night Schley took his squadron in shore until the ships were estimated to be at a distance of eight miles from the Morro, and then at sunrise on the morning of the 29th, with the *Brooklyn* in the lead, the squadron swept in and across the harbor at a distance not stated, but the ships were close enough to enable every man on deck to see clearly into the mouth of the harbor with the naked eye.

And every man on deck "definitely located" the Spanish squadron. "Right across the entrance of the harbor, but inside the Morro battery, lay the *Colon*, her white awnings glistening in contrast with her black hull, easily distinguishable by her peculiar rig of military mast between smoke-stacks. A little farther in lay another cruiser, one of the *Vizcaya* class." With glasses it was easy to see the crews walking idly about their decks.

Having had what an old sailor would call a severe look at the enemy, Schley steamed out to sea. The Spaniards did not fire a gun— they did not even beat to quarters on their ships. There was no necessity for their doing so.

Going ten miles out to sea, Schley stopped and scattered his squadron in blockading formation. And there the squadron remained idle for two days. Meantime the *New Orleans* had come from Sampson's squadron.

Then, on the 31st, he determined on making what he reported as a "reconnaissance." The reporters called it "a battle lasting fifty-five minutes."

Transferring his flag to the *Massachusetts*, Commodore Schley ordered the *Iowa* and the *New Orleans* into line, and soon after noon he left his blockading station and steamed in to attack the forts. Reports vary as to the location of his blockading station on that day —vary between six and ten miles off shore. At any rate it is certain that he *steamed in* to make the attack, and that when he had arrived at a range of 7,000 yards the *Massachusetts* opened fire. A range of 7,000 yards is just forty yards short of four land miles.

The batteries at once began replying, while the *Colon* joined them as soon as she could bring her men to quarters.

Having passed across the mouth of the harbor at a distance of four land miles from the forts, our ships turned out to sea in a wide curve and once more passed across the mouth, this time at a range of 9,000 yards, or more than five land miles. A private letter from an officer of the *Iowa* to the writer hereof says, that the range of this round was more than five sea-miles—" more than ten thousand yards." Let it stand at five land miles, but this much is certain: The strain on the carriages of the *Iowa's* twelve-inch guns—the strain due to the extreme elevation that was necessary for the great range—almost disabled them.

Only the *Colon* of the Spanish squadron had any real part in this battle, the others having gone behind Gorda Point.

The Spanish report of this encounter said:

"The American squadron, commanded by Commodore Schley, composed of large ironclads and cruisers, attacked the fortifications at the entrance of Santiago. Our ironclad, *Cristobal Colon*, closing the *mouth* of the port, and supported by the fire of the forts, repulsed the attack."

Schley's official report said:

"Made reconnaissance this afternoon, May 31st, with the *Massachusetts, Iowa,* and *New Orleans,* to develop the fortifications with their character. The fire was returned without delay by the heavy batteries to the east and to the west of the entrance; large calibre, long range. *The range was 7,000 yards;* reconnaissance developed satisfactorily the presence of the Spanish squadron lying behind island near inner fort, as they fired over the hills at random. Quite satisfied the Spanish fleet is here."

The italics are not in the originals.

Having told the dates and described the manner in which Commodore Schley became "quite satisfied" of the presence of Cervera in Santiago harbor, some little space must be given to events elsewhere.

The reports of Schley's movements reached Sampson as promptly as the make-shift despatch-boats could carry them, and Sampson hastened back from Nicholas Channel to Key West, where he could quickly communicate with Washington, and when there telegraphed (3 P.M., May 29th) "would like to start at once with *New York* and *Oregon* [for Santiago] arriving in two days. *I can blockade indefinitely.*"

Italics are not in the original despatch. Secretary Long replied: "Act at your discretion with the object of blockading Spanish division as soon as possible." Accordingly Sampson left Key West at 11 o'clock that night (May 29th), and, going over to the Cuban coast, picked up the *Oregon*, the auxiliary *Mayflower*,

The *Mayflower* on the Blockade.

Captain M. R. S. Mackenzie, and the torpedo-boat *Porter*, and went at a thirteen-knot gait around the east end of Cuba. This squadron reached Santiago early on the morning of June 1st, a remarkable run, all things considered. Captain Chadwick, of the *New York*, writes that "on passing the entrance we observed the *Cristobal Colon* and one of the *Vizcaya* class near the harbor entrance, but at 10.30 A.M. they shifted their moorings farther in and out of sight. . . . There was then a month of close blockade."

To follow now the movements of the *St. Paul* after she left Key West to scout for Cervera, we learn that she arrived off Santiago on May 22d and found the harbor unguarded by any American ship. As none of the Spanish ships was disposed to come out, Sigsbee threw overboard a target and proceeded to exercise his men (chiefly naval militia) with the five-inch guns the ship carried. Both ship and target were within range of the forts, but the Spaniards looked on quietly while the green gunners proceeded to show their natural ability by shooting the target to pieces.

For three days the *St. Paul* lay quietly off the harbor, and then, on the 25th, the British steamer *Restormel*, with 2,400 tons of good Cardiff coal for Cervera on board, was seen ploughing along toward the harbor at a twelve-knot gait. The *St. Paul* went after her in a hurry, and when she was within three miles of the Morro stopped her, as related above, and sent her with a prize crew to Key West. The most disgusted man afloat that day was the captain of the *Restormel*. He had not ended expressing his feelings when he reached Key West. That the Spaniards should have allowed an unprotected cruiser to carry off that good coal from under their guns was too much for the stomach of an Englishman.

Neither the shooting of the *St. Paul*, nor the attack "to develop the fortifications," was the first gun-fire that Santiago heard. On May 17th the auxiliary *St. Louis*, Captain Casper F. Goodrich, and the tug *Wompatuck*, Captain Carl Jungen, arrived off the port at night. The *Wompatuck* grappled a cable five hundred yards from shore, but her winch made so much noise that the Spanish sentries in the forts heard her, and two gun-boats came out of the harbor to see what was going on. The gun-boats were supposed to be torpedo-boats, and the Americans withdrew and waited for daylight. At 10 o'clock next morning they went in again. The Spaniards opened fire with two six-inch rifles and the smooth-bores, but the *St. Louis*, with her six-pounders, and the *Wompatuck*, with one three-pounder, drove the gunners from the rifles and the smooth-bores were not worth considering. A mortar battery (eight-inch modern mortars) got the range, after a time, and the *Wompatuck* had to leave, but she cut a hundred-fathom length from the cable before she

Captain C. W. Jungen.

turned her stern to the enemy. She was at work one-quarter of a mile from the beach for fifty minutes.

Going thence a few miles east to Guantanamo, the cable-cutters ran in there, and the *Wompatuck* got hold of a cable, but here the shore fire was hotter, while the *St. Louis* was unable to reach well with her little six-pounders, and she was compelled to order the *Wompatuck* out. Captain Goodrich had to signal a second order before she abandoned the attempt. Jungen was from the *Maine*.

Perhaps the most important fact about this cable-cutting expedition, is that the high-power cannon at Santiago were silenced by the six-pounders of the *St. Louis*, and the three-pounder of the *Wompatuck*. That is, the men were driven from their guns. The *St. Louis* fired one hundred and seventy-two shots, and the *Wompatuck* seventy-six. The *Wompatuck* was at work on the cable for fifty minutes on May 17th, and a total of two hundred and forty-eight of these tiny shells sufficed to protect her from the modern guns mounted on shore at the mouth of Santiago harbor, during that time.

CHAPTER XIV

THE BLOCKADE OF SANTIAGO

DISPOSITION OF THE SQUADRON—THE STORY OF HOBSON'S FUTILE BRAVERY—IT WAS ANOTHER PROOF THAT CULTURE AND COOL COURAGE GO HAND IN HAND—THE FORTS BOMBARDED—GOOD WORK OF THE *VESUVIUS*.

ADMIRAL SAMPSON having reached the station off Santiago and found Cervera still within, at once planned to hold him there permanently. It is easy to say that he succeeded, but wholly impossible for anyone who has had no such experience to fully understand the strain that the work involved. Nevertheless, even a landsman can gather some idea of the situation from the facts. Here was a harbor, the entrance channel to which was but three hundred and fifty feet wide at the narrowest point, while the cliffs on each side rose two hundred feet or more above it. In the night-shadows of these cliffs, that entrance was a very black hole. Within this black hole lay four cruisers rated as twenty-knot ships, with two destroyers that had made thirty knots—they could cover one sea mile in exactly two minutes. It was in the speed of these boats that the chief danger lay—the danger of a surprise. Who could tell at what minute of the night the lookouts would report the enemy's ships within easy torpedo range of ours?

In this emergency the Admiral had two courses to pursue, if he were to reduce the danger of a sudden night attack to the utmost limit. He could establish his squadron, which was soon increased to an ample number by the arrival of other vessels, in a wide arc off the mouth of the harbor at a distance of six miles or more. At that range he would be entirely safe from the guns on shore, and if an enemy's torpedo-boat came out, it would have to run across the high seas for at least twelve minutes before reaching one of our ships. In that time we should have many chances of picking her up by our search-lights.

Another plan for corking the bottle—by this time Cervera was said to be "bottled up" in Santiago—was to close in about the mouth at night, and keep the channel brilliantly illuminated with the search-lights. This "was a bold thing to do," says Captain Chadwick; "but it was in keeping with the whole habit of mind of our Commander-in-Chief, whose idea, constantly expressed in speech and act, was to be in close touch with the enemy."

Accordingly the whole squadron closed in to a range of two miles and a battle-ship picket was established every night. That is to say, two battle-ships ran in shore until within a mile or less of the Morro. Inside of these, three small auxiliaries were lined across the harbor at a distance of perhaps a half mile from the Morro. Inside of them, and but a quarter of a mile from the beach, three steam-launches, each armed with a one-pounder and four marines with rifles, went prowling to and fro.

As night came on one of the two battle-ships here lay with not a light showing, while the other turned her search-lights upon the harbor entrance. "The long and brilliant beam of light shone through the entrance and over the intervening hills as far as Santiago, six land miles distant," says Chadwick. "Every detail of the narrow cañon with cliffs two hundred feet high, forming the harbor entrance, was made visible as day, and the whole proceeding can only be properly described in the remark of the British Naval *Attaché*, who, on looking at it from the deck of the *New York*, exclaimed:

"'What a d——d impertinence!'"

Of such a character was the blockade established by Sampson within three days after his arrival, and maintained until Cervera's squadron was destroyed.

Now although the battle-ships took turns in this work, and it was reasonably certain that no projectile from the shore could pierce a vital part of anyone of them, their upper works, where the crews were obliged to sleep on account of the temperature, were made of such thin material that even a well-directed shell from a smooth-bore, might have been dropped among the sleepers on the pickets. As a matter of fact, the Spaniards never fired a cannon at the night pickets, but they peppered the launches with Mauser rifles, and it was expected that they would use their cannon—there was never an hour of the night, when the men on watch were not looking for the flash of a modern gun on shore. "Anxiety for their men told heavily" on the officers from the first night—the night of June 1st, after Sampson had arrived. Sampson foresaw this immediately on arrival, and his first effort to relieve the strain made the name of Hobson known throughout the world.

After reaching Santiago and taking one look at the narrow entrance to the harbor the possibility of sinking a ship there, to effectually close it, and so prevent Cervera's exit, was apparent to many of the officers of the squadron. Sampson, knowing the width of the channel, had considered the plan of sinking a ship in it while he was lying in Nicholas Channel, and in a despatch dated May 27th, had ordered Schley to sink the collier *Sterling* there, but Schley ignored the order. On the very day he reached Santiago, Sampson began to carry out the plan. There was the *Merrimac*. She had been sold to the Government at a price twice her value. She was a bad ship—she could serve the nation much better in blocking the channel than in any other way, and preparations to sink her into the channel were immediately begun. At the earnest request of Mr. Richmond Pearson Hobson, Assistant Naval Constructor, he was put in charge. He had been placed on the *New York* to watch her workings in actual war, and write a report thereon for the chief of his bureau. His knowledge of ships fitted him for the task, and he had already shown his courage, when he worked the range-finder on the *New York*, during the bombardment of San Juan de Porto Rico.

Lieutenant Hobson.

About two hundred men were employed in stripping the *Merrimac*—all that could be effectively used—for it was intended to send her in just before daylight next morning. However, after stripping her, it was necessary to fit her with torpedoes that would sink her instantly, when the time came, and this took so long that day had arrived on the morning of June 2d, before she was ready. Hobson was anxious to go then, but the Admiral ordered him to wait.

Meantime a crew of six men had been selected from among the hundreds that crowded aft to volunteer. They were Daniel Montague, Chief Master-at-Arms of the *New York;* George Charette, Gunner's Mate, first class, of the *New York;* J. E. Murphy, Coxswain on the *Iowa;* John P. Phillips, a machinist, Oscar Deignan, Coxswain, and Francis Kelly, a water-tender, all of the *Merrimac.* To this crew of six men Coxswain Rudolph Clausen, of the *New York* added himself by eluding the vigilance of the officers. Admiral Sampson refused to allow any other officer to go on the expedition, or any more men than were actually needed, on the ground of the extreme danger of the undertaking. He was not going to waste any lives.

At 3 o'clock on the morning of June 3d, these men headed away for the harbor. A steam-launch from the *New York*, under Naval Cadet Joseph W. Powell, followed to pick up the crew of the *Merrimac*, should they succeed in getting away from her after performing their work, in either the row-boat or the life-raft that had been provided for them.

It was a cloudy night, but because the channel was so narrow it was absolutely certain that the *Merrimac* would be discovered before she reached her destination, and that a heavy fire from the batteries of all kinds would enfilade her, while the sentinels and the troops encamped along shore were likely to spatter her

The *Merrimac* in the Entrance to Santiago Harbor.

deck with Mauser bullets as a tropical rainstorm would pelt her with drops of water. In short, there was not one chance in a thousand, apparently, for any of these men to live through that adventure, and yet they had eagerly volunteered for it, and one had stowed himself away on board without permission! Nor was the chance of Cadet Powell and his men much better, for it was his duty to follow the *Merrimac* to the mouth of the harbor, where he, too, would be as easy a target as the men on the ship, and there to wait until after daylight.

Getting his bearings by the outlines of the Morro against the sky, Hobson drove the old ship into the centre of the narrow channel. A hell of flame leaped out on both sides as she passed the Morro, while the *Vizcaya*, that was on guard just around the bend, began firing with her broadside battery. The Spaniards thought we were coming with our squadron to force the harbor, and all the guns, big and little, that would bear, and many that would not, were fired with feverish rapidity. Immediately the shots began to reach the ship, but no vital damage was done, and she held on her way until opposite Estrella Point.

Then the time to sink her had come, and Hobson pressed the electric button. Three of the torpedoes that were placed at her water-line exploded, tearing open her sides. The man at the anchor cut it loose, bringing up her head just opposite the point, while her stern swung slowly around with the tide.

It seemed for a moment that she must sink,

From a copyrighted photograph by J. C. Hemment.

The Spanish Prisoners who were Exchanged for Hobson being brought under American Escort with a Flag of Truce to the Meeting Place between the Lines.

as they wished, right across the channel, but she filled so slowly, that she lay lengthwise of the channel and well at one side before she finally struck the bottom. In describing what followed Hobson said afterward: "We were all aft, lying on the deck. Shells and bullets whistled around. Six-inch shells from the *Vizcaya* came tearing into the *Merrimac*, crashing clear through, while the plunging shots from the fort broke through her decks.

"'Not a man must move,' I said; and it was only owing to the splendid discipline of the men that we all were not killed. We must lie there till daylight, I told them. Now and again one or the other of the men lying with his face glued to the deck and wondering whether the next shell would not come our way, would say, 'Hadn't we better drop off now, sir?' but I said, 'Wait till daylight.' It would have been impossible to get the catamaran anywhere but on to the shore, where the soldiers stood shooting, and I hoped that by daylight we might be recognized and saved.

"It was splendid the way those men behaved. The fire of the soldiers, the batteries, and the *Vizcaya* was awful. When the water came up on the *Merrimac's* decks the catamaran floated amid the wreckage, but she was still made fast to the boom, and we caught hold of the edges and clung on, our heads only being above water."

At daylight the fire ceased and a Spanish launch came toward the wreck. Hobson and his men agreed to try capturing her and running for the open sea, but as she drew near a dozen marines aimed their Mausers at the Yankee heads, and Hobson saw that, in Western parlance, they had the drop.

"'Is there any officer in that boat to receive a surrender of prisoners of war?' I shouted. An old man leaned out under the awning and waved his hand. It was Admiral Cervera. The marines lowered their rifles, and we were helped into the launch.

"Then we were put in cells in Morro Castle. It was a grand sight a few days later, to see the bombardment, the shells striking and bursting around El Morro. Then we were taken into Santiago. I had the court-martial room in the barracks. My men were kept prisoners in the hospital." So ran Hobson's story.

Admiral Cervera was so much impressed by the gallantry of the *Merrimac's* crew that he sent an officer under a flag of truce to tell Admiral Sampson that all were uninjured and well, and that they should be well cared for. They were imprisoned in the Morro until after the first bombardment, when they were removed for safety to Santiago.

Hobson and his men were exchanged after a time (July 7th), and Hobson was sent north to arrange for work to be described farther on.

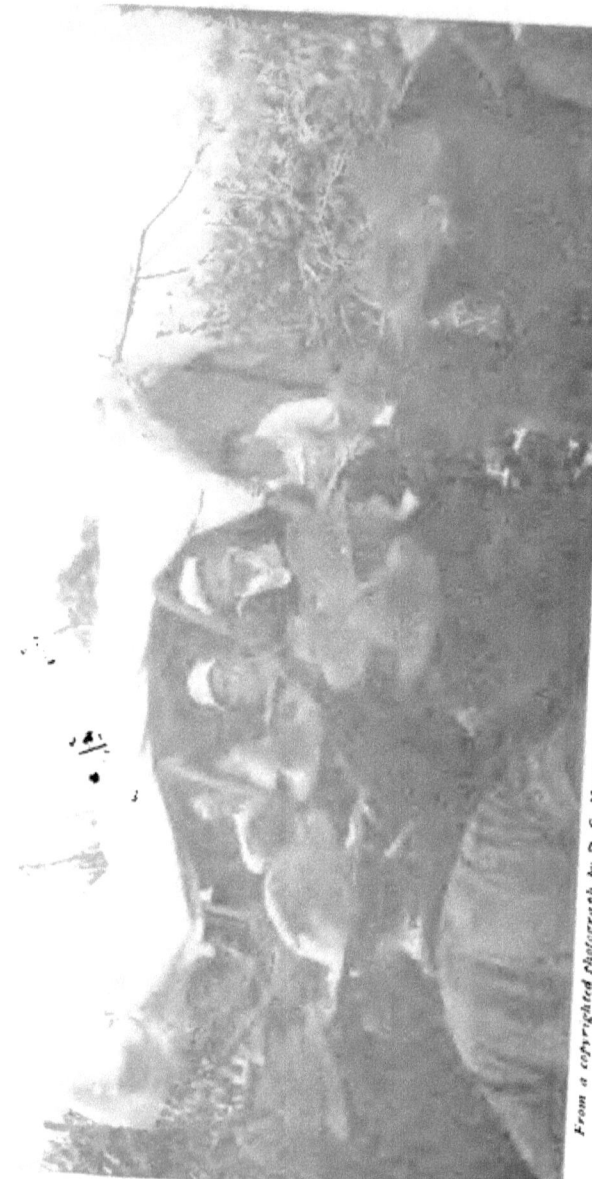

From a copyrighted photograph by J. C. Hemment.

Hobson's *Merrimac* Crew in the American Lines

The ovations which he received everywhere were notable, New York showing an especial appreciation by a public meeting in his honor.

At the risk of what may appear as a monotonous repetition it must be said that the significance of these demonstrations, like those following the victory of Admiral Dewey, was in this, that they proved the capacity of the people to appreciate real heroism. Dewey was honored because the people were able to appreciate a great sea captain; Hobson because they knew a courageous man when they saw him.

But that is not all that is to be said of Hobson and Powell, for they are simply representative men among the younger officers of the navy. A hundred others in the squadron were heart-sick because they had no such opportunity, and opportunity was all that was lacking to give us a hundred records like that of Hobson and Powell.

And there is one other fact about Hobson that is of importance. He has always been known as a typical student. He is what the old-fashioned sailor would call a "scientist."

The *Merrimac* having failed to sink as intended, Captain Chadwick says, "it was at once determined to injure the batteries so that a battle-ship might lie in close. This led to an attack on the batteries during the morning of June 6th. The ships formed in line at 6.40 o'clock. The careful reader will note that where a fleet was to be attacked, both at Manila and San Juan de Porto Rico, the work began at daylight. In the attacks on forts they always took the matter more comfortably. The squadron was arranged in two divisions. For an attack on the fortifications on the east side of the harbor the Admiral selected the *New York*, Captain Chadwick; the *Iowa*, Captain Evans; the *Oregon*, Captain Clark; the auxiliary cruiser *Yankee*, Captain Brownson, and the despatch-boat *Dolphin*, Captain Henry W. Lyon. For the west side he detailed the *Brooklyn*, Captain Francis A. Cook, with Commodore Schley in charge of the division; the *Massachusetts*, Captain F. J. Higginson; the *Texas*, Captain John Philip, and the auxiliaries *Suwanee*, Captain D. Delehanty, and *Vixen*, Captain A. Sharp.

Captain F. A. Cook on the *Brooklyn*.
From a copyrighted photograph by E. Muller.

The formation was completed well off shore, and then the two divisions steamed in, side by side. On arriving at a range of 4,000 yards the *New York* opened the battle with a shot from the eight-inch guns in the forward turret. The *Brooklyn* followed immediately. Then Sampson turned to the east, and Schley to the west, giving the other ships a chance, but both divisions continued on in shore to a range in some cases of less than 3,000 yards, while the *New York*, in an effort to shell out the forts lying well up the harbor entrance at Estrella Point, and even the Gorda Point, stood in until but 1,800 yards from the Morro.

It was a lowering morning in the rainy season. The rain-squalls came drifting along at sea with the clouds reaching down to the mountain-tops on shore and almost touching the old castle at the harbor mouth. The ships at times disappeared in the thick rain-squalls, but the hot red flame, and white smoke-clouds came booming out, as they continued their fire in spite of the obscurity.

Captain F. J. Higginson, Commanding the *Massachusetts*.

Eventually the *New Orleans* and the *Marblehead* were permitted to join the others, and then the squadron had a new experience, for when the *New Orleans* fired, only a flash was seen. She carried smokeless powder and there was no white cloud hanging about her to interfere with the men who were looking through the sights on her guns. This is a most important matter. We plume ourselves on the excellence of the work of our sailors, but we do not give them the full credit that they deserve, for we compelled them to fight with guns that were not the best, and with powder that was as bad as any, if not the worst, in the world.

According to Sampson's report, the firing began at 7.30 o'clock and ended at 10. The Spaniards woke up soon after it began and gave a fine exhibit of fireworks—an exhibit that served to strengthen the nerves of our men, even if it did not do any damage. The newspaper reports of the battle all mentioned the dash of the auxiliary *Yankee* with her Naval Militia crew, and of the *Suwanee*. The *Yankee* and *Texas* kept firing from their stern-guns long after the squadron was ordered out to sea.

The Spaniards reported sixteen men from the *Reina Mercedes*, including her second officer and an ensign, killed, and one officer and eleven sailors wounded, while two Spanish artillery lieutenants and one private were killed and three officers and twenty-one soldiers were wounded among the land force. A number of our shells passed over the hills, and fell in the city of Santiago, six land miles away. The forts were silenced. One gun was dismounted, but it did not appear that the forts were materially injured. Nevertheless, the effect of the bombardment was just what was wanted. As Captain Chadwick says, during the month that followed "not a shot was fired by the enemy at any one of the ships" doing blockade duty.

Yankee, Auxiliary Cruiser. Rated at 4,600 tons; speed, 15.5 knots. Battery, ten five-inch guns and four six-pounders.

It must be said, however, that other attacks were made on the alongshore fortifications after this one. Further than that, the *Vesuvius*, Captain John E. Pillsbury, here had her first real trial, and it is certain that her presence helped to keep the Spaniards quiet. The guns of this vessel could not be aimed with any certainty, and they are not of as long range as the dynamite guns supplied to the army during the war. Nevertheless, Captain Chadwick says:

"The watch described was varied frequently at night by the coughing up (for so it sounded) of a gun-cotton projectile from the *Vesuvius*, the explosion of which at times shook the earth for a radius of miles. I remember one of her earlier efforts, when lying asleep on the transom of the chart-house forward (my usual night resting-place) . . . I awoke conscious of a heavy jar to the whole ship's structure, which must have been transmitted from the point where the shell landed through the earth and up through the three hundred fathoms of water on the surface of which we were lying. . . . There is no question of the terrifying effect of these shells upon an enemy; so long as they were expected the men at the batteries remained away from their guns and under cover; and there is also no question of their great destructiveness. They ploughed great pits in the earth, and had they fallen fairly in a battery must have put the guns *hors de combat* for a time, at least."

The shells she fired contained two hundred and fifty pounds of gun-cotton, and men who saw where they landed say that "they made holes like the cellar of a country house." Could a new *Vesuvius* be built and armed under designs from Washington, we should have a ship for attacking land batteries that would be a real terror.

CHAPTER XV

THE MARINES AT GUANTANAMO

OUR FIRST ARMED FORCE TO MAINTAIN A HOLD ON CUBAN SOIL.—THE BAY CAPTURED BY THE *MARBLEHEAD* AND *YANKEE*—IT WAS HOT WORK FOR A WEEK—THE SPANIARDS IN THE BRUSH—ASSAULT ON A FUNERAL *CORTÉGE*—SPANISH WOODS STATION CAPTURED, AND CAIMANERA'S FORT DESTROYED—A TORPEDO IN THE PROPELLER OF THE *TEXAS*—GOOD HEALTH OF THIS FORCE ON SHORE.

Having given the Spanish batteries at Santiago harbor mouth an effective and discouraging proof of the skill of the naval gunners, the next care of the Admiral was to secure a harbor where any of his ships in need of coal or repairs might lie in safety regardless of the weather. For the hurricane season was at hand, and a shelter for these purposes was absolutely necessary to maintain the efficiency of the squadron on the blockade. And a harbor of the kind needed lay forty miles away to the east—Guantanamo Bay. It was a much better place for coaling ships than the Sand Key Roads at Key West, to which Schley had proposed to return to coal his squadron. A number of islands divide this bay in such a way as to form an inner and an outer harbor, but the outer bay affords a safe anchorage, while the water is deep (six fathoms or so) near shore, in places, and ships may even come almost to the beach.

On June 7th Admiral Sampson sent the *Marblehead* and *Yankee* to take possession of the outer bay—an honor which the *Yankee* received because her crew had run in so close to the batteries and had shown so much persistence in the bombardment on the 6th. The story of this war, it may be said, in passing, shows that the officers who displayed the most aggressive appetite for fighting and adventure were the ones who saw most real service.

As the two war-ships approached the entrance of the harbor they received a warm fire from a battery on shore near the telegraph station, while a gun-boat came out to lend a hand. But when McCalla and Brownson turned their guns loose, the gun-boat fled to the inner harbor, and the men of the battery to tall timber on the far side of the hill. It was only a skirmish, but it gave us a harbor as useful as was Port Royal to the Federal forces in the Civil War.

Here the *Marblehead* remained until June 10th, when a landing was effected by a force of marines. At the outbreak of the war—on

April 22d—the first battalion of marines sailed from the Brooklyn navy-yard on the transport *Panther*, Captain G. C. Reiter, for Key West. The battalion was under Lieutenant-Colonel Robert W. Huntington. It included five infantry companies of 103 men and officers each, and an artillery company (four three-inch rifles) of 117 men and officers. These were landed at Key West and remained there until Cervera was found, when they were at once forwarded to Santiago for the purpose to which they were now devoted.

On the morning of June 10th the *Panther* took them to Guantanamo Bay. The *Oregon*, the *Yankee*, the *Yosemite* (Captain W. H. Emory, with the Michigan Naval Militia to man her), the *Scorpion*, Captain J. P. Merrell; the *Dolphin*, Captain W. H. Lyon, and the storeship *Supply*, Captain R. R. Ingersoll, were also of the expedition. The bay was reached soon after dinner. There was no opposition from the shore, and to the inspiring strains of "There'll be a Hot Time in the Old Town To-night" the men pulled ashore in the small boats of the squadron. The landing was just inside the eastern point of the harbor. Color-Sergeant Richard Silvee, of Company C, raised the gridiron flag over the ruins of a blockhouse on the hill at 2.10 o'clock. The blockhouse had been eviscerated by the fire of the

Marblehead and *Yankee* on the 7th, but the flag-staff was still standing.

To prevent possible infection by yellow fever, an abandoned fishing-village on the

Port Guantanamo, or Cumberland Harbor.

point, and all other houses in the vicinity, were burned, and then the camp was established on the top of the bare hill overlooking the bay where the remains of the Spanish block-house stood. The encampment was named Camp McCalla, in honor of the energetic captain of the *Marblehead*. The naval forces afloat and ashore were enthusiastic over the landing.

To the honor of landing the first armed force on Cuban soil the marines added that of the first fight ashore with the Spaniards. The Spaniards had withdrawn from the beach through fear of the ships, but they merely retired to the brush beyond the coast-range hills and there awaited, in force, for what they deemed a favorable time for an attack.

During the 10th the marines were hard at work all day landing supplies and getting their camp in order, and they were tired enough to sleep soundly that night. Nevertheless, the Spaniards waited until the afternoon of the 11th. But when, at about 5.30 o'clock, they did get ready, the Spaniards were for once persistent enough to keep our men heated up for almost a week.

The trouble began immediately after a grizzled old Cuban ally came into camp on the run to say that the Spaniards were upon us. Three Mauser bullets followed the Cuban into camp. At that time some of our men were still at work in the camp, while fifty or so were bathing in the bay at the foot of the hill. As the firing began the bathers ran, half-naked, up the hill to join the command. Meantime, Colonel Huntington had his men at work, with the precision and regularity of veterans, firing by volleys into the brush whence the Spanish shots came, while three parties were sent out to beat up the brush in search of the enemy. In half an hour the firing was over for the

Picket Sentry, on Guard Duty, Protected from the Intense Rays of the Sun by a Thatch.

moment, but when one of the scouting-parties returned it lacked two of its men—Privates James McColgan and William Dunphy were left behind, shot dead. Then as night came on the attack was renewed. The smooth hill-crest where the camp lay showed clear against the sky, and the Spaniards from nearby hills, where they were covered by thick brush, were able to pour in a fire that at last became deadly. They were scattered in groups of from three or four to a dozen, but numbered, in the aggregate, several hundred. Our men could see nothing but the flashes of guns in the brush for a target, and were at a great disadvantage. Between 1 and 2 o'clock in the morning, during a specially fierce onslaught by the Spanish, Dr. John Blair Gibbs was killed while walking from the hospital-tent toward the remains of the block-house, but it is believed that he was killed by a shot from the revolver of a Cuban officer who was dancing around in the camp, wild with excitement, and firing in all directions.

Dr. John Blair Gibbs, the First Officer Killed on Cuban soil.

The next day (Sunday, June 12th) Colonel Huntington decided to move his camp down to a safer place near the beach, and that proved the hottest day's work that those marines saw during the war—hot in two senses, for the unclouded sun beat down fiercely, and the Spaniards poured in an unrelenting fire the whole day long. It appeared that the Spaniards had learned the Cuban trick of lashing green brush to their bodies, and covering their faces with green palm leaves. It was impossible for our men to distinguish a man so decked out in the brush. Moreover, the Spaniards were firing smokeless powder cartridges. The return fire of the Americans was, therefore, well-nigh at random; even that of the ships did not seem to be effective. If the Spaniards had been ca-

Tents of Officers on the Beach—Colonel Huntington's Tent in the Foreground.

pable marksmen, it is likely they would have wiped out the marines. As it was, two of our men—Sergeant-Major Goode and Private Tauman were killed.

A number of raids through the brush were made by our men, in one of which the party under Lieutenant Neville lost Sergeant Charles Smith. The ships in the harbor—including the *Texas*, that had come for coal, took a hand in the fighting by shelling the brush, but nothing seemed effective in driving off the musquito-like attack.

In the course of the day funeral services were held over the bodies of the dead. Chaplain Jones of the *Texas*, officiated. That a funeral service was in progress was obvious to everybody who could see the *cortège*, but the gathering of the men about the graves merely incited the Spanish to the fiercest onslaught of the day. It was not that they charged on our men then or at any time. They never did make a charge, though there were 2,000 of the Spaniards around the bay at one time. But they fired more vigorously during the funeral than in any other part of the day. A party of them located on the west side of the bay, from whom nothing had been heard theretofore, began working their Mausers then, although their shots fell into the bay.

Exasperated by such an infamous attack, our men went at the Spaniards with a will that for a time sent them skulking. A couple of Colt's machine guns had been landed, and these now began to sputter. Their shots flew like the water from a hose—in a steady stream, and whenever the gunners were able to locate a Spanish group, that group vanished; nevertheless it was like striking into a cloud of Adirondack punkies.

As night came on the Spaniards were still in force about the camp, and the scene, as each attack was made, was varied by the flashes of the *Marblehead's* search-light here and there over the chaparral, with shells from her guns flying through the beam to burst in the brush beyond. A dancing flame illuminated the

Within the Trenches at Camp McCalla.

muzzle of each machine gun incessantly, while the rifles of the marines spurted fire as fast as the men could handle the cartridge-clips. And that lasted the whole night through. From the days of Columbus down, the Americans have seen many remarkable fights in the brush, but never before anything like this.

On Monday the fighting went on in much the same fashion. It was not deadly, exactly. No one was killed on our side, at least, but it was wearing beyond any man's power of description. There was no rest either by day or night, and the marines at last saw that they were obliged either to clean out the Spanish forces from the entire region, or abandon the landing altogether. Fortunately it was learned from Cuban scouts that the Spaniards had a fighting base back between the camp and the sea. They had there a big water-tank with a windmill to pump water from a well into it, while a heliograph on a ridge served to keep open communications with the Spanish fort at the town of Caimanera on the upper bay. To capture this station was of the utmost importance, because there was no other drinking-water available for the Spanish nearer than the Caimanera fort.

On learning this fact (it was on the 14th), the marines went out in force. They found the Spaniards all through the brush, calling to one another from ridge to ridge by imitating the cuckoos of the region (as they had been doing since the 10th), but no decided stand was made until the crossing of a couple of trails near the Spanish signal station was reached. Even here the Spanish soon fled and were chased over the hills toward the sea, where the crew of the *Dolphin* saw them and drove them back.

The Spaniards, supposing that to surrender was to be killed anyway, ran hither and thither, buffeted by different companies of marines and the despatch-boat, while a small company of Cubans helped the fight with amazing good-will and courage. The Cubans at last captured a Spanish lieutenant with seventeen men, and the chase ended. Then some estimate of the losses sustained by the Spaniards was had. This officer said 68 men had been killed and about 200 wounded that day alone.

That their losses during the three days were much larger than those figures is certain. Our scouting parties found many bodies, but there was one sign of the dead that was everywhere present over the brush and that needed no inspection for confirmation. The sky was specked over with the black-feathered buzzards, and these gathered in flocks and came down swiftly to almost every place in the brush to which our fire was directed. The buzzard called to the land-crab and said, " We be of one blood—ye and I. Good hunting, all you below!" And the land-crabs replied " A full gorge to you! Come!"

Following the destruction of the Spanish base of operations in the woods came an attack on the Caimanera fort facing the upper bay. Captain John Philip of the *Texas* had charge of this expedition, and he was helped by McCalla of the *Marblehead* and Delehanty of the *Suwanee*. The *Texas* brought to, facing the fort at Caimanera, at 2 o'clock in the afternoon of June 15th, and opened fire with twelve-inch guns at a range of 2,400 yards. The other ships soon joined in, and after two or three shots that fell short, almost every one landed in the fort or the town. In reply the Spaniards fired three ineffectual shots and then fled. The fort was destroyed.

A remarkable incident in this little expedition up the bay was the discovery that the channel was mined. The engineer on watch in the engine-room of the *Texas* observed that one propeller had fouled something. An examination showed that it had picked up a harbor mine and jammed it against the sternpost. It was taken up on deck, where it was found to be of the kind designed to explode by contact. It was loaded and primed, but the barnacles had grown so thick on the contact plungers that they had failed to work. Two other torpedoes of the kind were knocked from their moorings by the *Marblehead*, and a dozen or so were taken up altogether later on.

With the destruction of the Spanish station in the woods and the Spanish fort at Caimanera the troubles of the marines came practically to an end. The Spaniards had had enough. But the marines remained as a guard over our naval base until the end of the war, living on shore constantly, and subject to all the vicissitudes of climate that the army had to endure before Santiago. However, the story they had to tell of life in Cuba was very different from

A Spanish Contact Mine Picked Up by the Propeller of the *Texas*.

that told by the soldiers. Our marines had their fight and their losses in battle, but they never had to complain of lack of food or medical supplies, or any other needful thing.

"Since the battalion left for Cuba," said one

of the officers of the Marine Corps, "it has not lost a man through sickness. The number of sick has at no time been more than two and one-half per cent.

"The marines landed at Guantanamo, only a few miles distant from Santiago, occupied the same soil, fought in trenches, and endured almost, if not quite, as many hardships as the soldiers. The marines have not complained of anything, and apparently have had no cause for complaint, as they were provided for in the best manner possible. Their health was carefully watched and the result speaks for itself.

"The officers had nearly all had experience in tropical countries, and they carefully watched the diet of the soldiers, the drinking-water, and everything that conduced to their comfort and welfare. When the tents were pitched the floors were put together and placed on rocks, a rock at each of the four corners, raising the floor slightly from the ground. This prevented the soldiers from coming into personal contact with the soil, and permitted proper drainage and ventilation of the tents."

To the honor of commanding our first armed force to make and maintain a landing in Cuba, Colonel Huntington added that of taking care of his men in a way unsurpassed in the history of the war.

"From the establishment of the Marine

Corps to the present time, it has constituted an integral part of the navy, has been identified with it in all of its achievements, ashore and afloat, and has continued to receive from its most distinguished commanders the expression of their appreciation of its effectiveness as a part of the Navy."—*Report of House Committee on Naval Affairs*, 39th Congress, 2d Session.

CHAPTER XVI

AUXILIARIES AND NAVAL MILITIA

THE SPOOK FLEET AND ITS EFFECT ON THE MOVEMENT OF THE ARMY—LANDING AT BAIQUIRI—KILLED BY A SHELL ON THE *TEXAS*—TWO GOOD FIGHTS AGAINST ODDS OFF SAN JUAN DE PORTO RICO—THE *ST. PAUL* AND THE *YOSEMITE* WITH THEIR UNTRAINED CREWS WERE A CREDIT TO THE NAVAL OFFICERS IN CHARGE OF THEM—FIRST AMERICAN FLAG RAISED OVER CUBAN SOIL—GOOD WORK ALONGSHORE.

ON June 20th came the army under General Shafter to land near Santiago, and, by capturing that city, compel the surrender or destruction of the Spanish squadron in the harbor. The naval opportunity of destroying the squadron as they lay in the mouth of the harbor in sight of the sea had been lost. The narrow and tortuous channel (remember it was but three hundred and fifty feet wide) had been filled with mines. The land works guarding the channel had been strengthened by landing guns from Cervera's ships. A dash into the harbor was now absolutely out of the question. But the army had been preparing for an invasion for weeks. The President's call for volunteers had produced the cheering spectacle of thousands of men crowding each other in their anxiety to enlist—thousands more than were needed. Many of these, with regulars to show them the way, had been gathered at Port Tampa, Florida, with a fleet of transports to carry them.

An army of 10,000 men was ready to embark by the 6th of June—one ship-load did embark in fact, but was recalled—when a curious thing happened. What has come to be known as the "Spook Fleet" was sighted by Captain W. H. H. Southerland of the auxiliary cruiser *Eagle*, in the Bahama Channel on the north coast of Cuba. At 9 o'clock at night, on June 7th, the *Eagle's* lookout reported a light and five minutes later another was seen. The *Eagle* went in chase and in a little time saw a squadron of four vessels. The *Eagle* was within a mile of these four vessels, for a half hour, but none of them answered her night signals. The *Eagle* then hastened to Key West and reported the facts. Shortly after her arrival the *Resolute*, Captain J. G. Eaton, came in and reported what were apparently the same four ships in the same locality and on the same night.

These reports stopped the embarkation of the 10,000 men at Tampa. The *New Orleans* and three other vessels were on that night en route to Santiago, but the fact that two of

Watching the Bombardment of Baiquiri, June 22, 1898, from the Transport *Yucatan*.

our ships failed to get responses to their signals was deemed good proof that the ships seen were Spaniards watching for our transports. The Spaniards had had the cruisers *Isabel II.*, and the *Alfonso XIII.*, the destroyer *Terror* and a number of gun-boats at San Juan de Porto Rico. It was entirely possible that these should have gone out to look for our transports. Anyway, the sailing of the army was delayed until the 14th, when 16,887 men got away, instead of 10,000, and the event showed that every man who went was needed. But the identity of the four ships, called spooks, remains unsolved at this writing. That four real ships were seen is, of course, not doubted. The two crews could not have been mistaken. As it was easy enough for lookouts to miss seeing the signals of the *Eagle* and the *Resolute*, it is probable that the ships seen were the *New Orleans* and her consorts.

On the arrival of the army off Santiago it was determined to make the landing at Baiquiri, a little port seventeen miles east of Santiago, where there was an iron pier, formerly used by an American firm for the shipment of iron ore obtained from a mine back in the country. There was also a beach fit for small boats in calm weather and a railway ran parallel with the beach to the vicinity of the Santiago Morro.

There was a block-house and a fort guarding the pier, and because the Spaniards were expected to make a stout resistance, a feint of landing at several places was ordered. Accordingly on the morning of June 21st, the *Texas*, Captain John Philip, the *Scorpion*, Captain Adolph Marix, and the *Vixen*, Captain A. Sharp, went to Cabáñas, a landing-place a few miles west of Santiago; the *Eagle*, Captain W. H. H. Southerland, and *Gloucester*, Captain R. Wainwright, to Aguadores; the *Helena*, Captain W. T. Swinburne, *Bancroft*, Captain R. Clover, and *Hornet*, Captain J. M. Helm, to Enseñada de los Altares, and the *New Orleans*, Captain W. M. Folger, *Detroit*, Captain T. H. Dayton, *Castine*, Captain R. M. Berry, and *Wasp*, Captain A. Ward to Baiquiri. The coal transports were sent to Cabáñas to carry out the feint there, but when the real attack on the shore batteries was begun it became apparent that no force of consequence was gathered anywhere to resist a landing. Very little reply was made to our bombardments east of Santiago, and 3,000 men were landed in small boats at Baiquiri the first day without special incident.

However, the *Texas* in carrying out orders to attack the batteries west of the harbor shelled the Socapa battery, where some modern rifles from the Spanish squadron were mounted. The Spaniards replied, and near the end of the attack one six-inch shell struck the *Texas* on the port bow. Passing through the plate that was perhaps an inch and a quarter thick, it struck a stanchion and exploded. Frank J. Blakely, an apprentice, was killed instantly, his body being cut so badly, that they had to call the roll to learn who was hit, while nine men were wounded. The bulk of the fragments of the shell struck the plating on the farther side of the ship, bulging it somewhat, but not breaking it.

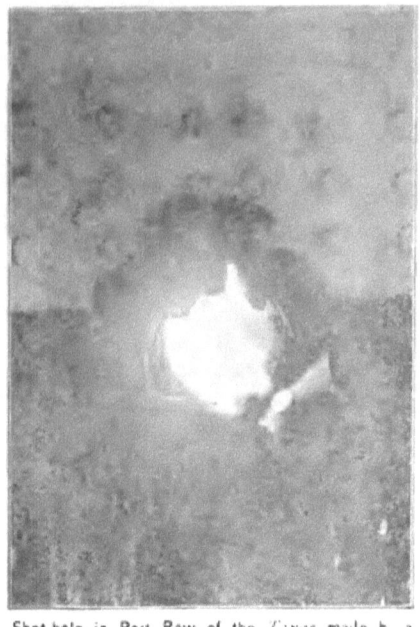
Shot-hole in Port Bow of the *Texas*, made by a Six-inch Shell (photographed from the inside).

The remaining troops were all landed by the 23d.

Meantime the Spanish strategists at Madrid had been preparing to divert our attention somewhat from Santiago by ordering a squadron of twelve vessels, of which the battle-ship *Pelayo* was the flag-ship, to sail for Manila and annihilate Dewey. It is certain, now, that this squadron was not fit for the voyage, let alone annihilating the Yankee Admiral, but they did eventually pass the Suez Canal. As a reply to this, we organized what we called our East-

Shot-hole Starboard Hammock Berthing, Midships in the *Texas*.

ern Squadron for an attack on the coast of Spain, of which something is said farther on.

The knowledge that the Spaniards had the destroyer *Terror*, and two or three other fighting ships at San Juan de Porto Rico during all these operations was not forgotten by Admiral Sampson, and as soon as he could spare a vessel, he ordered the port blockaded. The *St. Paul*, Captain Sigsbee, was chosen, because she was at once a good fighter and swift enough to carry news quickly to Santiago, should that be necessary. She reached her destination on June 22d, and had a fight on hand before the day was over. As told by the *War Budget*, a periodical printed on the *St. Paul*, the story runs :

"We came off the port early on the 22d. The weather was fair, the trade wind blowing fresh from the eastward and raising somewhat of a sea. At about 12.40 the third-class cruiser *Isabel II.*, or one of her class, came out and, steaming under the Morro until she was abreast of the batteries, commenced edging out toward us, firing at such a long range that her shots were ineffective. As her purpose evidently was to put us within fire of the batteries we took but little notice of her, lying still and occasionally sending in our largest shell at her to try the range. Soon afterward she dropped to the westward and the torpedo-boat destroyer *Terror*, or it may have been her sister ship the *Furor*, was sighted steaming along shore under the batteries. Captain Sigsbee watched her for awhile and worked along with her in order to separate her from the cruiser and keep her in the trough of the sea if she came for us. She then circled to get up speed and headed for us, firing straight as far as direction went, but her shots fell short. When within range of our guns the signal "Commence firing" was made, and for several minutes we let fly our starboard battery at her at from 5,500 to 6,000 yards, the shells striking all around her. This stopped her ; she turned her broadside to us, and her fire soon ceased. She then headed inshore to the southward and westward, going slow, and it was evident to all on board that she was crippled, drifting well leeward of the main harbor entrance. Off the Morro she flashed some signals to the shore, and afterward a tug came out and towed her into the harbor.

"All this time the cruiser was firing at us, and some of her shots and those of the *Terror* fell pretty close. The cruiser followed the *Terror* back toward the port, and soon afterward was joined by a gun-boat, and the two steamed under the batteries to the eastward. But when the *St. Paul*, making an inshore turn, seemed to be going for them, they returned to the harbor and we saw no more of them.

"The Spaniards seemed to have settled this whole matter in advance, as they wished to have it, for the townspeople came out on the bluffs to see the Yankee driven off or sunk, and the cruiser flew an ensign at her gaff almost as big as a maintopsail.

"The *Isabel* is bark rigged and carried four 4.7-inch breech-loading rifles, four 2.7-inch breech-loading rifles, eight machine guns, and two torpedo tubes. The *Terror* has two fourteen-pounders, rapid fire; two six-pounders, rapid fire; two one-pounders, automatic Maxims, and two torpedo tubes. Length, 220 feet; estimated speed, 28 knots.

"We know that the *Terror* was struck three times, and that one shot entering the engine-room killed an engineer and fireman. And from what we regard as trustworthy information, we are inclined to think that she was seriously damaged, requiring the assistance of tugs to keep her afloat."

The story is especially interesting because it shows how well Yankee Jack can write as well as how he can fight—shows the grade of intelligence of our man before the mast. The physical superiority of the Spanish force was great enough to have made victory easy for them, and they were so sure of it that the captain of the *Terror* made a speech in the plaza of the town before he went out in which he gave the enthusiastic audience the details of his plans for bringing the Yankee into port.

On June 28th the Porto Ricans saw another fight off San Juan, wherein the odds against us were still greater; in fact the handling of our ship, the *Yosemite*, Captain William H. Emory, was extraordinary. When morning came, that day, many rain-squalls were drifting alongshore with the trade wind, reducing the range of vision so much that a Spanish transport, the *Antonio Lopez*, with supplies for the town, was able to get within two miles of the *Yosemite* before she was seen.

At that time the *Yosemite* was slowly circling off the harbor, at a distance of five miles west-north-west of the Morro. The *Lopez* was heading in from the west, but on discovering the *Yosemite* she turned south toward the land, intending to skirt the reefs, and get under cover of Fort Canuelo, on the west side of the harbor.

The moment the *Lopez* was sighted the *Yosemite* dashed ahead at full speed, the men were sent to quarters, and in a few minutes they began firing their five-inch guns at a range of two miles. At that the guns of the Morro and Canuelo began to belch, and, curiously enough, they got and kept the range. And then came the cruisers the *Isabel II.* and *General Concha* from the harbor to aid in the attack. These two ships had seven guns of 4.7-inch calibre between them, besides smaller ones that were entirely effective against any ship like the *Yosemite*, and their fire combined with that of the forts was hot enough to have warranted Emory in seeking deep water at once. Moreover, the *Yosemite* was manned by inexperienced men (the Michigan Naval Militia). Nevertheless, the *Yosemite* held her course to head off the *Lopez* until she drove her hard on the reef, six miles from the Morro, and then she went hunting the Spanish war-ships, only to see a torpedo-boat coming from the harbor at full speed, sneaking along shore as if to get behind her.

By this time, however, the *Yosemite* had the range of the cruisers, and they turned back in haste, though keeping up a steady fire. Then the *Yosemite* had a chase after the torpedo-boat, but it got behind the stranded *Lopez* apparently uninjured.

At that the *Yosemite* opened once more on the *Lopez*, giving it, all told, two hundred five-inch shells, besides some six-pounders, and setting it on fire, after which the Spanish cruisers were driven out of sight behind the Morro. What with the forts, the cruisers, the torpedo-boat and the *Lopez* the *Yosemite* had a call for dextrous manœuvring that was unique in this war.

The *Lopez* was wrecked, but the Spaniards asserted that they saved twelve of the fifteen guns she was bringing, besides some ammunition. They got it from the wreck after the *Yosemite* was ordered away. The *Yosemite* kept her battle-flags flying all day, as she cruised off the Morro, in hope that the Spaniards would come out with their repaired *Terror*, and the other fighters seen in the morning, but it was a vain hope. If anyone had doubted the efficiency of our auxiliary cruisers manned by naval militia, the work off San Juan in June dispelled it entirely. With our naval officers in command, a few experienced seamen for petty officers, the auxiliaries did work that was within its limits quite as creditable as that done by the regular fighting ships. The genius of the nation can very well rest on the deeds of these emergency men for its reputation.

There were a couple of minor incidents in the naval history of the month on the Cuban coast that should have mention here. The auxiliary *Yankee* had a little brush with a gunboat and a shore battery at Cienfuegos, in which one man, S. B. Kennedy, was wounded.

Lieutenant Victor Blue, of the *Suwanee*, who had made a landing some time before on the north coast, to communicate with Gomez, the Cuban general, now made a complete tour of Santiago Bay, in order to locate exactly the Spanish squadron. For this he was especially commended by Secretary Long.

And then there was the hoisting of the first American flag on Cuban soil some weeks earlier, that has been so far overlooked. During the month of May the blockade was maintained chiefly by tugs and other small auxiliaries. The tug *Leyden*, Captain W. S. Crosley, was stationed off Cardenas, and about the middle of the month, after having driven the Spaniards from the light-house on the little coral island off that port, he landed and raised a thirty-foot specimen of the Stars and Stripes. He had no men to leave as a garrison, but the Spaniards, although they had repaired the gun-boats which were shelled by the *Wilmington* on the bloody 11th, were afraid to venture out to take the flag down.

Lieutenant Victor Blue of the *Suwanee*.

Meantime the blockade had been maintained by these small vessels of our fleet with what must be considered remarkable efficiency. Two Spanish vessels did manage to slip out of Havana, and one got in, while a vessel loaded with supplies for the Spanish army was reported at Manzanillo, a port on the south coast some distance west of Santiago. As to this port, no regular watch was maintained there, and at Havana the number of our vessels was very small, considering the work to be performed. On recalling the regularity of the trips of the blockade-runners at Wilmington during our Civil War, it is seen that our work on the Cuban coast was excellent. And it was the dreariest, most wearying, most heart-breaking work of the war. In addition to the blockade work proper, a number of expeditions of Cubans who wished to join the insurgents were landed, with ample supplies, under the guns of our vessels.

Then, to return to Santiago, Admiral Sampson had to report that Lieutenant Harlow, with two launches, one of which was commanded by Cadet Powell and the other by Cadet Hart, made a survey of the little harbor at Cabáñas on the 17th, and were "subjected to a heavy and continued fire at short range." The launches were struck seventeen times.

The *Vesuvius* ran into Santiago channel one night, passing clear around the sunken *Merrimac* to learn her exact position. Curiously enough, the Spanish did not see her on this trip.

On the whole, however, so far as decisive work was concerned, our ships in American waters had a quiet time for a month after Sampson reached Santiago. Neither the blockade, nor the fights off San Juan, nor the bombardments of the forts at Santiago (one of which occurred on July 2d) had any marked influence in ending the war. Nevertheless, our unrelenting persistence was having some effect, and our army was closing in on Santiago. We at least had the Spaniards everywhere on the defensive, and their situation was everywhere perilous. Cervera had been corralled, if we may use a Rough Rider's term, and he had now to choose between tamely submitting within and making a wild dash through the narrow gate.

And when he had considered the matter from every point of view—how at night the Yankee squadron was close in, but by day was farther off; that the Yankee battle-ships were slow and his cruisers fast; that while the Yankees were superior in weight, his destroyers, in the excitement of battle, might reduce the preponderance; that if he remained all would be lost, but if he ran he might save some—when he had considered all this and had discussed it with his captains he could come to but one conclusion: a dash for the open sea had to be made.

CHAPTER XVII

DESTRUCTION OF CERVERA'S SQUADRON

LUCK WAS WITH THE SPANIARDS, IN A WAY, FOR TWO OF OUR BIG SHIPS HAD LEFT THE BLOCKADE—THEIR SMOKE HAD EXCITED OUR SUSPICION AND OUR LOOKOUTS WERE ALERT—QUICK WORK WITH THE TORPEDO-BOATS AND TWO CRUISERS—EULATE'S VAIN EFFORT TO CATCH THE *BROOKLYN*—A RECORD RACE IN NAVAL WARFARE THAT ESTABLISHED THE FAME OF THE BULL DOG *OREGON*—HOW WAINWRIGHT'S DAY CAME AT LAST.

WHEN the morning of Sunday, July 3d, came, the conditions off-shore were much more in favor of the Spanish Admiral than he had had any reason to hope for. The battle-ship sentinels of Sampson's fleet during the fore part of Saturday night were the *Massachusetts* and the *Texas*, but some time after midnight the *Massachusetts*, being short of coal, was ordered away to Guantanamo to replenish her bunkers. She left the squadron at 4 o'clock; we had one less battle-ship than usual to guard the harbor when daylight came. Worse yet, in view of the accredited speed of the Spanish ships, we were also to be lacking the aid of our swift armored cruiser, the flag-

From a copyright photograph by J. S. Johnston, New York.

Massachusetts, First-class Battle-ship. Dimensions, 348 x 69; draft, 27; displacement, 10,288. Speed, 16.2 knots. Main Battery, four thirteen-inch, eight eight-inch, and four six-inch guns.

ship *New York*. On the day before (Saturday) the Admiral had arranged for a visit to the head-quarters of General Shafter under most extraordinary circumstances. Shafter had suggested that our squadron be forced through the unsurveyed and well-mined channel, three hundred and fifty feet wide, leading into Santiago Bay, and from his head-quarters, miles out of range of Spanish bullets, had said: " I am at a loss to see why the navy cannot work under a destructive fire as well as the army." Sampson saw that it was necessary to see Shafter " for a discussion of the situation and a more definite understanding." He accordingly arranged to go to Shafter's head-quarters on Sunday morning, and at 8.55 o'clock the *New York* left the guard-line and steamed away east to land the Admiral.

"The remaining vessels were in or near their usual blockading positions, distributed in a semicircle" (of which the Morro was the centre), "about the harbor entrance, counting from the eastward to the westward in the following order: The *Indiana*, about a mile and a half from shore; the *Oregon*—the *New York's* place was between these two—the *Iowa, Texas*, and *Brooklyn*, the latter two miles from the shore west of Santiago. The distance of the vessels from the harbor entrance was from two and a half to four miles, the latter being the limit of day-blockading distance. The length of the arc formed by the ships was about eight miles. . . . The auxiliaries *Gloucester* and *Vixen* lay close to the land, and nearer the harbor entrance than the large vessels, the *Gloucester* to the eastward, and the *Vixen* to the westward." So says Sampson's official report.

It was a beautiful Sunday morning, "fair and warm," with a "light breeze from north'ard and east'ard" [from private letter to author] beautiful alike without and within the harbor. On the sea, our ships in the wide arc, with their bows toward the harbor entrance, swayed gently to the lazy, trade-wind swell, with only a whiff of smoke coming now and again from their funnels, for steam was low and only enough coal was used to keep the furnaces ready for an emergency. "The steam at this time in the boilers was sufficient for a speed of five knots," according to one report, but it was not that of the *Oregon*. On the *Oregon*, Chief Engineer Milligan had been "'running a sweatshop'—keeping steam up for a ten-knot gait, regardless of the profanity of his shipmates."

In the harbor the Spaniards swung to the pull of the winches that were heaving in the cables, while huge volumes of smoke poured from their funnels—volumes so large as to make their commanders look aloft uneasily. On the sea our men, in the usual Sunday routine, washed themselves, and put on their best clothes, and blacked their shoes, to make ready for the tour of the inspecting officers; in the harbor the Spaniards, stripped to the waist, dumped coal into their furnaces, and sent up ammunition for all the guns, which they cast loose and loaded with the hurry and fume and noise of the unaccustomed when preparing for battle.

But while our ships were in perfect repose out at sea, their lookouts were nevertheless perfectly alert. Even when at 9.30 o'clock the regular call to quarters for Sunday inspection rang through the seemingly listless squadron, there were men in every lookout perch, and on

Chart of Santiago Harbor.

every bridge, whose eyes were never for an instant taken from the harbor of Santiago. Within half an hour smoke had been seen between the hills to the west of the harbor—the hills of Socapa point and Smith Cay, the island a half mile inside, behind which the Spanish squadron lay. The smoke had bulged its black head to view for only a moment, but a glimpse was enough for the lookouts, whose eager wish for the honor of first reporting the coming of the enemy had stirred them so that on the *Texas* the signal flags " 2-5-0," which should announce the news, were kept bent to the halyards, which a man held in hand, and the bulldog *Oregon* was prepared to growl by keeping a man at a loaded six-pounder with his finger on the trigger. At 9.30 the squadron lay at perfect ease, but with eyes wide open. At 9.31 the sharp bow of a Spanish cruiser was seen by every lookout on our ships, cleaving the water from behind Smith Cay, and on the instant every man of them bawled "The fleet's coming out," while the quartermaster on the *Texas* clawed his halyards to get his signal flags aloft, and the *Oregon's* gunner pulled the trigger of the lean six-pounder and fired the first shot of the battle. And then before the echo of that shot had come back from the hills, or ever the signals on the *Texas* had reached her truck, the electric gongs on every ship were clanging the call to clear ship for action, the officers on every bridge were jingling the bells in the engine-room for full speed ahead, and shouting to the engineers the inspiring news, while the men, breaking from the lines in which they had formed for inspection, ran, yelling for joy, and stripping their shirts from their backs, as they fled to gun-breech and stoke-hole. In two minutes, though five is speedy in ordinary times, the order to cast loose and provide had been obeyed, while the growing splash under the bows of the ships and the lengthening wakes astern, and the puffing volumes of smoke from the funnels, told how the men below had raked open their fires, and set the fans of the forced draft whirling, and were now spraying the coal over the glowing grate-bars. The Spaniards would fight at last, and we were driving our ships with the battle-flags at every peak, full speed to meet them.

Admiral Cervera, Commanding the Spanish Squadron.

It was at 9.31 that the first Spaniard showed her bow to our waiting squadron. She was the *Maria Teresa*, Cervera's flag-ship, and she was coming from behind Smith Cay, a little more than three-quarters of a mile within the Morro. And because of the lay of the shoals, she was obliged to run almost a half mile outside of that point, before she could turn, in her determined flight to the west. She was rated as a twenty-knot ship, but now it took her full five minutes to reach out to the open sea—to arrive within the closing coil of the Yankee squadron. Over to the east, and nearest of all, the *Indiana*, "with screws whitening the water astern" was heading for the Morro. A six-pounder on her superstructure, like that on the *Oregon*, awoke the echoes, and then the guns of every battery alongshore flamed in an attack upon her and all our ships to help the flying Spaniards. In five seconds more the *Maria Teresa*, still heading to the south to round the off-shore shoal, fired a great gun at the *Brooklyn* and a full broadside at the *Indiana*. The water around the *Indiana*, "was alive with the fall of projectiles," both from the shore batteries and the Spanish ship.

The guns of our entire squadron roared in reply, and then with her helm hard over, the *Maria Teresa*, with increasing speed, turned to the west to enter the pitiless gauntlet prepared for her; but hope was not yet lost, or ended. In her wake, at intervals of 800 yards, came the *Vizcaya* the *Colon* and the *Oquendo*, every one a terror in its physical strength and who could say what these combined might not accomplish?

With her first round the *Indiana* drove more than one projectile into the broadside of the *Maria Teresa*, but the Spaniard fled to the west, and the *Indiana* turned her guns upon the others in quick succession. "As the *Viz-*

From a copyrighted photograph by J. S. Johnston, New York.

Indiana, First-class Battle-ship. Dimensions, 348 x 69; draft, 27; displacement, 10,288. Speed, 16.2 knots. Main Battery, four thirteen-inch, eight eight-inch, and four six-inch guns.

caya came out I distinctly saw one of the *Indiana's* heavy shells strike her abaft the funnels, and the explosion of this shell was followed by a burst of flame, which for the moment obscured the afterpart of the stricken ship," says Commander Eaton, who saw the fight from the *Resolute*. But not the fire of one ship could stop the fleeing squadron. Each in her order turned west, with the *Colon* running inshore of those ahead of her, and then the boom and scream of gun and shell blended into a roar that none can describe, and none that heard it will ever forget.

Our firing began at a range of from two to three miles, but that range was quickly cut down to a trifle over a mile. And then, of all times the worst for them, came the torpedo-boat destroyers, the *Pluton*, "at a distance of twelve hundred yards" behind the *Oquendo*, and the *Furor* behind the *Pluton*. In the broad light of the day, with not even a haze of the smoke of battle to conceal them, came these two sneaks of the night. They had two miles of open water to cross before they could reach any of our battle-ships. The smaller guns of the *Indiana*, the *Oregon*, the *Iowa*, and the *Texas*, with some of their larger guns as well, were turned upon them, while Richard Wainwright, of the *Gloucester*, lay in wait to head them off. Wainwright was from the

Maine, and his day had come. He had boldly fired at the big cruisers as they passed, but when they were gone he slowed down, that his steam might rise to lift the safety-valve — that he might be ready — and then, as the destroyers cleared Socapa Point, he "steamed for them and was able to close at short range." What did it matter to him that he was "under the fire of the Socapa battery?" Or what thought would he give to the fact that he had six-pounders and the enemy twelves and more of them? Even before he had "closed at short range" his gunners had found their target, and within twenty minutes from his first shot the *Furor* turned, crippled like a wounded sea-bird, for a resting-place among the rocks on the beach, and there she arrived just in time to save her from sinking. The *Pluton*, alas! was snatched from his victorious grasp by a shell from one of the larger ships. Three ships claim the honor of that shot, and honor it was, for it was one of the largest size, and it struck the slender hull amidships, cutting it in two, and

Richard Wainwright, of the *Gloucester*.

down she went instantly in deep water—the first victim of the destruction that was abroad that day.

But although four of our big ships had turned their guns for the moment to stop the torpedo devils, they had in no wise neglected the flying

Gloucester, Converted Yacht. Formerly J. Pierpont Morgan's *Corsair*. Main Battery, four six-pounders.

cruisers. While yet the destroyers were afloat our shells were literally cutting the *Maria Teresa* to pieces. An eight-inch struck the shield of one of her 5.5-inch guns, passed through and exploded, ranging aft. "The effect of the explosion was terrific." Another entered the ship just under the after barbette, exploded on the gun-deck, ranging aft, with such damaging effect that "all the men in that locality must have been killed or badly wounded, while the beams were ripped and torn, the bulkheads were shattered," and, what was infinitely worse, the fire-main was cut by the fragments of the shell before they passed out on the farther side of the ship.

To the destructive effect of these shots was added the damage done by two twelve-inch shells that entered below the berth-deck, making one widened hole where they entered, exploding and completely wrecking the after torpedo compartment.

With these huge projectiles came a hail of five-inch and four-inch and six-pounder shells so numerous and so deadly that it is impossible to follow them in detail, but when they burst amid her splintering decks and bulkheads there was no water to quench the quick-spreading flames. Her men, driven from their guns by the sand-storm blasts of our ships, turned inboard to face death in a form still more terrible. There were piles of cartridges in the paths of the flames that were sure to explode; but worse than all that—worse even than the hurtling projectiles from our nearing ships—the fire was leaving the crew no foothold to stand upon. They had literally to choose between remaining where they would be burned alive and running for the beach, where they might have some hope of escape by swimming ashore.

With helm aport the *Maria Teresa* was headed for the land, and at 10.15 o'clock she drove, with fire reddening every port, and with a pall of smoke wrapping about her, hard and fast on the rocks "at Nima, six and one-half miles from Santiago Harbor entrance." She was still within the range of the shore batteries that had been worked in a futile frenzy to save her.

It was then that the heart of a typical Yankee naval officer appeared. The *Texas*, in her swift pursuit of the flying Spaniards, passed the stern of the *Teresa* as she struck the rocks, and our tars, with natural impulse, began to cheer. But Captain Philip, though the *Teresa* was wrapped from view in smoke, saw the horror upon her decks, and, turning to his men, said:

"Don't cheer. The poor devils are dying."

Meantime the full-steam rush of the other Spaniards had carried them past our battle-ships, because to get our boilers steaming at top pressure had been a work requiring time. Nevertheless, the last of the cruisers—the *Oquendo*—was well within our closing coil as she turned —so close, indeed, that never in the history of naval wars was a ship subjected to such a fire as that which flamed about her. For a time nearly every gun that would bear from four mighty battle-ships was aimed at her, and the effect "was terrific." Even as she came out an eight-inch shell struck the hood over the forward eleven-inch gun barbette, passed through, exploded instantly, and killed every one of the gun's crew. Three others struck her broadside, passing clear through above the armor belt. Still another pierced the side of the after broadside torpedo-room, and in bursting exploded the head of the torpedo there, and killed all of its launching crew. Another, probably from the *Indiana*, if its course be considered, " struck under the gun-deck, directly below the conning tower, ranging forward across the deck. Still another crashed through the superstructure, in front of the forward smoke-stack. These were the courses of the larger shells. Of the five-inch and smaller no account can be given, the number was so great, and as her crew testified afterward, it was the whizz and sting of the small projectiles —even of the six-pounders—that drove them wild. For these beat the roll of the death-march on the sides of the ship and piercing through, killed so many that blood swashed about the deck like water, and flowed in streams from the scuppers.

And then, as on the *Maria Teresa*, came the flames among the splintered bulkheads to complete the work of horror, and no man could stand longer at his post. Turning in the wake of the stricken flag-ship, the *Almirante Oquendo* drove flaming to the beach, and

striking at full speed, shoved her nose high on the rocks, while her stern settled down and with a crash she broke in two amidships. She had reached the land but a half mile west of her sister ship, the *Maria Teresa*—she was still within long range of a modern gun at the harbor entrance. It was exactly 10.20 o'clock, that she turned toward the beach. In just forty-nine minutes from the time we saw the bow of the first Spanish ship, we had utterly destroyed the two torpedo-boats and driven half of the cruisers ashore.

But two cruisers yet remained afloat, the *Vizcaya* and the *Colon*, and these were making a most desperate struggle to elude the clawing grasp of our squadron. From her location two and a half or three miles west of the harbor and two miles off shore when the Spaniards were seen, the *Brooklyn* was in the position of honor—the position wherein she, better than any other of our ships, might meet and destroy the flying cruisers. They had turned to the west, following closely the shore line, and must needs pass her, even if she remained in place, within a mile and a half.

Calling for full speed ahead, Commodore Schley steamed toward Morro Castle, while the skilful crew worked their guns with cool precision, until the *Maria Teresa* was in flames, beaten to death.

At that moment Captain Eulate, of the *Vizcaya*, seeing the fate that awaited him if he did not do more than his flag-ship had done, put his helm over and turned out to meet the *Brooklyn*, gun-muzzle to gun-muzzle, man fashion. Doubtless, too, he intended to ram her, if possible, and the supreme moment of the battle had come.

As the *Vizcaya* turned out to sea, Schley found himself for the instant heading inside of her—heading so as to reach in between her and the beach, and he concluded that if he continued on that course the *Vizcaya* would soon arrive so nearly abreast of him that she might use her ram, or at any rate a torpedo. To escape this danger he ordered the *Brooklyn's* helm hard a port—he brought up his ship so as to head straight at the *Vizcaya*, then crossed her bow at a distance too great for a torpedo, and continuing on the curved course, swept out to sea, with stern toward the Spaniards until entirely safe from both torpedo and ram. He did not attempt to make any use of his own torpedoes or well-built ram, but heading to the west, maintained a course nearly parallel with that of the Spaniards, and at a distance from them estimated at two miles.

Seeing that he had then no hope of overtaking the *Brooklyn*, plucky Captain Eulate headed the *Vizcaya* back to her old course

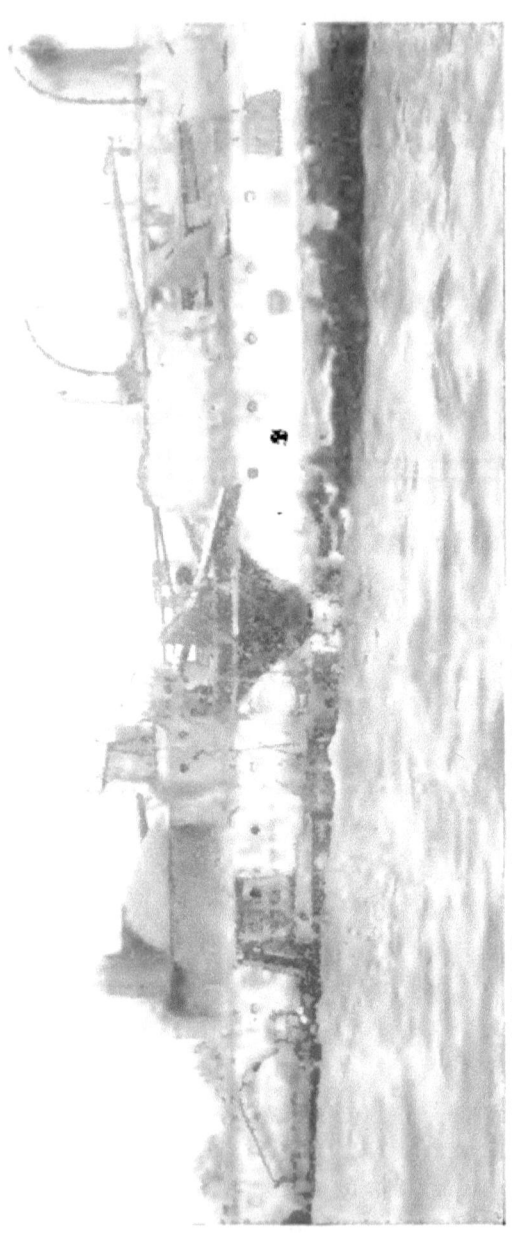

* From a photograph by J. C. Hemment, Copyright, 1898, by W. R. Hearst.

Almirante Oquendo, Infanta Maria Teresa, and *Vizcaya* (sister ships). Heavily-armored Cruisers (twelve-inch belt of steel). Dimensions. 340 × 65; draft, 21; displacement, 7,000. Speed, 20 knots. Main Battery, two eleven-inch, ten 5.5-inch guns.

along the beach and drove her ahead, hoping to escape the death-storm coming from the lowering battle-ships off his seaward quarter. The *Indiana*, because of her location, was left out of the fight when the last of the Spanish cruisers had been lost to sight in the cloud of battle, but the *Oregon*, the *Iowa*, and the *Texas*, with their growing pressure of steam, had been able to keep the range and even to close in. The *Iowa's* dash made men on our other ships think her Captain, "Fighting Bob" Evans, would succeed in ramming one of the flying cruisers, and the cruisers escaped that fate only because the *Iowa* had been so far out at sea when they appeared; but they could not escape her guns. And then there was the *Texas*. She had been called the "hoodoo" of the navy, because of many accidents she had endured, but now Captain John Philip, drove her toward the remaining Spaniards on a course that brought her to an easy range of the *Vizcaya*, while his guns' crews made her side flame unceasingly.

Last of all to be named, but never last in the service, came the *Oregon*. She had been lying farther to the east than any of our ships, save the *Indiana*, but with a burst of speed that astounded the whole squadron, she swept down to the westward as if to cross the track of the flying enemy. Beginning with the

Maria Teresa, as it led the way, and turning to the other two—the *Vizcaya* and the *Oquendo*—as they reached out to bear the brunt of the battle, she quickly joined with our other ships to annihilate the whole blood-and-gold squadron. By the time the *Teresa* and the *Oquendo* had been driven to the rocks, the *Oregon* had arrived at a close range with the *Vizcaya*. Indeed, after the *Vizcaya* had chased the *Brooklyn* out to sea, she had need to make haste in getting on her old course lest she suffer, at the bow of the *Oregon*, the fate she had hoped to inflict upon the *Brooklyn*. And the *Texas* was, as said, not so far away that her guns would not reach, while the *Brooklyn's* gunners, now that that ship had turned to parallel the course of the *Vizcaya*, were driving their shells into the Spaniard with unequalled accuracy, in spite of the range, and the end of Eulate's pride was soon at hand.

He had suffered from the fire of the *Indiana* and the *Iowa* in passing, but now the mortal blows were coming chiefly from the *Oregon* and *Brooklyn*. Not many were needed, it seems, for only three eight-inch, and four five-inch shell holes were found in her afterward, though two other holes may have been either five-inch or four-inch. The five-inch shells were all from the *Brooklyn*, for no other ship there had five-inch guns. Of the eight-inch shots no one can

From a photograph by J. C. Hemment. Copyright, 1898, by W. R. Hearst.

The Bow of the *Almirante Oquendo*. The smoke is from the vessel which was on fire when the photograph was taken.

tell which ship fired them, except that the one which struck just under the bridge and ranged forward must have come from a ship behind her, and was probably from the *Oregon*. But the large shells, as in the case of the other two, were really less distressful than the hail of smaller shot, and to the terror and loss that they inspired and inflicted was added the hell of flame that the shells started in the riven woodwork.

Eulate had won the honors of the day on his side, by driving the *Brooklyn* from his path, but he could not endure, nor could he escape, the storm that was upon him. Like the *Teresa* and the *Oquendo*, the *Vizcaya* was stricken like a deer on the runway, and staggering from the cramping wounds, turned aside to find a death-bed.

It was at 11.05 o'clock that she turned and at 11.15 her engines gave their last beat in landing her on the beach. She had sustained the flight for fifteen miles and rested at last, where her remains still rest, at Aserraderos.

But one of the Spaniards now remained afloat —the sleek, foxy *Colon*. She had skimmed along the beach inside of her bolder associates, and protected by their hulls, as the torpedo-destroyers should have been, had escaped with scarce a wound. And now that the *Vizcaya* was gone, she headed away for the west—to

Cienfuegos, to Havana—to any hole that would give shelter from the baying hounds that were upon her trail.

That was a record race in the annals of naval warfare. It was then that Milligan of the *Oregon*, went down into the stoke-hole to lend a hand beside the red-striped men who shovelled coal till the ship reached a speed of eighteen knots, though the pressure of forced draft and the climbing heat made each breath a gasp and each effort a weakening pain. It was then that the impatient junior officers begged for one shot until Captain Clark allowed it, and Milligan, black with coal, came upon deck to thank the captain, and say that his men were fainting below, but if they could hear a shot now and then they could live through and keep her going.

She was only a fifteen-knot ship in design, but now, in spite of the strain of the long voyage from the Pacific and in spite of the marine growths upon her bottom, with the bulging, roaring foam piled to the golden crest of her cut-water, she held her own with the flying pride of the Spanish navy.

And as she fired, the half-ton shells from Lieutenant Eberle's thirteen-inch guns struck nearer and nearer to the chase, so that hope fled faster than the whirling screws could drive it. For forty-eight miles the Spaniard held her

From a photograph by J. C. Hemment. Copyright, 1898, by W. R. Hearst.

Vizcaya Aground at Aserraderos.

way and then, lest a shell from the *Oregon* with the fire of the *Brooklyn*, out at sea, sink her, she turned in shore and was beached at the mouth of Rio Tarquino.

The battle was ended. We had swept the enemy from the sea, and Captain Philip, by a public act that portrayed the thought in the heart of every man in the squadron, called his men to the quarter-deck, and with bare head said:

Captain John Philip, Commanding the *Texas*.

"I want to make public acknowledgment here that I believe in God the Father. I want you all to lift your hats and from your hearts offer silent thanks to the Almighty."

CHAPTER XVIII

SEAMEN OF THE SQUADRONS CONTRASTED

STORY OF SPANISH TREACHERY ON A GOOD SHIP THEY HAD SURRENDERED TO US—CAPTAIN CHADWICK'S REMARKABLE SKILL IN HANDLING THE *NEW YORK*—OUR MEN AS LIFE SAVERS—UNDAUNTED IN THE PRESENCE OF FIRE AND EXPLODING MAGAZINES—ATROCIOUS CONDUCT OF CUBAN SOLDIERS—THE SQUADRONS COMPARED—REWARD OF A COMMANDER WHO BREAKS DOWN THROUGH OVERWORK.

In gathering up the loose ends of the story of the battle off Santiago it seems best to begin at the end and work backward. In this way we at least get one interesting view of the character of the enemy we whipped. Adolphus Kentreres, in an interview after the battle, is reported as saying:

"The projectiles of the *Oregon* began reaching us at 1 P.M., and that, together with the fact that it was not possible to fight with the after guns on account of the *Colon's* lack of large calibre pieces, and the certainty of being overhauled by the whole American squadron in a few hours, left no other remedy

From a Photograph by J. C. Hemment, copyright, 1898, by W. R. Hearst.

Cristobal Colon, Heavily-armored Cruiser (twelve-inch belt of steel). Dimensions, 328 x 59.7; draft, 24; displacement, 6 840. Speed, 20 knots. Main Battery, ten six-inch, six 4.7-inch guns.

than to run ashore in order to avoid useless sacrifice of life."

Whether he said it or not, it is true as far as it goes, but it does not tell, and no Spanish officer has yet told, the important part of the story. When the *Colon* turned to the shore her flag was hauled down and from that moment she was our ship. She was in perfect condition, having been hit by but eight unimportant shots; so far as known she had surrendered because of what her captain expected, not what the ship had received. Well, there was our ship in the hands of our prisoners, and they were driving her on the rocks, not to save their lives, as in the case of the other beaten ships, but to destroy the property they had surrendered to us through fear of losing their lives. And on to the shelving beach they drove her full speed. But that was not all. When once she was beached her engineer's crew were sent to open and break the sea-valves, and so let in the water to make sure of the treacherous work they had already begun. She was boarded by Captain Cook (with others) from the *Brooklyn*, to whom she was formally delivered. There is a story told among naval officers that when our men boarded the *Colon* they were met by the Spaniards with open wine-bottles in hand, and desired to drink, and that this was a ruse to keep our men from going below to close the broken sea-valves. It is added that the ruse succeeded in making some delay. Although this delay was contrary to the regulations we may be permitted to hope that the story is true. There were the Spaniards masking the destruction of our ship under the guise of hospitality, and there stood our men, easily blinded, because it was impossible for them to conceive such treachery even in a Spaniard. Once we found she was sinking every possible effort was made to save her, while the Spaniards looked smilingly on.

The ships that gathered near the *Colon* were the *Oregon*, the *Brooklyn*, the *Texas*, the *New York*, the *Vixen*, and the *Resolute*. The *Vixen*, though but a converted tug, had gone through the fight with six-pounders working, and was almost in at the death. The *Resolute*, Commander J. G. Eaton, was too far away at the start, but he followed the leaders to the end.

As night came on the long waves worked the *Colon* loose from her resting-place, and she was sliding slowly off to sink into deep water, when the *New York* steamed in, and putting her bow against the stern of the *Colon* pushed her around and upon the beach once more. Captain Chadwick handled his big cruiser with the ease and certainty that a harbor captain handles a tug-boat. As an exhibition of nautical skill and resourcefulness the act was unique. Nevertheless, the Spanish for the time succeeded in their purpose, for the *Colon* filled, and then turned over on her starboard side leaving only a part of her port quarter exposed. And there she lies at this writing (December 1, 1898), curiously enough, at the very spot where the ill-fated *Virginius* was going to land her filibustering expedition on that fatal night in 1873.

How the *New York* was found in the vicinity of the beached *Colon* is soon told. She had travelled away for eight miles on her mission to enlighten the general commanding the army, when the lookouts discovered that the blockaders and the forts at Santiago were in conflict, and that something enveloped in a cloud of smoke was just without the harbor. What that something was they could not see, but they could imagine well enough, and around turned the flag-ship with her engine-room bells jingling for full speed, and her crew hastening to obey the call to quarters. By the time she was half around they could see that Cervera was coming out. Never in the history of our navy were men more broken-hearted with disappointment. A determined, almost a desperate dash for a chance to join in the fight was made, and she arrived in time to make two long-range shots at the torpedo-boat destroyers and two at the *Oquendo*. Ensign Powell said afterward that he saw one of these four-inch shots strike one of the torpedo-boats, and there is no reason to doubt his eyesight. It was not the only shot that struck it, even among the larger projectiles, but it helped in the swift work of destruction.

Passing on swiftly in the wake of the flying Spaniards, the *New York* steadily gained on the leader—the *Colon*, and her crew had a growing hope of yet getting a shot at the cruiser when the last Spanish flag came down, and the fighting was ended for that day.

One more word must now be said of the *Oregon*. The prolonged labor of Captain Clark had broken his health, and after the battle he was condemned by a board of surgeons to leave his ship to recuperate. And that meant, really, that as a reward for his splendid services his pay was cut from $4,500 a year to $2,800.

The work of our men as life-savers was as worthy of praise as it was in battle. "So long as the enemy showed his flag they fought like American seamen; but when the flag came down they were as gentle and tender as American women," wrote Captain Evans. To this may be added the fact that they were required to show, and did show, as much bravery in the work of rescue as they did when behind their guns.

When it was certain that only the *Colon* was afloat, and that the *Oregon*, *Texas*, and the

From a photograph by J. C. Hemment, copyright, 1898, by W. R. Hearst.

The Bow of the Vizcaya.

Brooklyn were in hot chase, the *Iowa* turned to the blazing wrecks on the beach. So did the *Gloucester* when the destroyers were out of the way, while the *Indiana* was equally prompt in the humane work. And then the *Ericsson*, that was following with hot foot in the trail of the *Colon*, was ordered to turn ashore instead. There was need enough for all the help that could be given—need in one way at the wreck of the *Vizcaya* that is almost unbelievable. For she had run ashore at Aserraderos, where many Cubans were camped, and as her crew leaped from her burning deck unarmed to try for life in the breakers, the Cubans came to the beach and began to shoot the helpless sailors. It was atrocious—almost as atrocious as the acts of the Spaniards in shooting every Cuban they caught before we intervened, and in starving and slowly torturing the unresisting *reconcentrados*. But when our men arrived in small boats the shooting stopped instantly, and then began the heroic task of saving the wounded from the blazing decks.

There was "Fiddler" Trainor, as he was called by the newspaper reporters, a man of the *Iowa*—an average man among scores of others. He "shinnied" up a rope to the rail of the *Vizcaya*, although her plates were red with the glowing heat, and dragging three terrorized Spaniards from the upper deck, tum-

R. M. C. Hospital-ship.

bled them into the sea, where the boat's crew awaited to save them. The *Ericsson's* crew, from Captain Usher to the apprentice boy, showed equal courage, for the heat was exploding the ammunition that had been piled on the *Vizcaya's* deck, and firing her loaded guns on both sides, while it seemed absolutely certain that the magazines would be reached quickly by the flames. Nevertheless not a man of all the rescuers flinched, as the *Ericsson* came to beside her, and so hundreds of Spaniards were saved.

The care for the men of the *Maria Teresa* and the *Oquendo* was as unremitting as that beside the *Vizcaya*, nor was the peril less. The *Gloucester* had the honor of receiving the surrender of Admiral Cervera, who had reached the shore from his wrecked flag-ship. The prisoners were taken off shore, the *Iowa* receiving three hundred and three, the *Resolute* five hundred and eight and the *Harvard* six hundred and seventy-two. Some, who were severely wounded, died, and were buried with the honors due to their rank. Other wounded were placed on our hospital-ship *Solace*. Scores who were naked were clothed by the crews that received them. The crew of the *Colon* was divided among the ships that reached her.

First Ward—the *Keaf.*

It seems enough to merely mention the spectacle the burning ships afforded. Rarely has it happened that men of this day have seen a warship burn, but at Manila we saw a squadron on fire, and here off Santiago were two ships half a mile apart blazing fiercely, while a third was but a narrow span farther away. And when to the flame-splashed clouds of smoke arising from the three was added the volcanic blast of the exploding magazine on the *Oquendo* —who can adequately describe the scene? And there were heavy explosions of ammunition on all the three stranded Spaniards. I think the destruction of the *Maine* was then, at last, avenged man-fashion.

The following table, from the *Army and Navy Journal*, is believed to be a fair estimate of the number of guns engaged on each side:

United States.		Spanish.	
13-inch	4	11-inch	6
12-inch	4	6-inch rapid-fire guns	5
8-inch	18	5.5-inch rapid-fire guns	15
6-inch	7	4.7-inch rapid-fire guns	3
5-inch rapid-fire guns	6	12-pounders	4
4-inch rapid-fire guns	3	6-pounders	21
6-pounders	47	1-pounders	5
3-pounders	4	Hotchkiss, Rev. Cannon, 37 mm.	21
1-pounders	4	Max.-Nord.	4
Machine	8	Machine	7
Total	119	Total	91
The *Vixen* is not included.			

To determine the quantity of metal thrown, take the time allowed from fire to fire for the thirteen-inch gun as a unit; then in that length of time the weight of metal from each thirteen-inch gun would be 1,100 pounds; from four guns, 4,400 pounds. The allowed time from fire to fire for the thirteen-inch is 320 seconds, and for the twelve-inch it is 300 seconds; hence the weight of metal thrown by the twelve-inch in 320 seconds is 3,613 pounds. These quantities for other calibres are found similarly. Hence we have for the American guns:

13-inch	4,400	4-inch rapid-fire guns	1,584
12-inch	3,613	6-pounders	7,520
8-inch	12,000	3-pounders	384
6-inch	1,778	1-pounders	720
5-inch rapid-fire guns	3,840		

Total weight thrown in 320 seconds, 35,839 pounds.
Total weight thrown per minute, 6,720 pounds.

In determining this quantity for the Spanish guns, the same time allowances are used. The weights of projectiles are for common shell; the time unit is 300 seconds, being the interval from fire to fire of the United States twelve-inch gun.

11-inch	3,516	4.7-inch rapid-fire guns	1,440
6-inch rapid-fire guns	3,750	6-pounders	3,150
5.5-in. rapid-fire guns	10,277	1-pounders and R. F. G.	900
12-pounders	800	Max.-Nord	300

Total weight thrown in 300 seconds, 24,133 pounds.
Weight thrown per minute, 4,827 pounds.

It will be noted that the weight thrown each per minute was as 6,720 : 4,827 ; this is approximately as 139 : 100, therefore the fire

Shot-hole in the Smoke-stack of the *Brooklyn*.

of the United States ships, instead of being treble that of the Spanish ships, was one-third greater, and this small difference could not alone account for the disparity in results.

How great that disparity was appears on a moment's thought. The Spaniards were swept from the sea. Our ships received only the most trifling wounds. A shell exploded in the berth deck of the *Iowa* and ripped the deck and slashed about forcefully but in no way seriously. Another entered forward and broke up, without exploding, in the coffer dam. While the *Brooklyn* was in the track of the Spaniards she was struck by twenty shot besides pieces of shells. George H. Ellis, Chief Yeoman on the *Brooklyn*, was killed in the discharge of his duty and J. Burns was wounded.

Shot-holes in the Berth-deck of the *Brooklyn*.

In comparison with this loss of blood on our side, Admiral Cervera estimated his loss of life alone at six hundred men. The exact figures on their side can never be given, but a good estimate places their original force at 2,125 men, of whom nearly one-third were killed and the others made prisoners.

On a survey of the wrecks it appeared possible to save the *Maria Teresa* and the *Colon*. By the unwearied efforts of Naval Constructor Hobson, who returned to New York for wrecking apparatus, the *Maria Teresa* was floated in October, taken to Guantanamo, there partly repaired, and then sent North. *En route* a gale was encountered, and she was abandoned by her crew because her commanding officer thought she was about to sink. A few days later she was found on a coral reef off Cat Island, one of the Bahamas. Instead of sinking she had drifted sixty miles to a resting-place, and there she lies at this writing (December 1, 1898).

As an inspiration to our people, especially to our seamen, any one of these ships was worth twice the cost of a new one of equal power. It was a spirit of parsimony that allowed even the broken-backed *Oquendo* to lie on the rocks. She should have been taken off piecemeal, if need be, and at any cost, to be put together again and set afloat under the Stars and Stripes. The talk about the expense of saving these ships makes one wonder whether the Spaniards were wrong after all in their favorite appellation when describing us. The bravery of Hobson on the *Merrimac* was magnificent, but in his work on the wrecked ships, though it was in vain, he set an example that should stir the patriotism of his country long after he is dead.

A word only of the lessons we learned at Santiago seems necessary. The first tells of the deadly nature of wood in the construction of a war-ship. The second tells of the value of quick-firing guns—that we must develop, as soon as possible, long, high-power, quick-firing seven-inch or eight-inch guns for the broadside of our battle-ships, with ammunition hoists able to keep them supplied with cartridges. The third is the need for speed in our battle-ships, and that is one we have taken to heart. The fourth is the need of sheathing our ships with wood and copper to keep the bottoms clean.

Last of all is the lesson of the gunner's school. We had practised well at the target while at Key West, and our relative excellence when compared with the Spanish was well-nigh a hundred to one. But actually we fired more than 6,000 shots, and when we came to count the shot-holes in the wrecks we found a record that is shown by the following table compiled by the *Scientific American* from the official report of the Survey Board:

Size of Gun.	Number of Hits on each Vessel.				Total Hits by each Calibre of Gun.	Number of Guns of each Calibre in action.	Number of hits per Gun.
	Teresa.	*Oquendo.*	*Vizcaya.*	*Colon.*			
6-pounder	17	43	13	4	77	42	1.83
1-pounder	2	....	....	....	2	13	0.15
4-inch	1	7	4	2	12	3	4.00
5-inch	3	3	7	1	15	6	2.50
6-inch	1	1	....	1	3	7	0.43
8-inch	3	3	5	....	12	18	0.67
12-inch	2	....	....	....	2	6	0.33
13-inch	....	....	....	....	....	8	0.00
Totals	29	57	29	8	123	103	

To reach that number—one hundred and twenty-three hits—we counted even the tiny holes our six-pounders made in the smoke-stacks. Of course many hits were made in the burned up wood-work and on parts of the ships that were under water when our survey was made. But since we won a sweeping victory we may soberly face the facts. We made no more than three effective hits out of a hundred shots. And only two of our largest shots hit at all. What would we say of a trap-shot who killed but three birds out of a hundred?

CHAPTER XIX

CAPTURE OF GUAM AND MANILA

A BOMBARDMENT THAT WAS MISTAKEN FOR A SALUTE—THE EMPEROR-WILLIAM GERMANS WERE INCLINED TO MAKE TROUBLE, BUT DEWEY WAS A GOOD DIPLOMAT AS WELL AS A FIGHTER—OUR FRIENDS, THE BRITISH—NOTABLE VOYAGE OF TWO MONITORS.

The destruction of Cervera's squadron was the death-blow to Spanish power in America. The capture of Santiago and the conquest of Porto Rico were thereafter matters requiring brief time and small effort. But meantime something had been done on the Pacific. An expedition to aid Dewey at Manila was planned immediately after his great victory at Cavite and the capture of the forts at the mouth of the bay gave him full control of the water there. He might have taken Manila at any hour, but he had no landing force to control it if he took it, and that such a force was absolutely necessary for the safety as well as the control of the city, appears from a consideration of the fact that the Island of Luzon, like

Cuba, was in great part overrun with a horde of insurgents, whose character was as low as Spanish cruelty and greed had been able to make it. Even the hospital at Cavite had to be protected by our marines from insurgent outrage after we had driven away the Spanish forces.

Command of the forces to be sent to Manila was given to Major-General Wesley Merritt, and the first division of his troops, numbering over 2,500, sailed from San Francisco on May 25th, convoyed by the cruiser *Charleston*, Captain Henry Glass. The expedition sailed by the way of the Ladrone Islands, arriving there on the morning of Monday, June 20th. A little fortification, called Fort Santa Cruz, was found on a coral-reef at the mouth of Guam's Harbor (San Louis d'Apra), and the *Charleston*, on passing in, bombarded it, in the hope of having a small fight, but without avail, and she steamed on unmolested to the usual anchorage. Then came a small boat with the Spanish flag flying bravely above its stern, where were sitting Lieutenant Garcia Guiterrez, of the Spanish Navy, Captain of the Port; Señor Romero, health officer, and Francisco Portusac, a native of the island, who had been naturalized in the United States and had now come out to greet his countrymen and act as interpreter. But no interpreter was needed, for Captain Glass speaks Spanish, and to him Lieutenant Guiterrez said (vide the account of O. K. Davis, in New York *Sun*):

"You will pardon our not immediately replying to your salute, Captain, but we are unaccustomed to receiving salutes here and are not supplied with proper guns for returning them. However, we shall be glad to do our best to return your salute as soon as possible."

The reply of Captain Glass was short and surprising.

"What salute?" he asked.

The Spaniards looked at each other with raised eyebrows. It was odd that Captain Glass should ask such a question.

"The salute you fired," they responded together. "We should like to return it and shall do so as soon as we can get a battery."

Captain Glass smiled.

"Make no mistake, gentlemen," he said. "I fired no salute. Our country is at war with yours. When I came in here I saw a fort, and I fired a few small shells at it to unmask it, and see if there was any response."

The Spaniards were astounded. They had heard nothing of the war. Don José Marina, Governor of the group, was brought from Agaña, the capital, and with the garrison of two companies of soldiers was taken to the squadron; and on Monday, June 21st, Old Glory replaced the Spanish ensign over the group. On July 1st, the expedition reached Manila Bay.

Meantime Dewey had had some trouble in Manila Bay owing to the attitude of Admiral Diedrich, commanding a squadron of five warships sent there by the German Emperor. People who know what good citizens our German-Americans have been always, were unable to understand, at first, this act of Emperor William, but those who had met Germans in foreign countries knew all about the feeling which business antagonisms have created in German minds, both in Germany and elsewhere. The very fact that German-Americans are good Americans makes the Emperor-William Germans hate us. Admiral Diedrich disregarded the harbor regulations established by Dewey, by sending his launches scouting around the bay at night. He sent a ship (the *Irene*) to interfere with the attack of the insurgents on a Spanish post in a neighboring port (Subig Bay), and Dewey was obliged to send a couple of our ships there to drive the Germans away. He carried Captain-General Augustin to Hong Kong when that official was relieved of command by the Madrid Government and so prevented our taking an important prisoner. Finally, when we had increased our force by sending out the monitors *Monadnock* and *Monterey* (a notable voyage, that, by the way, though the *Monadnock* did not arrive in time), and by raising our land force to 10,000 men, and we were ready to take the city, he joined with two French ships in getting out of our range, on one side of the bay, while the English and the Japanese came to our side of the water and looked on with hearty cheers while we fought.

Monadnock, Twin-turret Monitor. D... ...s, 259.5 × 55.5; d aft. 15; displacement, 3,990. Speed, 12 knots. Main Battery, four ten-inch, two four-inch guns.

The British ships, were, it is said, under orders to join with us if the Germans interfered. In fact, here as elsewhere, during this war, the British were our steadfast friends. They increased their squadron as the German Emperor increased his at Manila, and there is no question but what they would have given us substantial support had the insolent interference of the Germans compelled Dewey to fire on them.

On July 19th a second force of Americans

arrived, and on the 25th, a third, with General Merritt himself in command. On August 4th came the monitor *Monterey*, Captain E. H. C. Leutze. The *Monadnock*, Captain W. H. Whiting, had been delayed, but she was expected any day, and preparations for an attack were made. The accession of General Jaudenes to the command in place of Augustin—a squirming Spanish effort for delay—was somewhat successful, and action was postponed from time to time, although there was some fighting in the trenches, until August 13th. Then Dewey ranged his ships before the Spanish forts, and at 9.30 o'clock in the morning the *Olympia* opened the battle. The firing lasted for over an hour, but there was no reply from the Spanish guns, and at 10.50 we stopped to ask by signal if the city had surrendered. They replied by asking for a conference. This was granted, with the result that the *Olympia* was able to signal at 2.30:

"The enemy has surrendered."

Flag-Lieutenant Thomas M. Brumby, of Admiral Dewey's staff, hoisted the American flag over the surrendered city. The navy's loss in the operations at Manila was nothing. The army saw some fierce little conflicts in the trenches, but the losses were small. It is not too much to say that Admiral Dewey, by his firmness, patience, and diplomacy in dealing with the Germans, and with the insurgents (who were to an exasperating degree obstreperous), and last of all with the Spaniards, showed his greatness as a commander quite as much as he did in that splendid dash when he destroyed the Spanish squadron.

CHAPTER XX

SURRENDER OF SANTIAGO AND AFTERWARD

DEADLY ACCURACY IN FIRING AT A TARGET FIVE MILES AWAY AND OUT OF SIGHT BEHIND THE HILLS—OUR SHIPS AT MANZANILLO, AND A POETIC TRIBUTE TO THREE OF THEM—THE CAPTURE OF NIPE—WHEN ENSIGN CURTIN OF THE *WASP* DEMANDED AND OBTAINED THE SURRENDER OF PONCE BY TELEPHONE.

ALTHOUGH the Spaniards in Santiago very quickly learned that Cervera's squadron had been destroyed, they showed a disposition to continue a stubborn resistance rather than an inclination to surrender, and in proof of this is the fact that late on the night of July 4th they sent their 3,000-ton cruiser *Reina Mercedes* to add to the obstruction made by the *Merrimac* in the channel inside the Morro. And it should be said here, that their stubbornness was due to a knowledge of the growing weakness in our army through the effects of fevers. They were not sure their torpedoes could keep Sampson out now that their squadron was gone. It happened that night that the *Massachusetts* and the *Texas* were on guard, the *Massachusetts* using her search-light on the channel, and the *Texas* lying by in the darkness. It was a matter of observation on the blockade that the men on the dark ship could see the channel better

The *Reina Mercedes* as She Lies at the Entrance to Santiago Harbor.
Reina Mercedes, Cruiser. Dimensions, 279 × 43; draft, 16.5; displacement, 3,090. Speed, 17.5 knots. Main Battery, six 6.2-inch guns.

than those on the one using the search-light. The *Texas*, not far from midnight, saw the bow of the *Mercedes* coming from behind Smith Cay, and both our ships began firing deliberately and with an accuracy that came now from experience. The *Mercedes* soon drifted, unmanageable, to one side of the channel, and grounded and sank, leaving a part of her deck still above water. She was hit by five of our largest shells.

The soldiers in the forts were on duty for the occasion, apparently, for they returned our fire as vigorously and as ineffectively as ever. An eight-inch shell from a mortar did fall on the *Indiana*, passing through to the berth-deck, where it exploded, with the effect of showing that eight-inch shells weighing but two hundred and fifty pounds are useless for such work. However, a fragment did dent the ward-room punch-bowl somewhat, and it was carefully preserved and mounted in silver, for use as a cover to the bowl it had so nearly ruined.

Another ship that was lost to the Spaniards about this time was the *Alphonso XII*. She sneaked from Havana on July 6th, but was headed off at Mariel, twenty-five miles west, by the *Castine*, Captain R. M. Berry, and overhauled by the *Hawk*, Captain J. Hood, the *Prairie*, Captain C. J. Train, and the *Badger*, Captain A. S. Snow, in the order named. She was driven ashore and set on fire by the attack. She was of about three thousand tons displacement, and had no mean battery (six six-inch and two three-inch guns), but she was no match for our auxiliaries. Her crew escaped ashore.

On July 10th, our squadron bombarded the city of Santiago. There had been truces and conferences between our land forces and the Spanish without avail, and the non-combatants were finally warned out. Then the *New York*, the *Brooklyn*, the *Indiana*, and the *Texas*, ranged up facing the hills, set their guns for a range of 9,000 yards and began firing on the city they could not see, but whose location was accurately plotted on the chart. In all one hundred and six shells (chiefly eight-inch) were fired, and all but three fell in the city. It is admitted that the terrible accuracy of this fire convinced the Spanish General Toral that he could not hold out much longer. The ships could with absolute certainty destroy the whole city.

On July 18th, at 7.30 o'clock in the morning, the *Wilmington*, with Captain C. C. Todd as senior officer, led the *Helena*, Captain W. T. Swinburne, *Scorpion*, Captain A. Marix, *Hist*, Captain L. Young, *Wompatuck*, Captain C. A. Jungen and the *Osceola* into the harbor of Manzanillo, that is found some distance west of Santiago. A right brave attack had been made on this port by the *Hist*, Captain Lucien Young, with the *Hornet*, Captain J. M. Helm, and *Wompatuck*, on July 1st. They faced five well-armed gun-boats, besides pontoons armed with six-inch muzzle-loaders, and succeeded in sinking one gun-boat, but were unable to destroy the entire force, and this last expedition was undertaken to complete what was then begun. There were a number of Spanish transports and gun-boats there, and Admiral Sampson had ordered that they be destroyed. The

A six-inch Gun on the Aft-deck of the Auxiliary *Hist*.

firing began at 7.50 o'clock, at a range beyond that of the field-pieces in some shore batteries found there, and continued for two and a half hours, during which the gun-boats *Maria Ponton, Delgado Perado, José Garcia, Cuba*, and *Española* were burned; the merchant steamer (blockade runner) *Purissima Concepcion* was sunk, and the *Estrella de Guantanamo*, the *Guardian*, and the *Sentinel Delgado* were shot to pieces.

Whereat, inspired by the brave deeds of the smaller auxiliaries in the first fight, Mr. Frank Taylor, an enthusiastic contributor to the *Army and Navy Journal*, broke into song:

> Why do our battle-ships scour the main,
> What need of big cruisers to thrash old Spain,
> When we have a surplus of Yankee pluck
> And the *Hist*, the *Hornet*, and *Wompatuck?*
>
> The Spaniards scoffed at our " Navy of tugs,"
> Manned by ignorant sailors and thugs;
> But a different tune is sung since they struck
> The *Hist*, the *Hornet*, and *Wompatuck*.
>
> A toast to brave Jungen, Helm, and Young,
> May their praises long and loud be sung;
> One foot on the table, boys, " Here's luck,"
> The *Hist*, the *Hornet*, and *Wompatuck*.

No attempt was made to reduce the batteries. As usual we suffered no losses, although at the last our ships had closed in to a half range for field-pieces.

Following the destruction of Cervera's squadron our new flying squadron, or Eastern squadron, as it was officially designated, was organized for a raid on Spain's coast, as an answer to her threat to send Camara's squadron to Manila. The *Newark*, Captain A. S. Barker, was made the flag-ship, and the *Iowa* and *Oregon*, with seven auxiliaries and transports were added. Commodore John C. Watson was put in command instead of Schley.

On July 21st, a raid was made on Nipe, on the north coast, nearly opposite Santiago. The *Annapolis*, Captain J. J. Hunker (senior officer), with the *Topeka*, Captain W. S. Cowles, our little ship purchased abroad, the *Wasp*, Captain A. Ward, and the *Leyden*, Captain W. S. Crosby, were in the expedition, with the two last named in the post of honor because of their light draft. The Spaniards vainly strove to stop them by exploding two mines in the channel as they entered. Then the forts began firing in Spanish fashion, but the gunners fled when we returned their fire. Last of all a small Spanish cruiser, the *Jorge Juan*, carrying three guns of 4.7-inch calibre and two of 2.8-inch, essayed a defence of the small fort near the town, but it took our men only fifteen minutes to sink her, and they were obliged to put out small boats to save her crew from

Commodore John C. Watson.

drowning. The small fort displayed a white flag when two shells had been fired into it.

Nipe was important because it was the supply port of the town of Holguin, where five thousand Spanish troops were stationed. As usual we suffered no damage.

Then Santiago surrendered and we moved on to Porto Rico. General Miles had come down to Santiago to take charge of our army, and thereafter everything pertaining to the army moved on as comfortably as everything moved afloat during the whole war. Richard Harding Davis in "The Cuban and Porto Rican Campaigns," says taking possession of Porto Rico was a "picnic," made so by the masterful powers of General Miles, and so it was.

The navy's part in the work was simple and even delightful. The expedition sailed from Guantanamo on July 21st. General Miles had 3,400 men in eight transports, and for an escort he had the *Massachusetts*, Captain F. J. Higginson, senior officer, with the *Columbia*, Captain J. H. Sands, *Yale*, Captain W. C. Wise, *Dixie*, Captain C. H. Davis, and *Gloucester*, Captain R. Wainwright. The Spaniards thought we would land at Fajardo, and were therefore surprised when they learned that we had landed at Juanica on the morning of the 26th. The Spanish force at the harbor made some little resistance, but the *Massachusetts* and *Columbia* shelled them, while the *Gloucester* ran close in, and with her small rapid-fire guns drove them off. She then landed a party who carried a machine gun. They were attacked as they hauled down the Spanish flag, but the Spanish could not face the blue-jackets, and soon fled to the country. The landing of the troops began in the afternoon.

From Juanica as a base, Miles made his way toward Ponce, the largest town near the south coast, while the navy went around to the harbor of Ponce to assist. Captain Higginson's official report has this to say of what followed:

"Commander Davis with the *Dixie, Annapolis, Wasp,* and *Gloucester,* left Juanica July 27th to blockade Ponce and capture lighters for use of army. City of Ponce and Playa surrendered to Commander Davis upon demand at 12.30 A.M. July 28th. American flag hoisted 6 P.M., 28th. Spanish garrison evacuated. Provisional articles of surrender until occupation by army:

"1. Garrison to be allowed to retire.

"2. Civil government remain in force.

"3. Police and fire brigade to be maintained without arms.

"4. Captain of Port not to be made prisoner.

"Arrived at Ponce from Juanica with *Massachusetts* and *Cincinnati,* General Miles and General Wilson and transports, at 6.40 A.M., 28th. Commenced landing army in captured sugar lighters. No resistance, troops welcomed by inhabitants. Great enthusiasm. Captured 60 lighters, 20 sailing vessels, and 120 tons of coal."

According to the work of Mr. Davis, previously mentioned, "the city of Ponce, which lies two miles back from the port, surrendered, officially and unofficially, on four separate occasions. It was possessed by the surrender habit in a most aggravated form. Indeed, for anyone in uniform it was most unsafe to enter the town at any time unless he came prepared to accept its unconditional surrender. In the official account sent to Washington by Captain Higginson, of the *Massachusetts*, the city of Ponce and the port surrendered to Commander Davis, of the *Dixie*, so General Miles reports— so history as it is written will report. But, as a matter of fact, the town first surrendered to Ensign Curtin, of the *Wasp*, then to three different officers who strayed into it by mistake, then to Commander Davis, and finally to General Miles. Ensign Curtin is a grandson of the war Governor of Pennsylvania. He is about the youngest-looking boy in the navy, and he is short of stature, but in his methods he is Napoleonic. He landed with a letter for the military commander, which demanded

Ensign Curtin of the *Wasp*.

the surrender of the port and city, and he wore his side-arms, and an expression in which there was no trace of pity.

"The Captain of the Port informed him that the military commander was at Ponce, but that he might be persuaded to surrender if the American naval officer would condescend to drive up to Ponce, and make his demand in person. The American officer fairly shook and quivered with indignation. 'Zounds,' and 'Gadzooks,' and 'Damme, sir,' would have utterly failed to express his astonishment. Had it come to this, then, that an ensign, holding the President's commission, and representing such a ship of terror as the *Wasp*, was to go to a mere colonel, commanding a district of 60,000 inhabitants?

"'How long will it take that military commander to get down here, if he hurries?'" demanded Ensign Curtin. The trembling Captain of the Port, the terrified foreign consuls, and the custom-house officials thought that a swift-moving cab might bring him to the port in half an hour. 'Have you a telephone about the place?' asked the Napoleonic Curtin. They had.

"'Then call him up and tell him that if he does not come down here in a hack in thirty minutes and surrender, I shall bombard Ponce.'"

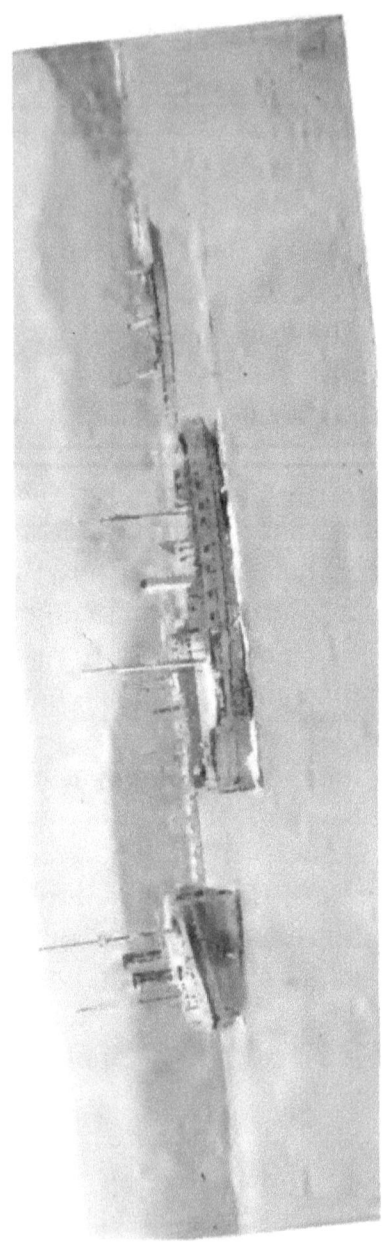

"This was the Ensign's ultimatum. He turned his back on the terrified inhabitants and returned to his gig. Four hacks started on a mad race for Ponce, and the central office of the telephone rang with hurry calls.

Port of Manzanillo.

"On his way out to the ship, Ensign Curtin met Commander Davis on his way to the shore. Commander Davis looked at his watch. 'I shall extend his time another half hour,' said Commander Davis. Ensign Curtin saluted, sternly, making no criticism upon this weak generosity of his superior officer, but he could afford to be magnanimous. He, at least, had upheld the honor of the navy, and he will go down in the history of the war as the middy who demanded and obtained a surrender by telephone.

"General Miles landed in the morning after Curtin had taken the place, and Mr. Curtin came ashore in the same boat with us. We asked him if he had already landed, and he replied, modestly, that he had, but he spared the commanding General's feelings by making no reference to his own part in the surrender."

Captain D. Delehanty, commanding the *Suwanee*.

The work of the navy was all but done. There was that irritating little port of Manzanillo, where we had had two fights, with excellent results afloat, but the forts and the town were still under the Spanish flag, and by orders of Admiral Sampson the *Newark*, Captain Albert S. Baker, assisted by the *Suwanee*, Captain D. Delehanty, the *Hist*, Captain L. Young, the *Osceola*, Captain J. L. Purcell, and the *Alverado*, a captured gun-boat, went to reduce the place. No such a ship as the *Newark* had ever been in that bay, but in spite of shoaling water, she steamed in to a range of 5,000 yards, and, with the others farther in, began a bombardment at 3.30 in the afternoon of August 12th, which was continued vigorously until 5.30, and thereafter with one gun every half-hour all night. The town was white with surrender-flags at daylight. It was the last fight of the war around Cuba. Before the sun was up the Spanish sent out a boat to announce that the protocol between the warring governments had been signed the day before, and hostilities were ended.

CHAPTER XXI

OUR NEW NAVAL PROGRAMME

VESSELS THAT WERE IN THE SHIP-YARD WHEN THE WAR BEGAN—TWO-STORY TURRETS AND BROADSIDE BATTERIES—SMOKELESS POWDER IN FUTURE, WITH GUNS THAT FOR THE MOMENT WILL LEAD THE WORLD—SHIPS TO REPLACE THE *MAINE*—THE NEW MONITORS—A TALE OF A TORPEDO-BOAT ON THE BLOCKADE—A SPLENDID FLOTILLA TO COME—A WORD ABOUT THE NAVAL ACADEMY.

THE breath of the sea comes once more to inspire the American nation as it did after the War of 1812. We began in halting fashion and under the spur of necessity, in the days after the Revolution, to build a navy. We were in the old days so full of the harbor-defence idea that we wasted much of our resources, but we did get a few ships afloat that were typical of our genius—got them afloat just in time to save the honor of the people. So in these late years we began in a way that was worse than halting to create a sea-power. We were still possessed with the idea that the way to resist aggression was to retire within our protected waters, and shoot at the off-shore enemy; the porcupine was still cherished rather than the eagle as a war emblem. Nevertheless, we did get commissioned just enough modern ships of war—enough when they were supplemented by half-antiquated monitors and many converted merchantmen—to enable our seamen to show their skill and valor. In a way, our inferiority in ships and guns, as compared with the best of European construction, was to the advantage of our sailors, for they swept the enemy from the sea in spite of all. We destroyed more than a score of the enemy's ships, including a squadron of the best kind of cruisers, all in open battle, and we lost just one man killed in doing it, where they lost more than a thousand. Never before was such work known in naval warfare, and yet it was done with material that was not the best in the world.

But when the whole truth is told we had done somewhat better than has appeared so far in this history, in the way of building a navy. For only those vessels have been described that had actual part in the fighting. We had laid down in the ship-yards five battle-ships, not yet described, at least two of which would have carried the flag to sea within six months, had the war lasted that much longer, and the three would have been ready within a year. These are the *Kearsarge* and the *Kentucky* in one

By courtesy of the "Scientific American."

Alabama, First-class Battle-ship. Dimensions, 368 x 72; draft, 27; displacement, 11,525. Speed, 16 knots. Main Battery, four thirteen-inch, fourteen six-inch guns.

class, and the *Alabama*, *Illinois*, and *Wisconsin* in another.

It is important to note the date when two of these ships were authorized by Congress, for the *Kearsarge* class was ordered on March 2, 1895, and yet they were not ready for the emergency that came upon us three years later. We might, in a case of distress, build a battleship in a year, as England has done, but the old motto of "slow and sure" is better, and we must look ahead for the needs of our navy in these days, when we must go to the crucible for steel, instead of to the forest for timber, if a ship is wanted. The *Alabama* class was ordered on June 10, 1896.

All of these five new ships are of one size in the hull—368 feet long, 72 feet wide, and with a maximum draught of perhaps 27 feet, when full loaded for sea. The Department places the displacement at 11,525 tons, when two-thirds loaded, but the fact is, when ready for battle, if ever they see real service, the displacement will probably be considerably more than 12,000 tons. Horse-power (10,000) to drive them sixteen knots is provided for, but we hope that they will do half a knot better, at least.

So far they are alike. In guns there is a remarkable difference. In arming the *Oregon* class we were somewhat over-burdened with the home-defence idea. We piled four turrets for eight-inch guns on each, along with the thirteen-inch gun turrets, for the purpose of increasing the weight of metal thrown. We thought we could thus throw two thirteen-inch shot and four eight-inch in a round either ahead or astern, while double that number could be thrown in a broadside, besides two six-inch shot and a hail of the smaller projectiles that, as we now know, are so tremendously effective against unarmored superstructures. But we were mistaken. It was at once seen to be impossible to fire the eight-inch guns fore and aft, because the blast of the gases would penetrate the openings in the thirteen-inch gun turrets, to the excruciating distress, if not the destruction of the men there. Stops are now placed on these turrets, so that the guns cannot come nearer than an angle of ten degrees to the keel.

In the *Kearsarge* class we tried the plan of building two-story turrets—a small turret for two eight-inch guns above the big turret for the two thirteen-inch guns, and we have every reason to believe that the system will work admirably. Although this gave us but four eight-inch guns where the *Oregon* has eight, we shall be able to fire as many guns of the two calibres in a broadside as the *Oregon*, and we shall fire two eight-inch dead fore and aft, where the

Oregon cannot fire one of that calibre. We have saved the weight of two turrets and of four eight-inch guns, apparently, in the design of the *Kearsarge* class, besides increasing the effective arc of the larger guns. What we saved thus we used in broadside guns. We put in fourteen five-inch rapid-fire guns where the *Oregon* carries but four six-inch guns—a very great increase in effectiveness, especially in case of such a battle as that off Santiago, where guns of eight-inch calibre and less did about all the work.

In designing the *Alabama* class we abandoned the eight-inch guns altogether, on the theory that they are better replaced with the six-inch rapid-fire guns. The *Alabama* class will carry fourteen of the six-inch rapid-fire guns in broadside, with two turrets of two thirteen-inch guns each.

This brings us to a brief consideration of the very latest development in guns, to which only mere references have been made hitherto. When we first began building modern rifles we quickly placed our weapons beside the very best in the world, but when 1897 came we were practically at a standstill, with a six-inch rapid-fire gun that had a muzzle energy of 3,200 tons; an eight-inch slow-fire gun with a muzzle energy of 8,011 tons, and a thirteen-inch gun with a muzzle energy of 33,627 tons. With guns of that efficiency we swept the Spanish from the sea, but we would better keep clear of

By courtesy of the "Scientific American."
Elliptical Turret of the First-class Battle-ship *Alabama*.

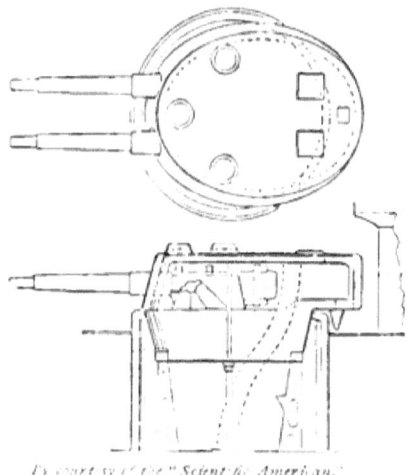

By courtesy of the "Scientific American."
Plan and Vertical Section through Elliptical Turret and Barbette.

the fool's paradise and not imagine we should have had such an easy time of it with other European peoples. For the British had developed a six-inch quick-fire gun with a muzzle energy of 5,373 tons, and the Germans had carried the rapid-fire principle in guns up to the calibre of 9.24 inches. The term rapid-fire means practically that the gun

By courtesy of "The Engineers' Magazine" Company, Boston.

Boilers of the *Kearsarge*.

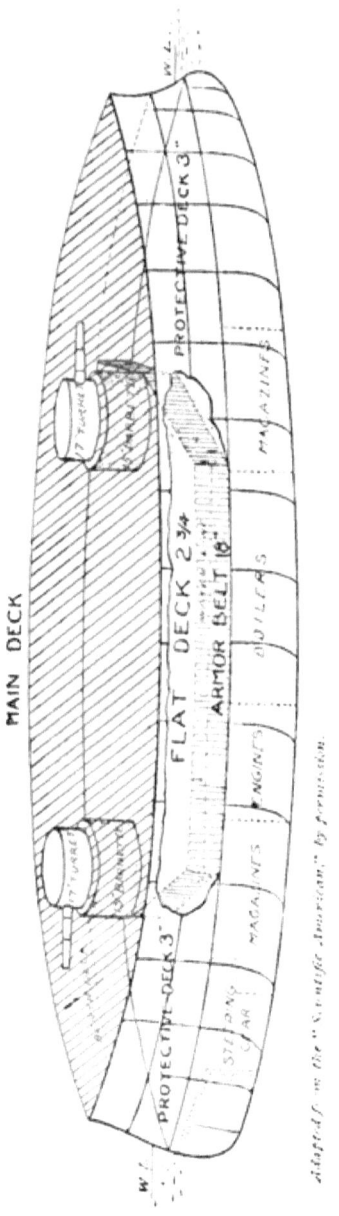

Outline Diagram of a Floating Steel Fort called a Battle-ship. *Adapted from the "Scientific American," by permission.*

can be fired nearly five times where the slow breech-loaders are fired once.

But what was of still greater moment was the development of the twelve-inch gun as the largest weapon for a battle-ship. We have thirteen-inch guns for our *Alabama* class. They weigh 60.5 tons and their muzzle energy is 33,627 tons. The contemporaneous British twelve-inch gun has a muzzle energy of 44,500 tons, although it weighs but 50.25 tons. Observe the saving in weight of gun as well as the enormous increase in power, for with the saving of thirteen tons in weight of gun, there is a saving in weight of ammunition for each shot, and thus many more charges can be carried. Nor is that all, for the lighter gun can be handled with greater speed and precision —we ourselves at Santiago landed two twelve-inch shot in the enemy, but not one of the larger calibre. We went into the war with Spain very far behind the standard of excellence in guns.

Captain Charles O'Neil, Chief of Ordnance.

But out of this war has come a new era for our navy. While we were providing for the needs of actual battle, we looked ahead for the needs of the future. We provided for three more battle-ships of a quality the best that our resources would permit. That was on May 4th. At the end of June plans for these were completed, which provided for ships not materially different from the *Alabama* class—a speed of sixteen knots, four guns of thirteen-inch calibre and fourteen of the six-inch rapid-firers—very good ships indeed. But while yet the builders were figuring on the cost came Sampson's victory off Santiago, with the wonderful record for speed made by the *Oregon*. The Department, as well as the nation, awoke to the need of speed in battle-ships, and at last, after the beast had curled there for more than ninety years, we took down the porcupine from the truck of our naval flagstaff and replaced it with the eagle. We threw overboard, so to speak, the idea that to cruise about our own coasts in slow, thick-armored, heavily armed ships was the best way to preserve peace, and we adopted the idea which Commander McCalla stencilled on the superstructure of the *Marblehead*—the idea that the best protection against an enemy's fire is an efficient fire of your own. We came to see that battle-ships fit for aggressive war were the best for coast defence, and we contracted for ships of a speed of eighteen knots, and a coal capacity sufficient for a fighting voyage to—well, say to any part of the world where a Subig-Bay incident may occur.

But that is not all to be said of them. We have been overhauling our gun construction. Captain O'Neil, while driving the naval gun-factory day and night to produce war material, found time to design new guns, from the four-inch up, and to plan a smokeless powder-factory at Indian Head, for which Congress provided the money.

We will begin with the powder. As now made our powder is not only smokeless, but it has raised the muzzle-velocity of the old one-

Projectile for a modern six-inch gun, weight, 100 pounds, powder, 50 pounds.

Projectile for an old-time six-inch smooth-bore, weight, 32 pounds.

Six-inch cast-iron gun, breech reinforced by extra thickness only.

Six-inch cast-iron rifle, breech reinforced by wrought jacket shrunk on.

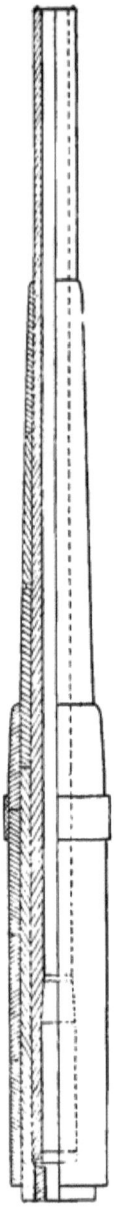

Modern six-inch rifle showing extra reinforcements.

The Evolution of the Six-inch Gun.

(Relative proportions are shown by the diagrams.)

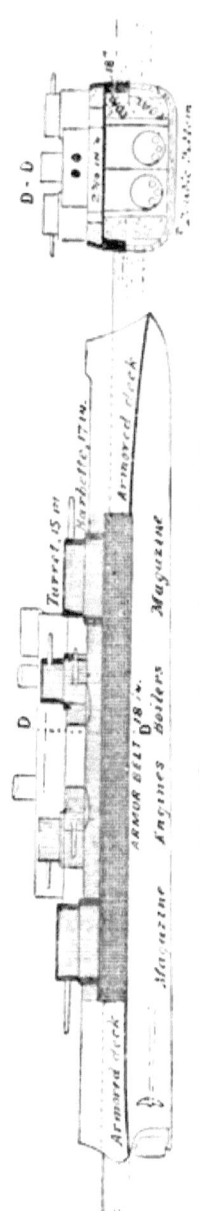

Diagram Showing the Armor Protection of a Battle-ship

hundred pound projectile from 2,200 feet per second (our very best) up to 2,600, while the new designs of guns, by lengthening the bore and increasing the size of the powder-chamber, increase the velocity up to 3,000 foot-seconds for all calibres.

To consider now the new twelve-inch gun as the largest weapon for our battle-ships, we find that it weighs 53 tons, or 10.5 tons less than the thirteen-inch gun, and yet it has a striking energy of not less than 48,000 tons, or nearly 15,000 tons greater than the thirteen-inch we have built for our *Alabama* class of ships. And it must be kept in mind that with this tremendous increase of power has come a great increase in the amount of ammunition the ship can carry, and a greater ease of manipulation, with a consequent increase of precision.

We have designed rapid-fire eight-inch guns with a proportionate increase of power, and the new style six-inch guns in the broadside of the newest ships will have a muzzle energy but a little under that of the eight-inch on the *Oregon*, while in real effectiveness, due to the speed and precision with which they can be fired, they will far surpass the old eight-inch. We hope we may not seem offensive when we say that the effectiveness of our new guns, all things considered, is for the moment ahead of the world.

With their speed and ability to make long voyages, and the power of their guns, our latest battle-ships will replace the *Maine* in a way worthy of the nation. They are to be named *Maine*, *Missouri*, and *Ohio*.

But the end is not yet in sight in the race for improvement in guns. The use of segments or staves for the core of the gun and to withstand the lengthwise strain, with square wire wound around them to withstand the centrifugal strain—this system has shown wonderful results, both here and abroad. The small size of the segments and of the wire insures an enormous elastic limit in the parts of the gun— say twice that of the old style of forged cylinders and jackets—while the possibility of flaws is eliminated absolutely. It is presumptuous for a landsman to prophesy in such a matter, and yet it may be said here that a time is likely to come when ten-inch rapid-fire guns in the turrets and eight-inch rapid-fire guns in the broadside will constitute the armament of a battleship.

Of armor-plate but a word need be said, or ought to be said. Though the use of armor

Kruppized Armor-plate Showing Effect of a Six-inch Projectile, Weighing 100 Pounds.

Tested at Indian Head Proving Ground, July 13, 1898.

is undoubtedly necessary in these days, the thought of it originated in the heart of a coward—in the heart of some old-time warrior, who made a shield or a coat of mail because he was afraid to meet the enemy with naked breast to naked breast. Neither barbettes nor conning-towers make brave men. Let us send our cadets to sea in torpedo-boats rather than battle-ships. We have used armor up to a thickness of eighteen inches, but now we can make it sufficiently effective with a thickness of but twelve or fourteen at most. This is particularly pleasing in two ways. In the first place we save much weight on the turrets and belt, which we are able to use for protecting our

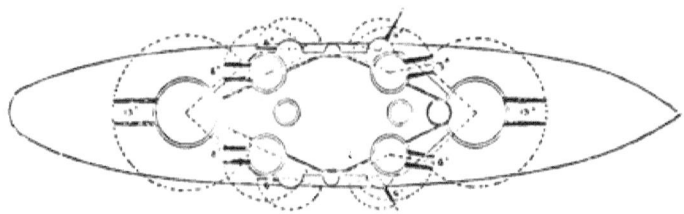

(Aft guns show maximum fire as originally proposed. Forward guns show maximum fire as finally modified.)

Deck Plan of the *Indiana*, *Massachusetts*, and *Oregon*.

broadside guns, and in adding to the power of the machinery. In the second place it shows us that our steel-makers, on whom we depend for our ships, are unsurpassed. We have come to a state of industrial development where we are building war ships for Russia and Japan, and supplying plates for a builder of merchant ships at Belfast, Ireland, as well. We can make the best quality of steel at a price to compete with the whole world, *thanks to the change of policy toward our navy that was inaugurated at the inception of the White Squadron.*

As a concession to the timorous souls who shiveringly carried their silver from New York to their country homes lest the Spaniards come and loot the town, we have ordered four harbor-defence monitors. It is not quite a sheer waste of money, even though a very light sea destroys the monitor's accuracy of fire. With the six already in commission we will have enough smooth-water fighters to give every needed aid to the forts about our largest harbors, and give a blockading force, should one ever come, something to think of. They are to be 225 feet long, displace 2,700 tons, draw 12.5 feet of water and are to be armed with two of the twelve-inch guns just described, with four four-inch rapid-fire guns, besides enough smaller ones to stand off torpedo-boat attack.

Of vastly more importance to the service was the appropriation for torpedo-boat destroyers and torpedo-boats. Sixteen of the destroyers are under contract, with twelve of the smaller boats. An interesting chapter might be written on the work of the torpedo-boats in the war with Spain. Some newspaper men of the class who shoot before the breech-block is closed, announced that the war with Spain, and especially the battle off Santiago, had proved the torpedo-boat worthless. The statement was distinctly and viciously untrue. One incident shall suffice to prove it untrue. In the blockade of Havana, Lieutenant John C. Fremont of the *Porter*, as he has told in *Harper's* for November, 1898, ran the *Porter* under the stern of the *New York*, and thence alongside to a range where he had her dead be-

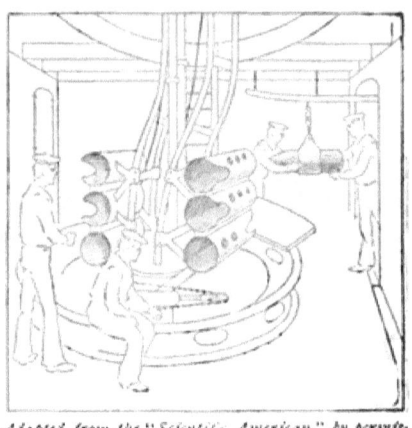

Adapted from the "Scientific American," by permission.

Indiana—Loading the Ammunition-hoists for Thirteen-inch Guns.

yond peradventure, being all the time well convinced she was a Spanish cruiser instead of his

Adapted from the "Scientific American."
Ramming Home the Charge in a Thirteen-inch Gun.

own flag-ship, and nothing but the fortunate discovery that the cruiser had three smoke-stacks instead of but two, as all the Spaniards had, prevented his sinking her then and there. The *New York's* lookouts did not see him until he had made the squadron signal three times; they failed, because the *Porter* was shrouded in the *New York's* smoke, and the quality of the signal-lamps was poor. It was the moment of greatest peril that came to any of our ships in the whole war. The men who guarded the mouth of Santiago harbor, and, under the strain, came to see torpedo-boat ghosts —the men who fired at a hole in the rocks, and at a trade-wind swell, and at a railroad-train ashore, each time thinking they saw a torpedo-boat—these men speak of the night "demons of the sea" with respect. We are to have a flotilla, modest in numbers, but of the best quality. The destroyers are to displace about 325 tons and show a speed of thirty knots, while the others are smaller in design and are rated at twenty-six knots, quite ample for the purpose.

There is one thing we might do for the improvement at once of the navy and the whole nation—we might make the Naval Academy free to all American boys who could pass the examination, and would serve in the navy before the mast, as need required, a reasonable number of years. We might fill every petty office and post on board ship—man every machine, as well as every gun with graduates of our Naval Academy. If we retained the present course of instruction—rather if we improved on it stead-

ily—we should then have crews of a grade of intelligence and self-respect hitherto undreamed of. In leaving the service, as the graduates who failed to get commissions might do, they would carry with them a training that would make them superior citizens, and we should soon have in them a naval reserve worthy of the name. We should remove absolutely the un-American barrier that now rises between the forecastle and the cabin.

When we think of it we know that a chief function of Government is the education of the young. A time ought to come, and so it will come, when every man who wears the naval uniform shall be known as an educated gentleman. But this is only to mention what is yet a long way ahead. It would cost much money to enlarge and maintain such a naval academy as would be required then, and we shall not use our national revenues for any such chimerical purposes as educating sailor-men until after we have finished improving the mouths of the Cattaraugus and the Cheesequakes Creeks.

To sum it all up, looking ahead as well as backward, we can see that we are not to have the largest navy in the world—we shall never need that—but we are to rank well in numbers and with the best in quality; never again shall our navy be quoted as the standard of inefficiency.

It was shameful that at the end of the nineteenth century of the era of Christianity, two nations were obliged to resort to a butchery of men before order could be restored where anarchy reigned, but let us face the truth. There was no other way. And if we will consider ourselves as well as the people whom we liber-

Firing a Six-pounder on the *Marietta*.

ated, we shall find that the war, as waged, was well-nigh an unmixed blessing. It is better to cultivate manhood under the blazing muzzle of a modern rifle, than to yield to the degrading influence of sordid pursuits. We had set up as our hero the man who " had made his pile " by legalized theft ; we had used our flag and our most beautiful natural scenery for hideous advertisements. And then came war, and for one brief span we brushed aside the muck and cheered men for what they were, and not for what they possessed. That alone was worth the pain, but it was not all.

By the Civil War we wiped away the curse of human slavery, and disintegrating States were blended into one great nation. With all its horror the effect of that war upon our people was most beneficent. And through the war with Spain we have been reminded that blood is thicker than water, and have learned that there can be no permanent peace on earth, and no substantial progress in real culture, until the one race that fully comprehends the meaning of Liberty and Justice is dominant beyond dispute.

INDEX

Aguadores, attack on, 280

Alabama authorized, 369; armament, 373, 376

Alfonso XII. at Havana, 72; wrecked, 352

Alfonso XIII. at San Juan, 279

Almirante Oquendo, 194, 195; attempts to escape, 298; destruction of, 307 *et seq.*

Alverado, Spanish gun-boat, 360

Ammen ram, the, 27

Ammunition, amount expended at Manila, 184, 185; at Santiago, 337, 338

Amphitrite ordered to Key West, 86; off Matanzas, 129; her unfitness, 130; ordered to San Juan, 196; in tow of the *Iowa*, 197; in battle line, 198

Anderson, Lieutenant E. A., at Cienfuegos, 142

Anglo-Saxon Race united, 102

Annapolis at Nipe, 356

Antonio Lopez attacked by the *Yosemite*, 285 *et seq.*

Argonauta captured by the *Nashville*, 136

Armor, improvements in, 382 *et seq.*

Army, at the outbreak of the war, 127

Army of Occupation, delay of, 276 *et seq.*; at Santiago, 290

Army and Navy Journal quoted, 84, 185, 336

Atlanta, plans of, 35 *et seq.*

Augustin, Captain-General, leaves Manila, 346

Autonomy in Cuba a failure, 63

Auxiliary Navy, the, 88 *et seq.*, 92, 287

Bache at Havana, 106

Badger overhauls the *Alfonso XII.*, 352

Bagley, Ensign Worth, of the *Winslow*, killed at Cardenas, 151

Bailey, Frank H., Chief Engineer of the *Raleigh*, at Manila, 191

Baiquiri, landing of the Army at, 279, 280

Baltimore, plans of, 45; joins Commodore Dewey, 154, 155; sails for Manila, 156 *et seq.*; at Subig Bay, 159; renews the fight, 172 *et seq.*; ammunition expended by, 184, 185; casualties on, 189, 190

Bancroft, gun-boat, 49; ordered north, 86; at Enseñada de los Altares, 280

Baker, Captain A. S., of the *Newark*, in the Eastern squadron, 353; at Manzanillo, 364

Bartlett, Captain John R., organizes a coast signal-service, 216

Battle-ship era, the, 54 *et seq.*

Battle-ships, our first, 55, 56; time required to build, 369; new ones building, 366 *et seq.*; need of greater speed in, 378

Beecher, Lieutenant Albert M., at the Washington gun factories, 92

Bernabe, Señor Luis Polo y, succeeds Dupuy de Lome at Washington, 69

393

Bernadou, Lieutenant John B., of the *Winslow*, at Cardenas, 144 et seq.; wounded, 150, 152; standing as an officer, 153

Berry, Captain R. M., of the *Castine*, at Baiquiri, 280; heads off the *Alfonso XII.*, 352

Blanco, Captain-General, succeeds Weyler, 63

Blandin, Lieutenant John J., died of injuries received on the *Maine*, 75

Blockade of Cuba proclaimed, 118, 119; a peaceful one not popular, 126; the only thing we could do, 127; disposition of ships for, 129, 130; effects of, 141 et seq.; of Havana, 288

Blocklinger, Lieutenant-Commander Gottfried, of the *Baltimore*, 155

Blue, Lieutenant Victor, of the *Suwanee*, his tour of Santiago Bay, 287

Boston, plans of, 35 et seq.; leaves for Manila, 156 et seq.; sent to Subig Bay, 159; returns the fire from El Fraile, 161; in the battle of Manila, 175; aground, 179; ammunition expended by, 184, 185; struck by a Spanish shell, 189

Bowen, Captain, of the *Virginius*, 17

Bowles, Asst. Naval Constructor, F. T., Secretary of Advisory Board, 32

Brooklyn a greater *New York*, 60; flag-ship of the flying squadron, 88; at Key West, 211; ordered to Cienfuegos, 212; in the attack on Santiago, 254, 255; position in the blockade, 293; advantages of, 311; in the battle of Santiago, 312; her effective fire on the *Vizcaya*, 316; helps in the capture of the *Colon*, 321; struck by shot and shells, 339; bombards Santiago, 353

Brownson, Captain of the *Yankee*, at Santiago, 254, 255

Brumby, Flag-Lieutenant Thomas M., at Manila, 163, 181; hoists the American flag over Manila, 349

Buenaventura, first prize of the war, 122 et seq.

Cabáñas, attack on, 139

Cables, cutting of, 14, 142 et seq., 237, 238

Caimanera fort, attack on, 270 et seq.

Calkins, Lieutenant C. G., of the *Olympia*, Navigator, at Manila, 163, 181

Caldwell, Flag Secretary at Manila, 181

Camachi, Señor Eloy, Cuban leader, 15; Navigator of the *Virginius*, 17

Camp McCalla, 263

Cardenas, blockade of, 129; the fight at, 145 et seq.; lives lost there, 153

Castillo destroyed by Dewey, 171, 179

Castine ordered north, 86; on the blockade, 129; joins the Flying Squadron, 221; at Baiquiri, 280; heads off the *Alfonso XII.*, 352

Cavite Point, forts on, 163, 164; reduced by Dewey, 175; batteries of, 182

Cervera, Admiral, ships of his squadron, 194, 195; enters Santiago Harbor, 212, 231, 232; his kindness to Hobson and his men, 250; his attempted flight, 297; destruction of his fleet, 298 et seq.

Chadwick, Captain French E., of the *New York*, on the *Maine* Board of Inquiry, 76; his article on the navy, 211; sees the Spanish ships in Santiago Harbor, 235, 236; at Santiago, 254, 255, 293, 328 et seq.; on the effects of the shots from the *Vesuvius*, 257, 258; his handling of his ship, 328

Chandler, William E., Secretary of the Navy, 31

Charette, Gunner's-mate George, in the *Merrimac's* crew, 244

Charleston, plans of, 45; sent to Manila as convoy, 344; captures Guam, 345

INDEX

Chester, Captain, in charge of the South American Squadron, 86
Chicago, plans of, 34, 35
Cienfuegos, cutting of the cables at, 141 *et seq.*
Cincinnati, cruiser, 49; ordered north, 86; on the blockade, 129; at Matanzas, 136; at Ponce, 358
City of Washington, survivors of the *Maine* taken to, 72
Clark, Captain Charles E., of the *Oregon*, remarkable run of his ship from San Francisco to Key West, 213 *et seq.*; at Santiago, 254, 293, 301 *et seq.*; compelled to leave his ship by ill-health, 330
Clausen, Coxswain Randolph, stowaway on the *Merrimac*, 244
Clover, Captain R., of the *Bancroft*, at Enseñada de los Altares, 280
Coghlan, Captain Joseph B., of the *Raleigh*, leaves for Manila, 156 *et seq.*
Colonel Lloyd Aspinwall, American steamer, seized by the Spaniards, 9–14
Columbia, commerce-destroyer, 60; with the flying squadron, 88; escorts General Miles to Porto Rico, 357; shells Juanica, 358
Concord leaves for Manila, 156 *et seq.*; sent to examine Subig Bay, 159; replies to the fire from El Fraile Island, 161; in the battle of Manila, 175
Converse, Captain George A., of the *Montgomery*, at Key West, 86; at San Juan, 205
Cook, Captain Francis A., of the *Brooklyn*, at Santiago, 254, 312 *et seq.*
Corregidor Island, 159; defences on, 160
Cowles, Captain William S., of the *Fern*, at Key West, 86; at *Nipe*, 356
Cristobal Colon sailed without her largest guns, 195; discovered at Santiago, 231; replies to the fire of Schley's ships, 233; comes out of the harbor, 298, 301; her run for freedom, 319, 320; runs ashore, 320; scuttled by her crew, 327 *et seq.*
Crosley, Captain W. S., of the *Leyden*, raises the Stars and Stripes at Cardenas, 288
Cuba, valued by Spain only as a source of revenue, 2; the condition of, a sufficient cause for war, 83, 84, 185, 186
Cuba, Spanish gun-boat, burned, 354
Cuban Army numbers exaggerated, 5
Cubans, revolts of, 3
Cubans made what they are by Spain, 7
Curtin, Ensign, of the *Wasp*, his demand for the surrender of Ponce, 359 *et seq.*
Cushing, on the blockade, 129
Davis, Captain C. H., of the *Dixie*, escorts transports to Porto Rico, 357
Davis, Richard Harding, his "The Cuban and Porto Rican Campaigns" quoted, 357; his account of the surrender of Ponce, 359 *et seq.*
Dayton, Captain James H., of the *Detroit*, at Key West, 86; coolness of, at San Juan, 205; at Baiquiri, 280
Dayton, Ensign, sent as boarding officer to the *Panama*, 140
Deignan, Oscar, in the *Merrimac's* crew, 244
Delehanty, Captain D., of the *Suwanee* at Santiago, 254; at Manzanillo, 360
Delgado Perada burned, 354
DeLome, Dupuy, Spanish Minister at Washington, his letter regarding President McKinley, 68; resigns, 69
Detroit, 49; at Key West, 86; on the blockade, 129; captures the *Catalina*, 132; before San Juan, 198; in the bombardment, 203; effectiveness of her small guns, 204; her narrow escape, 204; at Baiquiri, 280
Dewey, Commodore George, sails

for Manila 156 *et seq.*; his
plan of attack, 157; without a
battle-ship, 160; enters Manila
Bay, 161; leads the attack, 163
et seq.; "When you are ready,
you may fire, Gridley," 167; his
conduct of the battle, 168 *et
seq.*; gives his men a rest, 171
et seq.; the fight renewed, 172
et seq.; tactics used by, 175,
176; his report of the battle,
179 *et seq.*; his ships in range
for five hours, 182; strength of
his squadron compared with the
Spanish, 182 *et seq.*; damage
done to his ships, 189; his debt
to his engineers, 191; early
naval experiences, 191; his success like that of Perry's, 192;
receives the thanks of the President and the American people,
ib.; his trouble with the German
Admiral, 346; bombards defences of Manila, 348

Diedrich, Admiral, **interferes at
Manila,** 346, 347

Dienaide, T. M., reports, says the
officers of Schley's fleet were
convinced that Cervera was not at
Cienfuegos, 224; the fleet expected a dash into Santiago Harbor, 227

Dillingham, Lieutenant, executive
officer of the *Nashville*, 123

Dispatch-boats, need of, in the
war with Spain, 38

Dixie escorts transports to Porto
Rico, 357

Dixon, Chief-Engineer Albert F.,
on the auxiliary navy board,
88

Doddridge, Ensign John A., of
the *Boston*, shell exploded in his
room, 189

Dolphin, dispatch-boat, plans of,
37, 38; prejudice against, 38;
on the blockade, 129; in the attack on Santiago, 254; at Guantanamo Bay, 261, 269

Don Antonio de Ulloa, bravery
of her crew, 170

Don Juan de Austria, burned at
Manila, 179

"Don't cheer, the poor devils are
dying," 307

Dupont, in the blockade off Matanzas, 129; joins the flying
squadron, 224; damaged on a
reef, 226

Dyer, Captain Nehemiah M., of
the *Baltimore*, at Hong Kong,
154; at Manila, 159, 172 *et seq.*

Eagle joins the flying squadron,
225; reports a strange fleet, 276;
at Aguadores, 280

Eaton, Captain J. G., of the *Resolute* reports a strange fleet, 276

El Correo burned at Manila, 179

Ellis, Chief-Yeoman George H., of
the *Brooklyn*, killed at Santiago,
339

Emory, Captain W. H., of the
Yosemite, at Guantanamo, 261;
his fight with a Spanish fleet off
San Juan, 285 *et seq.*

Engineers, heroism of, 150, 171;
conduct of, during the battle of
Manila, 190, 191; splendid record on the *Oregon*, 213, 214; spirit of, shown, 214, 219, 220; how
they worked at Santiago, 320

Ensenada de los Altares, attack on,
280

Entwistle, James, Chief Engineer
of the *Olympia* at Manila, 191

Ericsson on the blockade before
Havana, 129; lives saved by, at
Santiago, 333, 334

Española, Spanish gun-boat,
burned, 354

Estrella de Guantanamo shot to
pieces at Manzanillo, 354

Eulate, Captain, of the *Vizcaya*,
his dash for the *Brooklyn*, 312;
compels her to change her course,
ib.; his plucky effort to escape,
315

Evans, Captain Robley D.
("Fighting Bob"), of the *Iowa*,
story of, regarding the *Maine*,
81, 82; his remarks on receiving
Schley's order to sail for Key
West, 228; at the bombardment
of Santiago, 254; his efforts **to
ram** one of the Spanish **cruisers**
at Santiago, 315

INDEX   397

Everett, Lieutenant-Commander W. H., of the *Mangrove*, captures the *Panama*, 140, 141
Fern, at Key West, 86
Fernald, Naval Constructor, F. L., 32
Filibustering expeditions, our efforts to prevent them, 61, 62
Fish, Hamilton, Secretary of State, his demands regarding the seizure of the *Colonel Lloyd Aspinwall*, 10, 11, 12
Fletcher, Lieutenant Frank S., his good work at the Washington gun factory, 92
Flying squadron, formation of the, 88
Folger, Captain W. M., of the *New Orleans*, at Baiquiri, 280
Foote, off Cardenas, 129; fired on while scouting, 133
Ford, John D., Chief Engineer of the *Baltimore* at Manila, 191
Fremont, Lieutenant John C., of the *Porter*, his article on torpedo-boats cited, 385 *et seq.*
Fry, Captain Joseph, of the *Virginius*, 20; executed by the Spaniards, 21
Furor wrecked by the *Gloucester*, 302
Gatewood, Assistant Naval-Constructor Richard, 32
General Concha whipped by the *Yosemite*, 285 *et seq.*
General Lezo burned at Manila, 179
Gibbs, Dr. John Blair, killed at Guantanamo, 265
Glass, Captain Henry, of the *Charleston*, takes Guam, 344, 345
Gloucester, the, at Aguadores, 280; position of, before Santiago, 293; in the battle, 302; receives the surrender of Admiral Cervera, 335; escorts transports to Porto Rico, 357; shells the Spanish at Juanica, 358
Goode, Sergeant-Major, killed at Guantanamo, 266
Goodrich, Captain Casper F., of the *St. Louis*, assists in the cutting of the cables at Santiago and Guantanamo, 237, 238
Grant, General, his lack of aggressive interest in the *Virginius* affair, 22
Gridley, Captain Charles V., of the *Olympia*, sails for Manila, 156 *et seq.*; goes into the conning-tower, 163
Guam, capture of, 344, 345
Guantanamo Bay, losses at, 153; the cables cut at, 238; marines at, 259-376
Guardian shot to pieces at Manzanillo, 354
Gun-fire, remarkably small number of hits in the fight at Santiago, 342
Guns, numbers engaged on both squadrons at Santiago, 336; our slow progress in the making of large ones, 58-60; latest developments in, 373 *et seq.*
Hall, Passed Assistant-Engineer Reynold T., of the *Petrel*, at Manila, 191
Hampton Roads, head-quarters of the flying squadron, 88
Harlow, Lieutenant, surveys the harbor at Cabáñas, 289
Hart, Cadet, under fire in Cabáñas Bay, 289
Harvard brings orders to Schley to remain at Santiago, 228
Havana, American residents of, threatened, 64; attitude of Spaniards in, toward the destruction of the *Maine*, 72, 73; blockade of, 129
Hawk, sent to join the flying squadron, 222, 223; overhauls the *Alfonso XII*, 352
Helena, gun-boat, ordered to Key West, 87; on the blockade, 129; captures the *Miguel Jover*, 131; at Enseñada de los Altares, 280; at Manzanillo, 353
Helm, Captain J. M., of the *Hornet*, at Enseñada de los Altares, 280; at Manzanillo, 353
Henderson, Chief-Engineer, 32
Hercules, captured at Manila, 179
Herman Cortes, Spanish war-ship,

seized the *Colonel Lloyd Aspinwall*, 9
Higginson, Captain Francis J., of the *Massachusetts*, at Key West, 86; at Santiago, 254, 351, 352; escorts General Miles to Porto Rico, 357; his report of the work of the navy at, 358 *et seq.*
Hist at Manzanillo, 353, 360
Hobson, Assistant Naval Constructer Richmond Pearson, put in charge of the *Merrimac*, 243; takes her into Santiago Harbor, 244 *et seq.*; discipline of his men, 249; taken prisoner, 250; made a public hero, 253; his efforts to save the Spanish ships, 340, 341
Hodgsdon, Captain Daniel B., of the *Hugh McCulloch*, sails for Manila, 156 *et seq.*; in the battle, 161 *et seq.*
Hood, Captain J., of the *Hawk*, overhauls the *Alfonso XII.*, 352
Hornet, at Enseñada de los Altares, 280; at Manzanillo, 353
Howell, Commander J. A., 32
Hudson, at Cardenas, 144 *et seq.*; rescues the *Winslow*, 152
Hugh McCulloch, at Manila, 161
Hunker, Captain J. J., of the *Annapolis*, at Nipe, 356
Huntington, Lieutenant-Colonel Robert W., in command of marines at Guantanamo, 261 *et seq.*; his care for his men, 273
Illinois, authorized, 369; armament of, 373, 376
Infanta Maria Teresa, 194, 195; the first of the Spanish ships out at Santiago Harbor, 297; fires at the *Brooklyn*, 298; destruction of, 303 *et seq.*; floated, but lost in a gale on the way north, 340
Ingersoll, Captain R. R., of the *Supply*, at Guantanamo, 261
Indiana put into commission, 49; mistakes in, 58; at Key West, 86; at Cienfuegos, 129; ordered to San Juan, 196; ready for battle, 198; on the morning of July 4th, 295; heads for the Morro, 298; fires on the *Teresa*, *ib.*;

hits the *Vizcaya*, 301; falls behind in the chase, 315; struck by an eight-inch shell, 352; in the bombardment of Santiago, 353
Insurgents, no systematic efforts made by Spain to hunt them, 6
Intervention, demand for, 1–7
Iowa, 58; at Key West, 86; before Havana, 129; bound for San Juan, 196; tows the *Amphitrite*, 197; in battle line, 198; begins the attack on San Juan, 203; casualties on, 206; joins the flying squadron, 221, 224; at Santiago, 232, 233, 254, 293, 301, 315, 333, 339
Irene, German war-ship, at Manila, 346
Iris, distilling ship, 92
Irwin, Ensign Noble E., wounded at Manila, 190
Isabel II., 279; whipped by the *Yosemite*, 285 *et seq.*
Isla de Cuba, Admiral Montojo, transfers his flag to, 169; burned, 179
Isla de Luzon burned at Manila, 179
Isla de Mindanao burned at Manila, 179
Jaudenes, General, succeeds Augustin at Manila, 348
Jenkins, Lieutenant Friend, killed on the *Maine*, 75
Jones, Chaplain, of the *Texas*, holds a funeral service under fire at Guantanamo, 267
Jorge Juan sunk at Nipe, 356
José Garcia, Spanish gun-boat, burned, 354
Juanica, landing of the troops at, 357 *et seq.*
Juch, Richard, Chief Engineer of the *Boston*, at Manila, 191
Jungen, Captain Carl, of the *Wompatuck*, helps cut the cables at Santiago and Guantanamo, 237, 238; at Manzanillo, 363
Kansas escorts the *Virginius* from the harbor of Colon, 17, 20
Kearsarge, authorized, 369; double turrets of, 370; advantages of, 373

INDEX

Kelley, Francis, one of the *Merrimac's* crew, 244
Kelley, Lieutenant-Commander J. D. J., on the auxiliary navy board, 88
Kellogg, Lieutenant Frank W., of the *Baltimore*, wounded at Manila, 190
Kentreres, Adolphus, of the *Colon*, his account of the battle of Santiago, 324
Kentucky authorized, 369; double turrets of, 370; advantages of, 373
Key West, the squadron gathered at, 86
Kindelberger, Assistant-Surgeon, of the *Olympia*; commended by Dewey for remaining with his ships though relieved, 180
Kuenzli, Ensign H. C., takes the prize *Argonauta* to Key West, 136
Lamberton, Captain Benjamin, of the *Olympia*, 163; commended by Dewey, 180, 181
Lee, Consul-General, his recall demanded, 84
Leutze, Captain E. H. C., of the *Monterey*, arrives at Manila, 348
Leyden tug at Cardenas, 288
Long, John D., Secretary of the Navy, his efforts in behalf of peace, 67
Lyon, Captain Henry W., of the *Dolphin*, at Santiago, 254; at Guantanamo Bay, 261
McCalla, Captain Bowman H., Commander of the *Marblehead*, the legends about his ship at the beginning of the war, 54, 55; at Key West, 86; at the cutting of the cables at Cienfuegos, 141; assures Schley that the Spanish fleet was not at Cienfuegos, 225; at Santiago, 255; at Guantanamo Bay, 266, 262, 268
McCarty, Captain of the *Colonel Lloyd Aspinwall*, protests against seizure of his ship, 9; held as a prisoner, 10
Maceo, General, killed by the Spaniards, 6
McGuire, Captain S. E., of the *Windom*, at the cutting of the Cables off Cienfuegos, 141, 144
Machias on the blockade of Cardenas, 129; in the fight at, 145 *et seq.*
Mackenzie, Captain M. R. S., of the *Mayflower*, 235
McKinley, President, his first warning to Spain, 63, 64
Magruder, Ensign Thomas P., boards the *Buenaventura*, 123
Mail, the, of London, interview with Admiral Montojo quoted, 186, 187
Maine, the first armored ship of American design, 47; plans of, 48, 49; never appreciated, *ib.*; an honor to the flag, 49; compared to earlier ships, *ib.*; her large sail-power, 51; sent to Havana, 67 *et seq.*; believed to be our most powerful ship by the Spaniards, 70; moored at a strange buoy, 70; blown up, 71 *et seq.*; number of men lost, 75; court of inquiry appointed, 76; the official report on, 76, 79 *et seq.*; her destruction a deliberate act, 80; her condition as revealed by Ensign Powelson, 82; destroyed through Spanish connivance, 83; destruction of, avenged, 336
Maine, the new, 377 *et seq.*, 381
Manila, Dewey's victory at, 154–193; the city taken, 348 *et seq.*
Mangrove on the blockade, 129; captures the *Panama*, 140
Manzanillo, reduction of, 363 *et seq.*
Marblehead, 49; at Key West, 86; on the blockade, 129; joins the flying squadron, 222, 225; discovers the Spanish fleet at Santiago, 231; in the attack on Santiago, 255; takes possession of Guantanamo Bay, 260, 262, 268
Maria Ponton burned, 354
Mariel, blockade of, 129
Marines, the, at Guantanamo, 261 *et seq.*; the first armed force on Cuban soil, 273
Marix, Lieutenant-Commander Adolphe, of the *Scorpion*, 123; Judge Advocate of the *Maine*

court of inquiry, 76; at Manzanillo, 353; at Cabáñas, 280
Marquis del Duero burned at Manila, 179
Martin, Paymaster John R., of the *Boston*, at Manila, 191
Massachusetts, 57; defects in, 58; at Key West, 86; in the flying squadron, 88; held at Hampton Roads, 196; at Key West, 211; ordered to Cienfuegos, 212; sails to the south of Cuba, 221; goes in to attack the Santiago forts, 232; in the attack on Santiago, 254; helps sink the *Reina Mercedes*, 351, 352; escorts transports to Porto Rico, 357; at Ponce, 358
Matanzas, blockade of, 129; defences of, 133, 134; bombardment of, 134, 139
Mayflower in the blockade before Havana, 129; joins Sampson's fleet, 235
Maynard, Captain Washburn, of the *Nashville*, at Key West, 86; at Cienfuegos, 141
Men behind the guns, preparation of, for their work, 99; types of, 138
Menell, Captain J. P., of the *Scorpion*, at Guantanamo, 261
Merrimac, collier, joins the flying squadron, 221; made ready for her entrance into Santiago Harbor, 243 *et seq.*; her crew, 244; her mission accomplished, 245 *et seq.*
Merritt, Assistant-Engineer Darwin R., lost on the *Maine*, 75
Merritt, Major-General Wesley, in command of the forces sent to Manila, 344
Metal, amount thrown by both squadrons in the battle of Santiago, 337, 338
Miantonomoh, guns and armor of, bought abroad, 46; ordered to Key West, 86
Miles, General, arrives at Santiago, 357; sails for Porto Rico, *ib.*; success of his expedition, 358 *et seq.*

Milligan, Chief-Engineer Robert W., of the *Oregon*, his fine record, 215; kept steam up in the *Oregon* ready for a dash, 294; goes into the stoke-hole of the *Oregon* to lend a hand, 320
Minneapolis, 60; in flying squadron, 88, 226
Mirs Bay, Dewey assembles his fleet at, 156, 157
Missouri, the, 377 *et seq.*, 381
Monadnock, sent to Manila, 346, 348
Monitors, new ones ordered, 384
Morrillo Castle, at Matanzas, 134
Morro Castle, at San Juan, 200, 203; at Santiago, Hobson and his men confined in, 250
Montague, Chief Master-at-arms Daniel, one of the *Merrimac's* crew, 244
Monterey, goes to Manila, 347, 348
Montgomery, cruiser, 50; at San Juan, 196, 198, 205
Montojo, Spanish Admiral in command at Manila, 158; loses his flag-ship, 169; transfers his flag to the *Isla de Cuba*, *ib.*; expected to meet Dewey in the open sea, 185; an interview with, regarding his ship, 186, 187; his report on the loss of life on the Spanish side, 189
Murphy, Coxswain J. E., on the *Merrimac*, 244
Nanshan, transport, with Dewey's squadron, 156
Nashville, at Key West, 86; off Mariel, 129; captures the *Argonauta*, 136; overhauls the British cruiser *Talbot*, 137; assists in the cutting of the cables at Cienfuegos, 141, 142
National vanity, danger of, 43
Naval Academy, a wider use of, suggested, 386 *et seq.*
Naval militia, their good work in the war, 256, 286
Naval officers, value of their writings in educating public opinion, 28

INDEX

Naval strength, its dependence upon ship-building facilities, 47
Navy, new, beginning of the, 27 *et seq.*; building new ships under false pretences, 27; results of the Rodgers report, 28; difficulties to be overcome, 32; our first steel ships, 34 *et seq.*; cruisers and battle-ships, 43-60; plans for ships bought abroad, 44; imperfections in, 45; home-made steel provided for, 46; the *Maine* one of the first important ships, 47 *et seq.*; the *New York* and other cruisers, 49 *et seq.*; battle-ships, 54 *et seq.*; power of, not appreciated by Spain, 60; new ships building, 266 *et seq.*
Neville, Lieutenant, at Guantanamo, 266
Newark, flag-ship of the Eastern Squadron, 355; at Manzanillo, 364
Newcomb, Lieutenant F. H., at Cardenas, 144 *et seq.*; goes to the rescue of the *Winslow*, 152
New Orleans, joins Schley at Santiago, 232; ordered into line for an attack, 232; in attack on Santiago, 255; her effective fire, 256; at Baiquiri, 280
Newport, ordered to Key West, 87; on the blockade, 129
New York, 49; contract for, signed, 50; plans of, 50, 51; her military masts, *ib.*; armament of, 52; launched, 53; her official trial, *ib.*; her fine performance, 53, 54; at Key West, 86; captures the steamer *Pedro*, 128; before Havana, 130; at the bombardment of Matanzas, 134; returns the fire at Cabáñas, 139; starts for San Juan, 196, 197; takes the *Terror* in tow, 197; in battle line, 198; casualties on, 206; in the attack on Santiago, 254 *et seq.*; away from the fleet on the morning of July 4th, 293; returns and joins in the chase of the *Colon*, 328 *et seq.*; fires on Santiago, 353; her narrow escape from being blown up by the *Porter*, 385 *et seq.*
Niagara, transport, 196
Nipe, raid on, 356
North Atlantic Squadron, at Key West, 86; disposition of ships for blockade duty, 129
Norton, Assistant Engineer H. P., ordered to assist in designing new ships, 32
Ohio, 377 *et seq.*, 381
Olympia, sails for Manila, 156 *et seq.*; in the battle of Manila, 163 *et seq.*; struck by Spanish shells, 189; in the attack on the city of Manila, 348
O'Neil, Captain Charles, his good work at the Washington gun factory, 92; his improvements in guns and powder, 378
Oregon, battle-ship, 57; errors in, 58; her remarkable run from San Francisco to Key West, 213-220; joins Sampson's fleet, 235; in the attack on Santiago, 254; goes to Guantanamo Bay, 261; before Santiago, July 4th, 293; kept her steam up expecting a chase, 294; fires a gun announcing the coming of the Spanish fleet, 296; in the battle, 301, 315, 316; her race after the *Colon*, 320, 321; member of the Eastern Squadron, 355; defects in the type, 370
Osceola, her adventure with the *New Orleans*, 138; at Manzanillo, 353, 360
Panama, captured by the *Mangrove*, 139, 140
Panther, takes marines to Guantanamo Bay, 261
Paris, American liner, transferred to the Navy, 91
Patterson, John F., purchaser of the *Virginius* for the Cuban Junta, 15
Pedro, prize captured by the *New York*, 128
Pelayo, Spanish battle-ship, 281
Personnel of the Navy, high standing of, 28; act concerning the advancement of the, 42

Petrel, leaves for Manila, 156 *et seq.*; in the battle, 175; called the "Baby Battle-ship," 176

Philip, Captain John W., of the *Texas* at Key West, 86; at Santiago, 254, 255; shells the Socapa battery, 280; "Don't cheer, the poor devils are dying," 307; gives public thanks for victory, 323

Phillips, John, on the *Merrimac*, 244

Pillsbury, Captain John E., of the *Vesuvius* at Santiago, 257, 258

Pizaro, Spanish man-o'-war, at Colon, 17

Pluton, sunk at Santiago, 302, 303

Ponce, capture of, 358 *et seq.*

Poor, Admiral, at Havana, 9, 14

Porter, on the blockade of Havana, 129; ordered to San Juan, 196; ready for battle, 198; joins Sampson's fleet, 235; nearly torpedoes the *New York*, 385 *et seq.*

Porto Rico, occupation of, 357 *et seq.*

Potter, Lieutenant-Commander William P., of the *New York*, on the *Maine* court of inquiry, 76

Powder, the great value of the smokeless kind, 378 *et seq.*

Powell, Cadet Joseph W., in charge of the launch sent to pick up the crew of the *Merrimac*, 244, 246; with the survey party at Cabáñas, 289

Powelson, Ensign W. V. N., his discovery regarding the condition of the *Maine*, 82

Prairie, overhauls the *Alfonso XII.*, 352

Prisoners of war, those taken in Spanish ships expected to be shot, 132

Prize money, naval officers would have the dividing of, abolished, 141

Prizes, capture of, 128 *et seq.*

Protocol, the, signed, 364

Purcell, Captain J. L., of the *Osceola*, 138; at Manzanillo, 360

Puritan, ordered to Key West, 80; her unfitness for blockade duty, 130; at the bombardment of Matanzas, 134

Purissima Concepcion, sunk at Manzanillo, 354

Quesada, General M., 15

Rainy season in Cuba, the dangers of, 127

Raleigh, cruiser, 49; sails for Manila, 156 *et seq.*; in the battle, 175; ammunition expended by, 185

Ransom, George B., chief engineer of the *Concord*, at Manila, 191

Rapid-fire guns, value shown at Manila, 170; at Santiago, 341

Rapido, captured at Manila, 179

Reconcentrados, the, 4; Spain's promise to relieve, a sham, 63

Rees, Executive Officer Corwin P., with Dewey, 163

Reid, Captain, of the *Kansas*, his attitude toward the *Virginius*, 19

Reina Christina, destroyed at Manila, 168, 169

Reina Mercedes, sunk at Santiago by the *Massachusetts* and the *Texas*, 351, 352

Reiter, Captain G. C., of the *Panther*, 261

Resolute, at Santiago, 301

Restormel, captured by the *St. Paul* as she was taking a cargo of coal to Santiago, 226, 227

Roach, John, builder of the *Chicago*, *Atlanta*, *Boston*, and *Dolphin*, 41

Roberts, Don Lopez, Spanish Minister at Washington, 10; his reply to Secretary Fish, 11

Robeson, Secretary of the Navy, his influence in retarding naval progress, 33

Rodgers, Captain Frederick, a member of the board for the purchase of auxiliary ships, 88

Rodgers, Admiral John, head of the board appointed to consider the needs of the Navy, 27

Rodgers Board, the, 27; results of the report of, 28, 31; recom-

mendations by, 33 *et seq.*; value of the new navy, 36
Roelker, Past-Assistant Engineer L. R., ordered to assist in the designing of new ships, 32
Roosevelt, Theodore, Assistant Secretary of the Navy, his energetic preparation of the Navy for war, 67
St. *Louis*, American liner, transferred to the Navy, 91; helps in the cable-cutting at Santiago and Guantanamo, 237, 238
St. *Paul*, American liner, transferred to the Navy, 91; at Key West, 211; sent on scout duty, 212; joins the Flying Squadron, 226; takes the *Merrimac* in tow, 228; guards the entrance of Santiago Harbor, 236; blockades San Juan, 283; her fight with the *Terror*, 283 *et seq.*
Sampson, Captain W. T., of the *Iowa*, member of *Maine* court of inquiry, 76; his "Naval Defence of the Coast," 150; plans for an assault on Havana made by, 127; his search for Cervera, 194; ordered to San Juan, 196; his ill-assorted fleet, 196, 197; transfers his flag to the *Iowa*, 198; formation of his squadron, 198, 199; sends up the signal for attack, 200; the bombardment, 203 *et seq.*; his ships not fully manned, 206; his slow return to Key West, 211; goes to the Nicholas channel in search of Cervera, 212; his order to Schley regarding the blockade of Cienfuegos, 221; notifies Schley that the Spanish squadron is probably at Santiago, 222; sends further order to Schley to go to Santiago, 223; hurries to Santiago, 234, 235; his plans to hold the Spanish fleet, 239 *et seq.*; ordered Schley to sink the *Sterling* in the harbor, 243; decides to use the *Merrimac*, *ib.*; bombards Santiago, 254 *et seq.*: his report of the engagement, 256;

disposition of his fleet on the morning of July 4th, 291 *et seq.*; leaves the fleet to visit General Shafter, 293; joins in the chase of the *Colon*, 328 *et seq.*; bombards Santiago again, 353
Sands, Captain J. H., of the *Columbia*, escorts transports to Porto Rico, 357
San Francisco, Spanish steamer, towed the *Colonel Lloyd Aspinwall* to Havana, 10
San Juan, supposed to be the objective point of Admiral Cervera, 196; the city from the sea, 200; bombardment of, 203 *et seq.*; would have surrendered if the attack had continued, 206; blockaded by Admiral Sampson, 282
Santiago, cutting of the cables at, 237, 238; blockaded by Admiral Sampson, 239–258; bombardment of, 254 *et seq.*; mines in the harbor, 275; disposition of the fleet on the morning of July 4th, 291 *et seq.*; the destruction of Cervera's fleet, 297 *et seq*; bombarded by the fleet, 353; surrender of, 350 *et seq.*
Sargeant, Lieutenant Nathan, on the auxiliary navy board, 88
Saugus, 14
Schley, Captain W. S., in command of the Flying Squadron, 88; ordered to Cienfuegos to look out for Admiral Cervera, 211, 212; sails for the south of Cuba, 221; arrives off Cienfuegos, 224; convinced that the Spanish squadron was in the harbor, 224, 225; leaves for Santiago, 226; his unexpected order to sail for Key West, 227; makes no effort to learn whether Cervera was in Santiago Harbor, 228; complains of difficulties in coaling, 229; ordered to remain at Santiago, 230; takes his fleet nearer shore, 231; steams back to sea, 232; steams in to attack the forts, 232; his report of, 234; declines to meet the *Vizcaya* on even terms,

312; his chase of the *Vizcaya*, 316 *et seq.*

Scientific American, quoted on the number of shot-marks on the Spanish ships, 341, 342

Scorpion, converted yacht, goes to the assistance of the *Nashville*, 138; with the Flying Squadron, 321; sent to Santiago for news, 224; at Guantanamo Bay, 261; at Cabáñas, 280; at Manzanillo, 353

Scott, Ensign E. P., at Manila, 181

Scott, Lieutenant H., throws a tow-line to the disabled *Winslow*, 152

Search-light, test of, at Santiago, 351

Secondary batteries on our first battle-ships, 56

Sentinal Delgado, shot to pieces at Manzanillo, 354

Severn, United States ship, 14

Shafter, General, leaves to take possession of Santiago, 275 *et seq.*; delayed by reports of a strange fleet, 276 *et seq.*; wanted the Navy to force Santiago channel, 292

Sharp, Captain A., of the *Vixen*, at Santiago, 254; at Cabáñas, 280

Sheathing for ships, need of, 341

Shufeldt, Commodore R. W., member of Advisory Board appointed by Secretary Chandler, 32

Sicard, Rear Admiral, appoints a board of inquiry to investigate the destruction of the *Maine*, 76

Sickles, General Daniel, United States Minister at Madrid, calls on Sagasta in the *Colonel Lloyd Aspinwall* case, 11, 12; his final demand, 13, 14; recalled on account of his demands in the *Virginius* affair, 22

Sigsbee, Captain Charles D., of the *Maine*, 67; his despatch regarding the destruction of his ship, 72; transferred to the *St. Paul*, 211; reports capture of the *Restormel*, 226, 227; his fight with the *Terror* off San Juan, 283 *et seq.*

Silvee, Color-Sergeant Richard, raised the Stars and Stripes at Guantanamo, 261

Smith, Charles, master of the *Virginius*, 18

Smokeless powder, the great value of, shown, 256

Snow, Captain A. S., overhauls the *Alfonso XII.*, 352

Solace, hospital-ship, 92

Spain, early origin of the war with, 1; fortunes made by her officials in Cuba, 2; cruelty of her soldiers, 5; thought we wouldn't fight, 26; attitude toward our efforts in Cuba, 64; contempt for the United States shown, 8, 24, 69, 70; treachery of, revealed in the *Maine* case, 82, 184; her financial condition at the beginning of the war, 85; her opinion of our Navy, 85, 86; stubborn in defence, 103; ignorance of our power, 126; her rule in Cuba, 156–162; her squadron at Manila, 183; gunnery of her troops at San Juan, 206; loss at Santiago, 339, 340; end of her power in America, 343

"Spook Fleet," the, 276

Steers, Henry, ship architect, member of Advisory Board appointed by Secretary Chandler, 32

Stickney, J. L., correspondent of the New York *Herald*, commended by Dewey for service at Manila, 181

Subig Bay, strategical advantages of, 158

Sun, the, quoted on the battle of Manila, 188

Supply, store-ship, at Guantanamo Bay, 261

Sutherland, Captain W. H., of the *Eagle*, reports a strange fleet, 276, at Aguadores, 280

Suwanee, in the attack on Santiago, 254; at Manzanillo, 360

Swinburne, Captain William T., of the *Helena*, captures the *Miguel Jover*, 131; at Enseñada de los

INDEX

Attares, 280; at Manzanillo, 353
Talbot, British cruiser, overhauled by the *Nashville*, 137
Target-practice, value of, proved at Santiago, 341
Tawresey, Naval Constructor I. G., on the Auxiliary Navy Board, 88
Taylor, Captain Henry C., of the *Indiana*, at Key West, 86; at Cienfuegos, 129; at San Juan, 198; at Santiago, 293 *et seq.*, 353
Ten-Year War, the, 8, 9
Terror, ordered to Key West, 86; unfitness of, for blockade duty, 130; in the fleet ordered to San Juan, 196; taken in tow by the *New York*, 197; in line for battle, 198
Terror, Spanish torpedo-boat, at San Juan, 279; whipped by the St. Paul, 283 *et seq.*
Texas, her foreign plans had to be radically altered, 45; built at Norfolk, 47; her efficiency proved the value of the *Maine*, 49; at Key West, 86, 211; with the Flying Squadron, 88, 196; ordered to Cienfuegos, 212; sails to the south of Cuba, 221; in the attack on Santiago, 254; at Guantanamo, 266; picks up a mine with her propeller, 271; shells the Socapa battery at Cabáñas, 280; struck by a six-inch shell, 281; her position before Santiago, 293, 294; signals that "the fleet's coming out," 296; in the battle, 307, 315, 316; helps sink the *Reina Mercedes*, 351, 352; bombards Santiago, 353
Todd, Commander Chapman C., of the *Wilmington*, in the fight at Cardenas, 145; in the attack on Manzanillo, 353
Topeka, at Nipe, 356
Toral, General, Spanish commander at Santiago, 353
Tornado, Spanish gun-boat, takes the *Virginius* to Santiago, 20
Torpedo-boat destroyers, new ones building, 384

Torpedo-boats, value of, tested, 384 *et seq.*
Tracy, Secretary of the Navy, his instructions regarding the new battle-ships, 54
Train, Captain J. C., overhauls the *Alfonso XII.*, 352
Trainor, "Fiddler," of the *Iowa*, rescues sailors from the *Vizcaya*, 333
Trochas, the, 5
Velasco, Spanish war-ship, burned at Manila, 179
Very, Lieutenant Edward, member of Advisory Board, appointed by Secretary Chandler, 32
Vesuvius, on blockade duty before Havana, 129; her value shown at Santiago, 257, 258; runs into Santiago channel to investigate, 289
Virginius affair, the, 14-24
Virginia Seymour, tug that took Cubans out to the *Virginius*, 15
Vixen, joins the Flying Squadron, 225; at Cabáñas, 280; before Santiago, 293; in the battle, 328
Vizcaya, the, 195; fires on the *Merrimac*, 246; follows the *Maria Teresa* out of Santiago Harbor, 298; hit by a shell from the *Indiana*, 301; makes a dash for the *Brooklyn*, 312; runs ashore, 319; rescue of her crew, 333
Volunteers, their quick response to the President's call, 275, 276
Vulcan, repair ship, 92
Wainwright, Captain Richard, of the *Gloucester*, at Aguadores, 280; in the battle of Santiago, 302 *et seq.*
Walker, Captain Asa, of the *Concord*, leaves Hong Kong for Manila, 156 *et seq.*; in the battle, 161, 175
War, our preparations for, 64, 67; might have been avoided, 82; $50,000,000 appropriated for defence, 85; money used for aggressive purposes, 86; declared by Spain, 155; with Spain a

necessity, 390; message, the, 103–114
Ward, Captain A., at Baiquiri, 280; at Nipe, 356
Wasp, at Baiquiri, 280; at Nipe, 356
Watson, Commodore John C., in command of the Eastern Squadron, 356
Weyler, Governor-General of Cuba, known as the Butcher, 2; beginning of his rule, 3; cruelty of, 6; effect of his atrocities on our Government, 62; his reliance on the ravages of the Cuban climate, 127
White Squadron, the, 25–42
Whiting, Captain W. H., of the *Monadnock*, arrives at Manila, 348
Whitney, Secretary, went abroad for plans for new ships, 44; his work in building up the home steel industry, 45, 46
Wilder, Captain Frank, of the *Boston*, leaves for Manila, 156 *et seq.*; volunteers to remain in command of his ship at Manila, though relieved, 180; his coolness under fire, 190
Wilmington, ordered to Key West, 86; before Havana, 129; at Cardenas, 145 *et seq.*; at Manzanillo, 353
Windom, at the cutting of the cables off Cienfuegos, 141, 144
Winslow, Lieutenant C. W., in command of the cable-cutting expedition at Cienfuegos, 142; wounded, 144

Winslow, on the blockade off Matanzas, 129; at Cardenas, 145 *et seq.*; disabled, 150; rescued by the *Hudson*, 152; casualties on, 152; goes to Key West under her own steam, 152
Wisconsin, authorized, 369; size of, *ib.*; armament of, 373, 376
Wise, Captain, believed Cervera to be at Santiago, 226; escorts troops to Porto Rico, 357
Wompatuck, ordered to San Juan, 196; ready for battle, 198; at Manzanillo, 353
Wood, Captain Edward P., of the *Petrel*, sails for Manila, 156 *et seq.*; takes his ship in close to the batteries at Manila, 176
Wood, dangers of, on war-ships, 341
Woodford, Stewart L., Minister to Spain, demands Weyler's removal, 62
Wounded, care of the Spanish, at Santiago, 335
Yale, auxiliary cruiser, joins the Flying Squadron, 226; escorts troops to Porto Rico, 357
Yankee, in the attack on Santiago, 254 *et seq.*; at Guantanamo, 261, 262; at Cienfuegos, 287
Yosemite, auxiliary cruiser, at Guantanamo, 261; her fight with the Spaniards off San Juan, 285 *et seq.*
Young, Captain L., of the *Hist*, at Manzanillo, 353
Zafiro, with Dewey's squadron, 156

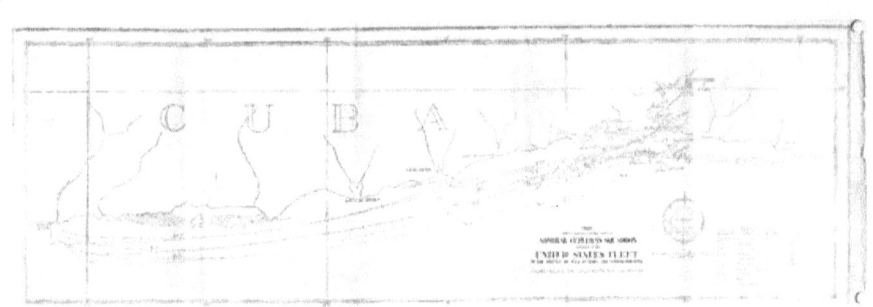

www.ingramcontent.com/pod-product-compliance
Lightning Source LLC
Chambersburg PA
CBHW051737300426
44115CB00007B/598